IMMO STORIES

WISDOM TO NOURISH YOUR MIND AND SOUL

J. P. VASWANI

HAY HOUSE

HAY HOUSE INDIA

Australia • Canada • Hong Kong • India
South Africa • United Kingdom • United States

Hay House Publishers (India) Pvt. Ltd.
Muskaan Complex, Plot No.3, B-2 Vasant Kunj, New Delhi-110 070, India
Hay House Inc., PO Box 5100, Carlsbad, CA 92018-5100, USA
Hay House UK, Ltd., Astley House, 33 Notting Hill Gate, London W11 3JQ, UK
Hay House Australia Pty Ltd., 18/36 Ralph St., Alexandria NSW 2015, Australia
Hay House SA (Pty) Ltd., PO Box 990, Witkoppen 2068, South Africa
Hay House Publishing, Ltd., 17/F, One Hysan Ave., Causeway Bay, Hong Kong
Raincoast, 9050 Shaughnessy St., Vancouver, BC V6P 6E5, Canada

Email: contact@hayhouse.co.in
www.hayhouse.co.in

DADA VASWANI'S BOOKS
Visit us online to purchase books on self-improvement, spiritual
advancement, meditation and philosophy. Plus audio cassettes, CDs,
DVDs, monthly journals and books in Hindi.
www.dadavaswanisbooks.org

ISBN 978-93-81398-92-0

Printed and bound at
Rajkamal Electric Press, Sonepat, Haryana (India)

Other Books by J. P. Vaswani

OTHER BOOKS BY J. P. VASWANI

25 Stories for Children and also for Teens
Break the Habit
It's all a Matter of Attitude!
More Snacks for the Soul
Snacks for the Soul
The Heart of a Mother
The King of Kings
The Lord Provides
The Miracle of Forgiving
The One Thing Needful
The Patience of Purna
The Power of Good Deeds
The Power of Thought
Trust Me All in All or Not at All
Whom do you Love the Most
You can Make a Differenc

In Hindi:
Jiski Jholi Mein Hain Pyaar (Dada J.P. Vaswani
    His Life and Teachings)
Pyar Ka Masiha (Pilgrim of Love)
Sadhu Vaswani: Unkaa Jeevan Aur Shikshaayen
    (Sadhu Vaswani His Life and Teachings)
Aalwar Santon Ki Mahan Gaathaayen
Brindavan Ka Balak
Santon Ki Leela
Bhakton Ki Uljhanon Kaa Saral Upaai
Dainik Prerna (Daily Inspiration)
Krodh Ko Jalayen Swayam Ko Nahin (Burn
    Anger Before Anger Burns You)
Prarthna ki Shakti
Shama Karo, Sukhi Raho
Safal Vivah Ke Dus Rahasya (10
    Commandments of a Successful Marriage)
Atmik Jalpaan (Snacks for the Soul)
Atmik Poshan (More Snacks for the Soul)
Bhale Logon Ke Saath Bura Kyon? (Why Do
    Good People Suffer?)
Mrutyu Hai Dwar... Phir Kya? (Life After
    Death)
Chahat Hai Mujhe Ik Teri Teri! (Hindi Booklet)
Ishwar Tujhe Pranam (Begin the Day with God)

In Marathi:
Krodhala Shaanth Kara, Krodhane Ghala
    Ghalnya Purveech (Burn Anger Before Anger
    Burns You)
Sufi Sant (Sufi Saints of East and West)

Jyachya Jholit Aahay Prem (Pilgrim of Love)
Mrutyu Nantar Che Jeevan (Life after Death)
Karma Mhanje Kay? Samjun Ghayaych?
    Karma (What You Would Like To Know
    About Karma)
Yashasvi Vyavahik Jeevanchi Sutre (10
    Commandments of a Successful Marriage)

In Kannada:
Burn Anger Before Anger Burns You
Life After Death
Why do Good People Suffer
101 Stories for You and Me
Tips for Teenagers

In Telugu:
Life after Death
Burn Anger Before Anger Burns You
What you would like to know about Karma

In Spanish:
Mas Respuestas de Dada (Dada Answers)
    Todo es Cuestion de Actitud! (It's all a
    Matter of Attitude)
Mas Bocaditos Para el Alma (More Snacks
    for the Soul)
Bocaditos Para el Alma (Snacks for the Soul)
Inicia Tu Dia Con Dios (Begin the Day with
    God)
Cita Diario Con Dios (Daily Appointment
    with God!)
El Buen Cuidado De Las Hijos (Good
    Parenting)
L'Inspiration Quotidienne (Daily
    Inspiration)
Aprenda A Controlar Su Ira (Burn Anger
    Before Anger Burns You)
Queme La Ira Antes Que La Ira Lo Queme
    A Usted (Burn Anger Before Anger
    Burns You)
El Bein Quentu Hagas, Regresa (The Good
    You Do Returns)
Mata al miedo antes de que el miedo te mate
    (Kill Fear Before Fear Kills you)
Encontro Diario Com Deus (Daily
    Appontment With God)
Sita Diario ku Dios (I Luv U, God!)
Vida despu'es de la Muerte (Life After Death)

Mas Cerca Oh Dios De Ti ! (Nearer My God To Thee)

Tiene Dios Favoritos? (Does God Have Favorites?)

Lo Que a Usted Legustaria Saber Sobre el Karma (What you would Like to Know about Karma)

101 Historias Paraa Ti Y Para Mi (101 Stories for You and Me)

Simplemente Vegetariano (Simply Vegetarian)

10 Mandamientos Para Un Exitoso Matrimonio (10 Commandments of Successful Marriage)

Maneje su Vida Momento a Momento (Management Moment By Moment)

Deje De Quejarse Y Empiece a Agradecer! (Stop Complaining Start Thanking)

Asi Nos Han Ensenado! (Thus I have been Taught)

Tu Puedes Marcar La diferencia (You Can Make A Difference)

In Arabic:
Daily Appointment with God
Daily Inspiration
Thus Spake Sadhu Vaswani

In Chinese:
Daily Appointment with God

In Dutch:
Begin De Dag Met God (Begin the Day with God)

In Bahasa:
Life After Death
Musnahkan Kemarahan Sebelum Amarah Memusnahkan Anda (Burn Anger Before Anger Burns You)
A Little Book of Success
A Little Book of Wisdom
Menulis Di Atas Pasir (It's all a Matter of Attitude)

In Gujrati:
It's all a Matter of Attitude
Ishwar Se Dainik Bhet (Daily Appointment with God)
Life After Death
Flowers & Fruits

In Oriya:
Snacks for the Soul
More Snacks for the Soul
Why Do Good People Suffer
Burn Anger Before Anger Burns You
Pilgrim of Love
Life after Death
Prathna Ki Shakti

In Russian:
What you would you like to know about Karma
Burn Anger Before Anger Burns You

In Sindhi:
Why do Good People Suffer
Burn Anger Before Anger Burns You

In Tamil:
Why do Good People Suffer
Burn Anger Before Anger Burns You
Snacks for the Soul
It's all a Matter of Attitude
More Snacks for the Soul
Secrets of Health and Happiness
10 Commandments of a Successful Marriage
Kill Fear Before Fear Kills You
Daily Appointment with God

In Latvia:
The Magic of Forgiveness

In French:
Burn Anger Before Anger Burns You

Dada J. P. Vaswani is one of India's greatly beloved and revered spiritual leaders. He is the life-force at the helm of the renowned Sadhu Vaswani Mission, an international, non-profit, social welfare and service organization with its headquarters in Pune, and active centres all over the world.

Born on 2 August 1918, at Hyderabad-Sind, Dada was a brilliant scholar, who turned his back on a promising academic career to devote himself to his uncle and Guru, Sadhu Vaswani, a highly revered modern day saint. Today, the Master's mantle has fallen on Dada, whom devotees and admirers look upon as the representative of God on earth; a mentor and guardian of deepest values and spiritual aspirations.

Dada J. P. Vaswani is deeply imbued with the liberal and tolerant spirit of the Hindu faith that he was born into, and firmly believes that there are as many paths to the Divine, as there are human aspirations. Each one of us can take our own untried, untested, unchartered paths to reach God, and God will meet us half way. This all-encompassing, humane and broad outlook makes him acceptable to aspirants all over the world, who perceive him as a non-sectarian, non-judgemental teacher and guide in whom they can repose their faith.

A staunch advocate of vegetarianism, Dada has made it his life's mission to spread the message of reverence for all life, as advocated by Gurudev Sadhu Vaswani. Under his inspired leadership, the Sadhu Vaswani Mission has made dedicated and sustained efforts to offer various service programmes encompassing the fields of spiritual progress, education, medical care, women's empowerment, village upliftment, relief and rehabilitation, animal welfare, rural development and service of the underprivileged and disadvantaged sections of society. Dada firmly believes in the words of his Master: 'Service of the poor is worship of God'.

A fluent, powerful and witty speaker and an inspired writer, Dada has authored over a hundred books and booklets, and is the youngest 95-year-old that you can ever meet. His rapport with the youth is truly amazing. He is at home on the world's most eminent fora, as well as in gatherings of students and young professionals, who find his personal magnetism, humility and aura irresistible. Spiritual leader, educationist, philosopher and mystic, Dada J. P. Vaswani represents the very quintessence of India's wisdom and universal spirit.

CONTENTS

CONFUCIANISM

HINDUISM

ISLAM

JAINISM

JUDAISM

SIKHISM

SUFISM

TAOISM

ZEN BUDDHISM

ZOROASTRIANISM

EPILOGUE
Sadhu Vaswani

FOREWORD

ℛELIGION HAS THREE ASPECTS: VALUES, RITUALS AND SYMBOLS. MORAL and spiritual values are common to all traditions and the symbols and practises – those rituals and customs that form a way of life within a religion – are what distinguish one tradition from another and give each of them their charm! The symbols and practises are like the banana peel and the spiritual values the banana. However, people in every tradition have thrown away the banana and are holding onto the peel.

The crisis facing the world today is fundamentally one of identification. People identify themselves with limited characteristics such as gender, race, religion and nationality, forgetting their basic identity as part of the universal spirit. These limited identifications lead to a conflict both globally and on a personal level.

Every individual is much more than the sum of these limited identifications. The highest identification we can have is that we are part of Divinity; then comes the identity that we are human beings and members of the human family. In this divine creation, the whole of the human race is united as one family. While the external practises and rituals may be different across religions, the inherent values and wisdom are common in all of them and this is the common thread that can unite this human family.

Dada J. P. Vaswani has been working ceaselessly for many decades to bring people from diverse backgrounds together and unite them through his universal teachings; this book is another effort in this direction. Stories have always been a very effective and entertaining way to transmit deep wisdom through the ages. This collection of stories strings these little gems from various faiths with the common thread of wisdom. I am sure the readers will enjoy soaking in the knowledge that the following pages carry.

Gurudev Sri Sri Ravi Shankarji,
Art of Living, Bengaluru

11

AUTHOR'S PREFACE

*L*ET ME BEGIN WITH THE TYPICAL COUNTER OFFENSIVE KNOWN AS devil's advocacy:

Who will read a book of stories from the scriptures in an age where five- and six-year-olds go around with tabs and gaming devices and their teenage siblings are watching YouTube videos, while their parents and elder family members (who really ought to know better) are watching the idiot box with the utmost concentration that they are capable of?

I am an indefatigable optimist. I believe that some good things in human civilization will always survive the test of time, no matter how tough our times may be. Love, laughter, compassion, understanding and storytelling – these may be threatened, they may seem to some people old fashioned and irrelevant; but they will always be with us, lighting up our darkest moments, bringing hope and good cheer to people when they need it most.

Why do we need stories, when the great scriptures are there with us? The simple answer to this question is: why do we need the proverbial spoonful of sugar to make the medicine go down children's throats? It is not that children or impatient adults cannot grasp great values and truths when they are put across to them; it is just that a story is a speaking picture and it helps all of us relate to the universal predicaments and the common human values that characters and situations in the story depict for us.

13

Let us take India. We have the Vedas, probably the world's oldest revealed scriptures. Why then did Veda Vyasa, the Adi Guru who split the Vedas, also give us the two great epics and the eighteen puranas?

It is said that Lord Vishnu Himself manifested his divinity through Veda Vyasa, for the purpose of codifying the Vedas. This classification of the Vedas was accomplished by Vyasa and later, the different branches and sub-branches (sakhas) evolved for each Veda over a period of time. It is said that the gods themselves came to hear the original classification of the Vedas from sage Vyasa, taking the form of his distinguished disciples: for they were well aware that it was Lord Vishnu who had manifested Himself in human form, to accomplish this monumental task for the benefit of His devotees. Thus we have the sloka:

Vyaasaya Vishnurupaaya Vyaasaroopaya Vishnave
Namo Vai Brahmanidhaye Vasishtaaya Namo Nama:
(I salute Vyasa in the form of Vishnu, and Vishnu in the form of Vyasa; for he was the progeny of sage Vasishta; and the embodiment of the true knowledge of Brahman [The Supreme Spirit].)

We know too, that in chapter ten of Bhagavad Gita 'Vibhuti Yoga', Lord Sri Krishna confirms this, when he says, 'Of all the sages, I am Vyasa' (*Muneempaayanam Vyasa*).

We are told that when Vyasa was preparing to leave his physical form and depart from this earth, Maharishi Narada went to him and urged him to write the eighteen puranas. Narada told the sage that his task in life would remain unfulfilled if the puranas were not written. Vyasa accepted his advice and composed the ancient puranas, also setting up the system of teaching them through kathas – the oral tradition of narratives. Thus, his writings filtered down to every level of society, from the highly learned pundits down to the illiterate peasants. This was Veda Vyasa's great contribution to the Sanatana Dharma – he took the Vedic religion and its great concepts right into the homes and hearts of the masses. We owe him a deep debt of gratitude for the same.

This is what our great immortal stories are all about: taking the great religious truths and precepts right into the homes and hearts of the people! For this purpose, in the service of this cause, our immortal stories are a treasure that we cannot and must not lose!

Looking back over my own lifetime, I can see how the tradition of storytelling is being metamorphosed into something new and strange. Children of my generation were privileged to listen to stories directly from the loving words of grandmothers, mothers, aunts and uncles. Teachers in colleges and schools too, were adept at storytelling to reinforce whatever they taught.

When time became a precious commodity at home and in school, we saw comic books, picture story books appearing on the scene, with illustrated synoptic accounts of the same great stories. Mothers and fathers, of an earlier generation, felt that they had done their duty by the children, when they presented them with a set of Amar Chitra Katha comic books!

Later came the age of movies, and then televised scriptures and epics. Our children saw Rama, Krishna, Moses and Mary in the form of actors who portrayed them effectively on the small screen and its larger version, the silver screen.

I am deeply grateful to the TV epics and to Amar Chitra Katha for keeping a great tradition alive. But I would be pained to think that we are losing out on the age-old mode of 'connectivity' in the family: the art of storytelling and the practise of sitting and listening to stories.

This book of immortal stories from the great faiths of the world is a small and humble step to interest my readers in this wonderful art form of storytelling. The book brings together stories from the great scriptures and parables narrated by the Avatara Purushas and prophets, as well as incidents from the great souls of the East and West. My fond and humble hope is that it may rekindle, at least in some of my readers, the desire to read more and pass on the same to their children. For, as Gurudev Sadhu Vaswani constantly reminded us, children are our greatest treasure. In our constant pressure to earn a livelihood or amass wealth (to leave to these same children) let us not lose sight of the best heritage that we can ensure for them: the wealth of values and ideals that must always govern human conduct.

The stories from the scriptures and from the lives of the great ones, articulate values and precepts that are vital to our well-being and moral growth. They offer us memorable characters caught in unique experiences which we relate to, because of their human interest. We can enter into the experience of the story, even as the original teachers and students featured in the stories did. The stories are meant to promote reflection, absorption, assimilation and as a sequel, enlightened action and awakened awareness.

The stories take us back to the times when avataras and men of God walked this earth, and lived and moved amongst us, as one of us. God, in His great wisdom, sent them to live amongst us, not to prove any point, not to demonstrate His omnipotence, but for our benefit and our betterment as human beings. What if we are no longer in Satya Yuga? The records and the testimony of the great ones are still available to us. All we have to do is to enter into the spirit of the stories we read, and the great ones come alive for us. Can we ask for more?

I hope that these stories will bring out the best in all of us – such as the virtues of gratitude to God; compassion for our fellow beings; forgiveness of others' trespasses against us, understanding and empathy with others; and the aspiration to seek the goal of this human birth and attain it.

This book is dedicated to the lotus feet of Gurudev Sadhu Vaswani who taught me to see the One behind the many.

J. P. Vaswani

BAHÁ'ÍSM

BRIEF INTRODUCTION

 HISTORIANS AND SCHOLARS OF RELIGION AGREE THAT THE Bahá'í faith is the world's youngest independent religion. Its founder Bahá'u'lláh (1817-1892), lived and preached his faith in times that are still in people's living memory. Today, over five hundred million people all over the world owe allegiance to this faith. The word Bahá'í is both a noun and an adjective, used respectively to describe the faith, and also a follower of the faith. The term Bahá'ísm is not generally encouraged, and Bahá'í faith is the preferred choice.

A new or independent religion does not arise in a vacuum. Thus, Buddhism and Jainism grew out of Hinduism; they were in one sense, reactions to Hinduism in their own historical and social context. Similarly, Jesus Christ was born a Jew, and followed the Jewish faith before his teachings evolved into the new religion of Christianity. We can also say that Buddhism and Christianity acquired their independence and distinct identity only when they moved out of the land of their origin, into the wider world arena, and became the accepted faith of 'outsiders' other than Indians or Jews. This is true of the Bahá'í faith too. It may be said to have originated in the matrix of Islam, although it subsequently became quite independent of the originating religion.

The new faith first began in Persia or Iran. From there, it spread to many neighbouring countries like Turkey, Russia and Northern India. Some Jews, Christians and Zoroastrians embraced the new faith, although its early followers were predominantly Muslim. Many of its ideas were drawn from the Holy Quran, although they differed in matters of interpretation.

The Bahá'í faith is unique in this respect – that it unreservedly accepts the validity of other faiths and world religions. Bahá'ís believe that Abraham, Moses, Zoroaster, Buddha, Krishna, Jesus, and Muhammad are all equally authentic messengers of one God. The teachings of these divine messengers are seen as paths to salvation which contribute to the 'carrying forward of an ever-advancing civilization'. But they also believe that these series of interventions by God through His messengers has been progressive with relation to human history, each revelation from God evolving from the previous one, each more complex than those which preceded it, and each preparing the way for the next.

Any discussion of the origins of the Bahá'í faith must begin with the mention of the great forerunner, who called himself as 'The Bab', meaning 'Gate', based on a Shia Muslim concept. In 1844, The Bab announced to his few faithful followers that he was but the latest in a long line of spiritual leaders whose task it was to proclaim the advent of God's messenger upon this earth. He also spoke repeatedly of 'He whom God shall make manifest', a Messiah whose coming had been proclaimed by all of the world's scriptures. In his book, the *Bayán,* The Bab described the messianic figure as 'the origin of all divine attributes', and stated that his command would be equivalent to God's command. This prediction was widely recognized as being fulfilled by Bahá'u'lláh, the founder of the Bahá'í faith.

Unlike most other prophets and visionaries before him, the founder of the Bahá'í faith took up the pen and paper himself, to write down for posterity, the revelation that he received. Over the next forty years, thousands of books, tablets and letters were written by him, or dictated to believers and followers who served as his secretaries. These form the core of the sacred scriptures of the faith he founded.

Humanity is seen as essentially one, though highly varied; its diversity of race and culture are seen as worthy of appreciation and acceptance. Doctrines of racism, nationalism, caste, social class and gender-based hierarchy are seen as artificial impediments to unity. The Bahá'í teachings state that the unification of humankind is the paramount issue in the religious and political conditions of the present world.

The following principles are frequently listed as a quick summary of the Bahá'í teachings, according to Abdu'l-Bahá:

- Unity of God
- Unity of religion
- Unity of humankind
- Equality between men and women
- Elimination of all forms of prejudice
- World peace
- Harmony of religion and science
- Independent investigation of truth
- Universal compulsory education
- Universal auxiliary language
- Obedience to government and non-involvement in partisan politics
- Elimination of extremes of wealth and poverty

The central theme of Bahá'u'lláh's message is that humanity is one single race, and that the day has come for its unification in one global society. One of the purposes of the Bahá'í faith is to help make this possible. Keeping with this philosophy, Bahá'ís come from a wide range of ethnic and cultural backgrounds.

There is no clergy in the Bahá'í faith. Because the human race has entered upon the age of its maturity, each individual is able to explore the revelation of God and to decide on the issues of life through prayer, reflection, and consultation with others. To make this possible, the Bahá'í scriptures have so far been translated into some 800 different languages. The way of life which Bahá'ís seek to cultivate, therefore, is one that encourages personal development. Daily prayer and meditation free the soul from conditioned patterns and open it to new possibilities.

Throughout the critical first century of the faith's existence, the provisions laid down by Bahá'u'lláh have protected the Bahá'í community from sectarianism, and have enabled it to adapt itself to the requirements of a rapidly evolving civilization.

The sufferings which their own fellow believers have experienced as victims of religious persecution have particularly sensitized Bahá'ís to Bahá'u'lláh's teachings on human rights. The Bahá'í International Community participates actively in United Nations consultations dealing with minority rights, the status of women, crime prevention, the control of narcotic drugs, the welfare of children and the family, and the movement toward disarmament.

The Bahá'í faith teaches that true religion promotes unity, and that unity is the fundamental prerequisite for the achievement of global peace. 'The well-being of mankind,' Bahá'u'lláh said, 'along with its peace and security, are unattainable unless and until its unity is firmly established.'

The Puppet Show

Dedicate the precious days of your lives to the betterment of the world.

– Bahá'u'lláh

$$\times\!\!\times$$

THERE WAS FOOD IN ABUNDANCE; MUSIC FILLED THE AIR; LIVERIED servants went about hither and thither, attending to the needs of the hundreds of guests.... There was a grand wedding celebration on in the luxurious family mansion of Mirza Buzurg, a prominent dignitary in the royal court of Persia. He had been in the service of the Shah of Persia as a minister and then as a governor. His wife Kadijih Khanum had ensured that the wedding celebration of their eldest son was suitably grand and lavish. Her younger son, Mirza Hussain Ali Nuri, was fascinated by all the ceremonies that were going on. But what enthralled the young lad above all else was the puppet show that had been arranged for the entertainment of the guests. He watched in amazement as the story unfolded before his eyes, and under the careful handling of the master puppeteer.

The story was set in a royal palace. The courtier puppets await the arrival of the king anxiously, having made grand preparations for his welcome. Some puppets sweep and mop the floor; other puppets decorate the palace with flowers; yet others lay out a red carpet for the king.

Soon, the puppet king arrives and sits on the throne. His soldiers drag a robber into the court, and request the king to punish him. Imperiously, His Majesty orders the thief's head to be severed from his body; the executioner arrives immediately with a huge butcher's knife and the robber is beheaded!

All of a sudden, a puppet messenger arrives to warn the king that enemies have entered his kingdom, and are likely to attack the palace any minute. The king orders his general to mobilize the army and prepare for war. And so the show went on. Young Hussain Ali watched it all in amazement, until it ended in thunderous applause from those present.

The audience dispersed. But the young lad stood rooted to the ground, unable to take his eyes off the puppet stage. What did he see? In a matter of minutes, the master puppeteer left the hall, carrying a small bag with him. 'Can you tell me what you are carrying in this bag?' the little boy asked him. 'All the puppets you saw on that stage a few minutes ago are now packed into this bag,' the man replied. 'And in this bag they will remain until I pull them out for the next show.'

Hearing this, the child was astonished. So this was what it was all about! In a flash it dawned on him that this world was also like an elaborate puppet show – and all of us are puppets, talking, laughing, planning, plotting, and absorbed in our petty lives. We do not even pause for a moment to realize that the show must soon come to an end – and back to the bag we must return. Then and there, the child made a mental resolve: life is too short; time is too precious; our sojourn upon this earth is ephemeral; therefore, I must not waste my time.

The young boy who watched the puppet show and learnt this valuable lesson was none other than the great founder of the Bahá'í faith. A mere puppet show was enough to make Bahá'u'lláh realize how illusory and transient were the trappings of earthly glory.

Bahá'u'lláh would write of this incident later: 'Ever since that day, all the trappings of the world have seemed in the eyes of this youth akin to that same spectacle. They have never been, nor will they ever be, of any weight and consequence, be it to the extent of a grain of mustard seed. Erelong these outward trappings, these visible treasures, these earthly vanities, these arrayed armies, these adorned vestures, these proud and overweening souls, all shall pass into the confines of the grave, as though into that box. In the eyes of those possessed of insight, all this conflict, contention and vainglory hath ever been, and will ever be, like unto the play and pastimes of children.'

Thought for Reflection

Gurudev Sadhu Vaswani often said that the best offering you can make to God is the tears of love and devotion. The gift of tears is what the Lord appreciates the most. We make all kinds of offerings to the Lord. In temples and in churches, people donate money, goods, clothes and food. How many of us offer to Him, the gift of tears?

Most of us are caught up in the entanglements of this world. We are enslaved by what the world has given us – pleasure, possessions, power – so much so that we do not even feel the need for God. But we forget a vital truth: if this earth is a shadow, how can we build upon it? What is there that we can be attached to in this world of transience? How then can we shed tears for Him?

It is only after much wandering that this realization dawns on man – that he is living a life of separation from God. He begins to feel that his wandering has taken him far away from God – and this realization brings tears to his eyes.

It is then that he decides that he must begin his journey back to God, for this is the only journey that will make his life worthwhile. When he embarks on this journey, out of the depths of his heart will arise the cry: 'Beloved, take the wanderer home!' and unbidden tears will flow out from his eyes.

Bahá'u'lláh and the Village Boy

Do not be content with showing friendship in words alone, let your heart burn with loving kindness for all who may cross your path.

– Bahá'u'lláh

Those were dark days for Bahá'u'lláh and his family. Just over a year after being exiled to Baghdad, Bahá'u'lláh was forced to withdraw to the mountainous wilderness of Kurdistan, where he lived alone for two years. He spent his time reflecting on the implications of the divine purpose to which he had been called. It was indeed, a period reminiscent of Moses' withdrawal to Mount Sinai, Jesus' 40 days and nights in the desert, and Muhammad's retreat to the cave on Mount Hira.

One day, near a village in the mountains, Bahá'u'lláh saw a young boy weeping bitterly. The great spiritual leader, always compassionate for anyone in sorrow, especially if it were a child, said to the young lad, 'Little man, why art thou weeping?'

The boy looked up at the one who spoke, and saw a *dervish*! 'Oh Sir!' he said and he fell to weeping afresh. 'The schoolmaster has punished me for writing so badly. I cannot write, and now I have no copy! I dare not go back to school.'

'Weep no longer. I will set a copy for thee, and show thee how to imitate it. And now thou canst take this; show it to thy school master.'

Then and there, writing paper and a quill were borrowed from the lad's school satchel and the copy of the writing exercise was made and given to the boy. His tears were wiped away with a kind smile and a loving gesture and the boy was sent off to school.

When the schoolmaster saw the writing which the boy had brought, he was astonished, for he recognized it as being of royal penmanship, this amazing script. 'Who gave this to thee?' said the master. 'He wrote it for me, the *dervish* on the mountain,' the boy replied, truthfully.

'He is no *dervish*, the writer of this copy, but a royal personage,' said the schoolmaster. This story caused many of the village people to set out to find this one, of whom many wonderful things were said. So great was the throng which pressed in upon him, that he had to go further away; again and again, he moved from place to place, hiding himself from the crowds, in the caves of the mountains, and in the desert places of that desolate land.

[Source: http://susangammage.com/bahaistories/quotepage. php?Stories%2FBaha%27u%27llah+-+Sulaymaniyyih%3B+]

THOUGHT FOR REFLECTION

Speak softly. Be humble. Be pure.

No matter what your status in life; no matter how rich and powerful you are; no matter how influential your connections may be, be humble. Treat all those below you with kindness and gentleness.

Why should we be humble? Because God resides within every one of us. He is richer than us, he is more powerful than us. He is more intelligent and is wiser than we are. He is omnipotent, omnipresent, and omniscient. His divine beauty, art, intellect, knowledge and ability are supreme. We are like a speck of dust, insignificant before His power and magnificence. And yet, He comes to live in the humble abode of our heart. Should this not teach us to be humble?

QURAT-UL-AIN 'TAHIRIH': A WOMAN AHEAD OF HER TIME

You can kill me as soon as you like, but you cannot stop the emancipation of women.

– Qurat-ul-Ain

Qurat-ul-Ain (Solace of the Eyes) or 'Tahirih' (The Pure One) are both names bestowed on Fatimah Baraghani, one of the most amazing women who was a committed and intense follower of the Bab; and a poet and theologian in her own right. She was one of the first believers of the Babi faith, and her life, her work and the manner of her death have made her one of the immortal figures associated with Bahá'u'lláh.

Fatimah was the daughter of Mulla Muhammad Salih Baraghani, who came from a very prominent family of Persia in those times. Though she belonged to a very conservative family and her father himself was a strict cleric with rigid views, he actually broke with tradition to tutor his daughter personally in theology, jurisprudence, Persian literature, and poetry. She was also permitted to take up Islamic studies and was able to grapple with issues related to religious law. Her father permitted her to sit behind a curtain and listen to the classes he conducted for his male students. Her ability to recite the Quran from memory was lauded by her teachers, and she exceeded the boys of the school in intelligence and grasping ability. Her father affectionately called her 'Zarrín Táj' (crown of gold) and lamented the fact that she was not a son to him. Thus, Fatimah reaped the benefits of learning encouraged by her father and her uncles, who were powerful clerics well connected with the Shah's court. Perhaps it was the scholarship that she received in those formative years that led her to radical views on religion and society in later life. This, combined with her strong views on women's status in society, impelled her to move towards the breakaway sect of the Bab.

Radical, free in thinking, intelligent and sharp witted, Fatimah was also a charismatic young woman, admired for her great physical beauty and charm. When she was around thirteen years of age, her father made her enter into a betrothal with a young man he chose for her. This was a marriage 'arranged' by her uncle and father, and by the age of fourteen, she was married to her cousin, Muhammad Baraghani. The marriage was not successful, although two sons and a daughter were born to the couple. Fatimah, as we saw, was renowned even at that young age for her beauty as well as her scholarship and her literary abilities; but the latter virtues were not regarded as desirable in a wife. Her husband did not like her literary pursuits or her thirst for learning.

In the library of her cousin, Javad Valiyani, Fatimah was first introduced to the radical writings of the Shaykhi Movement that was spreading rapidly in Iraq. Javad warned her that her father and uncle were opposed to these views, but she was increasingly influenced by what she read, and began to correspond with the leaders of the Movement in Iraq, to whom she posed questions on religious matters that troubled her. Siyyid Kazim, one of the leaders of the Movement, was greatly impressed by her intense interest in theological matters and was particularly pleased that he had such a devout student from the powerful Baraghani family.

At the age of twenty-six, Fatimah began to take greater control of her own life. She separated from her husband, and persuaded her father to permit her to undertake a pilgrimage to Karbala; the real reason for the trip was that she was very keen to meet her teacher in person. Unfortunately, Siyyid Kazim died before she could meet him; but his widow permitted Fatimah to set herself up in her home and teach Kazim's views to men from behind a curtain; as it was unthinkable in those days for a woman to appear before men in public, leave alone teach them. In this matter at least, she had to follow protocol. She was also allowed free access to all Kazim's unpublished works, and she spent a lot of time reading and assimilating his views. Her presence in Karbala and the role she had chosen for herself as a teacher created a controversy in the city, and the wrath of the male clergy forced her to withdraw from teaching for a while.

She now began correspondence with the Bab, who was well-known among followers of the Shaykhi sect and soon converted to his new faith. She became the seventeenth chosen member of his 'Living Circle', the select band of close followers whom he chose as his initial disciples. As the only woman in this group, she was often compared to Mary Magdalene, considered as Christ's Thirteenth Apostle. But Fatimah never ever met the Bab face-to-face; in distant Karbala, she remained one of his most ardent disciples and her teaching of the new faith led many people to embrace Babism.

The American Bahá'í scholar Martha Root says of her: 'Picture in your mind one of the most beautiful young women in Iran, a genius, a poet, the most learned scholar of the Quran and the traditions; think of her as the daughter of a jurist family of letters, daughter of the greatest high priest of her province and very rich, enjoying high rank, living in an artistic palace, and distinguished among her friends for her boundless, immeasurable courage. Picture what it must mean for a young woman like this, still in her twenties, to arise as the first woman disciple of the Bab.'

The Shiah Clergy of Karbala could not tolerate her conversion and her attempt to preach Babism. She was forced to leave the city, and one account states that she was stoned as she left for Baghdad. Here she started making public statements about the new faith and entering into scholarly debates with the clergy. This was thought to be highly unbecoming for a woman; especially one coming from an orthodox family like hers. However, she had many devoted women followers who thronged to hear her. The Shiah clergy of Iraq finally decided that since she was a Persian by birth, she should be sent back to the country of her birth.

Her father, uncles and brothers were deeply distressed by her radicalism and felt that she was bringing disgrace upon the family. They repeatedly requested her to recant her views and live by the tenets of orthodox faith; but this she refused to do. On her return to her family, she refused to live with her husband and took up residence in her brother's home. Her husband divorced her and her uncle disowned her; but she refused to give up her new faith. Unable to reconvert her, the orthodox clergy now began to accuse her of immorality. She protested that she was chaste and virtuous; her father believed her, but he was broken hearted that his brother had taken such a violent dislike to her.

Radical Shaykh views and Babi ideas were fast spreading in Persia at this time. There was unrest and disquiet in the public mind. Her uncle, a die-hard conservative who was intolerant of the new ideas, was murdered on account of his fanatic views and her husband openly blamed her for inciting hatred against him. He eventually forced the authorities to arrest her. She protested her innocence, but she was vilified and accused until the real murderer finally surrendered to the authorities. But her free days were now over; she was allowed to return home, but she was virtually under house arrest and her movements were constantly watched.

Her life was in danger now, and it was Bahá'u'lláh who arranged for her escape to Tehran. As believers of the Bab, they belonged to a common secret fraternity, and were in contact with each other. He had, as yet, not begun his own mission, and like Fatimah and many others, he was also a secret follower of the Bab. Fatimah was brought to Tehran and he allowed her to stay in his home, under the care of his wife. It was here that she developed a special affection for his son Abdul Ba'ha, who was then a small boy of three. Later, Abdul Ba'ha would write about her contribution to the composite Babi-Bahá'í faith and pay the most eloquent tribute to her in his book, *Memorials of the Faithful.*

While she was in Tehran, she expressed the desire to undertake a journey to Shiraz, where the Bab was imprisoned, to see the Messenger of God. But Bahá'u'lláh persuaded her to give up the idea as it could prove to be dangerous for her.

At long last, she and other Babis were given an opportunity to assert the expression of their faith, when the historical conference of Badasht was organized, and in part sponsored by Bahá'u'lláh. Here, many Babis met each other for the first time. The decision was made at this conference that there must be a complete break from the rituals and customs of the orthodox faith and the Shari'a law and a conversion to Babist beliefs and practises. Pressing for an armed rebellion to save the Bab and to break away from Islam, Fatimah removed her veil in public in a gesture of rebellion and defiance. This caused anger and revulsion among many men, and had serious repercussions.

Up until now, she had always been lauded as an epitome of purity and virtue. Now they accused her of being a loose and immoral woman.

When she first appeared unveiled among men, people screamed in horror at the sight; and it is said that one man was so horrified that he cut his own throat and fled the scene, with blood pouring from his neck. This act of unveiling was so controversial that it caused many Babis to give up the new faith. Vilified and slandered, Fatimah stood her ground bravely; and it was then that the title *Táhirih*, was bestowed on her by Bahá'u'lláh. The Bab, who heard about this incident, endorsed the title that had been bestowed on her.

Following a public outcry, *Táhirih* was arrested and taken to Tehran. The Shah was much impressed by her beauty and advised her to give up her faith so that he could pardon her and set her free. Some accounts even record that the Shah offered her a special place in his harem, if she recanted. This she refused to do; and for the next four years, she was put under house arrest in Tehran. She asserted before the court that she had a viewpoint and a belief, and it was no crime to hold to the same. She continued to speak to people who came to hear her and preached her radical views to them. She openly denounced polygamy, the veil and other restraints put upon women. While women were thrilled with her views, the orthodox clergy warned the Shah that she was becoming far too influential, and her heretic views were spreading fast among the people. They convinced him that she had to be put to death, for that was the only way to stop her.

Táhirih spent her last days in fasting and prayer. On the day of the execution, she was taken out into the garden at the dead of night and strangled with her own veil. Her body was dumped into a well and stones were thrown upon it.

She was no more than thirty-five when she met her cruel death, and her three children were orphaned. Eduard Polak, the Shah's European physician, who was an eyewitness to the execution, wrote about it thus: 'I was witness to the execution of Qurret el ayn [*sic*], who was executed by the war minister and his adjutants; the beautiful woman endured her slow death with superhuman fortitude.' Later, Abdu'l-Bahá who had been very fond of her in childhood, eulogized *Táhirih* as a 'woman chaste and holy, a sign and token of surpassing beauty, a burning brand of the love of God.'

THOUGHT FOR REFLECTION

I am afraid that for many generations we have been treating women as objects, commodities to be traded or exchanged, as weaklings in the control of men. If I sound harsh, consider what dowry is; do we not 'sell' our sons and brothers to the highest bidders who can offer us the maximum dowry? Do we not treat our daughters like objects which have to be marketed in marriage? Some people even refer to a woman as a doormat or a housemaid or unpaid servant and caretaker!

But let me say to you, woman is a shakti. Woman is a reservoir of power. It was with prophetic vision that Gurudev Sadhu Vaswani proclaimed: 'This century belongs to women. The woman soul will herald the beginning of the new age – a new civilization based on service, sacrifice, compassion and love. The new civilization will be based on selflessness.'

Yes! A new world is in the making! The man-made world has proved to be a broken, bleeding world, crumbling beneath its own burden. Man has blundered, for man has believed in force and violence. Even marriage at one time was marriage by capture. Man has had his chance. Now woman gets her chance; she is called upon to build a new world. She is a symbol of 'shakti'. Shakti is not force; shakti is the energy which integrates peoples, nations and communities.

Gurudev Sadhu Vaswani genuinely believed that the woman is the centre of social integration. He said that the woman has the shakti to rebuild the shattered world, in the strength of her intuitions, her purity, her simplicity, her spiritual aspirations, her sympathy and silent sacrifice. And therefore he asserted: The woman soul will lead us upwards, towards God.

Abdu'l-Bahá: His Father's Son

My name is Abdu'l-Bahá [literally, Servant of Baha]. My qualification is Abdu'l-Bahá. My reality is Abdu'l-Bahá. My praise is Abdu'l-Bahá. Thraldom to the Blessed Perfection [Bahá'u'lláh] is my glorious and refulgent diadem and servitude to the entire human race my perpetual religion... No name, no title, no mention, no commendation have I, nor will ever have, except Abdu'l-Bahá. This is my longing. This is my greatest yearning. This is my eternal life. This is my everlasting glory....

– Abdu'l-Bahá

ABBÁS EFFENDI WAS THE ELDEST OF THREE SURVIVING CHILDREN of Bahá'u'lláh and his wife Ásíyyih Khánum. Abbas's father had chosen to keep away from the life of politics and power. He led a life of quiet contemplation, simply doing as much good as he could in the service of the poor. Abbas's early life was luxurious and peace-filled. He was born and grew up in an environment of privilege, wealth, and love. As the grandson of the wealthy and influential Mirza Buzurg, he was brought up in the family's Tehran homes and country retreats, which were luxuriously appointed and beautifully decorated. He and his siblings had every advantage that a privileged noble family could offer.

But tragedy struck the family when the authorities began to persecute the Bab's followers. When a few of these radicals, mad with grief over the execution of the Bab, attempted the assassination of the Shah, Bahá'u'lláh, who had nothing whatever to do with the plot, was arrested under suspicion, and imprisoned in a notorious dungeon, known as the Black Pit. His home was looted and the family had to seek refuge in a rented home in a back alley, a far cry from their palatial residence. Young Abbas, who was just recovering from an attack of tuberculosis, was forced to endure separation from his beloved father. Apart from this emotional trauma, he also had to face deprivation, isolation and attacks and insults from other children in the neighbourhood.

One day, his mother sent him to his aunt's house to borrow some money to buy food for the family. On the way back, he was chased and stoned by street urchins, who called out 'He is a Babi! He is a Babi!' He was stoned and abused; he sought refuge in a neighbour's house, where he was forced to stay until darkness fell. But when he came out, the boys were still waiting to hound him and chase him! He ran as fast as he could, reaching home to collapse in exhaustion. The anxious mother, who had been waiting all afternoon for his return, asked him repeatedly, 'What happened? Why are you so panic-stricken?' But the young lad could not utter a word in reply.

Abbas was taken by friends of the family to visit his father in prison. The visit left him scarred emotionally. He would write later, 'We entered a small, narrow doorway, and went down two steps, but beyond those, one could see nothing. In the middle of the stairway, all of a sudden we heard His blessed voice: "Do not bring him in here" and so they took me back. We sat outside, waiting for the prisoners to be led out. Suddenly they brought the Blessed Perfection (Bahá'u'lláh) out of the dungeon. He was chained to several others. What a chain! It was very heavy. The prisoners could only move it along with great difficulty. Sad and heart-rending it was!'

He was fortunate that his beloved father was released from prison four months later; but the family lands and property were confiscated and they were banished from Persia, and forced to seek refuge in Iraq, which was then under the Ottoman empire. Abdu'l-Bahá, who was just nine years old at that time, was destined to never see his native land again.

It was a trying time for the whole family. The father was in very poor health after his long incarceration in the Black Pit. The mother was pregnant; all of them were grieving for their beloved child, Mihdi, the baby of the family who had to be left behind in Persia, as he was too weak to travel. The mountain roads to Baghdad were treacherous and covered in snow, and they were ill-equipped for the hard winter with very few supplies and inadequate winter clothing. When they finally reached Baghdad five months later, they were ill and exhausted.

It was not a peaceful life that awaited them here. Local dissension forced Bahá'u'lláh to leave the family and seek refuge in the mountains of Kurdistan. The family had to endure two more years of separation from him; but when Bahá'u'lláh returned two years later, there was a period of relative quiet and peace. By now Bahá'u'lláh was acknowledged as the leader of the small but growing Babi community.

Abbas was not sent to school in Baghdad, but was privileged to receive personal instructions from his father. He read and memorized Babi teachings with fervour. Soon, he was acting as a secretary, scribe, and personal assistant to his father. When he was barely nineteen, his father sent him to negotiate with troublesome authorities in Baghdad, who were not very well disposed towards Babis. He was also at this time, engaged in transcribing his father's sacred writings. When they were forced to move to Anatolia in Turkey, it was he who made all the travel arrangements, attending to the comforts of every member and also taking care of his father's needs. After four years of exile in Constantinople, the family was banished once again, to Adrianapole. Abbas now took on the name of Abdu'l-Bahá, meaning the servant of Bah'a.

When Bahá'u'lláh publicly proclaimed his mission in Adrianople, he gradually withdrew from the general public, leaving Abdu'l-Bahá to manage the affairs of the family and of the Bahá'í exiles. Thus Abdu'l-Bahá became his father's representative in all matters except those internal to the Bahá'í community.

For the next forty years, the family was virtually under house arrest in the city of Acre. Here, even as he was shouldering serious responsibilities, he witnessed the death of his brother, and the constant suffering of the other exiles who had followed his father. Amidst all this pain and suffering, he maintained his courtesy, his smiling demeanor, his attitude of selfless service, his devotion to the cause, his positive spirit and his sense of humour. In 1872, after his release from two years of harsh confinement in the citadel of Acre, Abdu'l-Bahá, at the behest of his father, married Munírih Khánum, whose father had been a distinguished early Babi from Isfahan. Over the years, the couple had nine children – seven daughters and two sons; only four of their children, all daughters, survived to adulthood.

As early as in the years at Adrianapole, Bahá'u'lláh had named his son his spiritual successor. Inscribed in the *Tablet of the Branch (Súriy-i-Ghusn)* are the Prophet's own words: 'Render thanks unto God, O people, for His appearance; for verily He is the most great Favour unto you, the most perfect bounty upon you; and through Him every mouldering bone is quickened. Who so turneth towards Him hath turned towards God, and whoso turneth away from Him hath turned away from My Beauty, hath repudiated My Proof, and transgressed against Me.'

Following the death of the Master, there was a revolt by Mírzá Muhammad Alí, Bahá'u'lláh's brother, and his band of followers who attempted to violate the provisions of Bahá'u'lláh's testament and tried to usurp Abdu'l-Bahá's authority. This was a cause of great anguish to the new leader and his faithful supporters. But the community reunited behind him, after an initial period of strife and disturbance.

Abdu'l-Bahá travelled extensively in Europe and North America, promoting the spread of the Bahá'í faith in the West, the proclamation of its principles, and the firm establishment of Bahá'í communities on the two continents. In his numerous addresses to western audiences, he effectively demonstrated the relevance of his father's teachings to many contemporary issues and problems.

The last few years of his life were spent in extensive correspondence with Bahá'í followers all over the West as well as in personal interaction with thousands of pilgrims who came to visit the holy shrines of the Master in Acre. This had the effect of deepening the understanding of recent converts and veteran Bahá'ís alike. He also supported and strengthened their efforts to establish an organizational framework for the Bahá'í faith and provided inspiration for its expansion.

Abdu'l-Bahá passed away in Haifa at the age of seventy-seven in the early hours of the morning on November 28, 1921.

THOUGHT FOR REFLECTION

What is it that the Guru does for us? What is it that we can get from no one but him?

The Guru creates us anew. We are reborn in the spirit, when we surrender to him. He is much more than an 'instructor', 'adviser' or 'professor'. He is an enlightener with a transforming power. Spirituality is, as we have seen, a tremendous *shakti*. And the Guru's *shakti* lies in this – that he leads forth the disciple not only towards liberation – but towards himself, so that the disciple becomes a teacher in his own right.

Vignettes from the Lives of the Baháʼí Masters

Hear no evil, and see no evil, abase not thyself, neither sigh and weep. Speak no evil, that thou mayest not hear it spoken unto thee, and magnify not the faults of others that thine own faults may not appear great; and wish not the abasement of anyone, that thine own abasement be not exposed. Live then the days of thy life, that are less than a fleeting moment, with thy mind stainless, thy heart unsullied, thy thoughts pure, and thy nature sanctified, so that, free and content, thou mayest put away this mortal frame, and repair unto the mystic paradise and abide in the eternal kingdom for evermore.

– Baháʼuʼlláh

The Conference at Badasht

THE CONFERENCE OF BADASHT WAS HELD IN JULY 1848, IN A village at some distance from Tehran. Eighty-one of the Bab's most distinguished followers came together in this Conference. The principal participants were Baháʼuʼlláh, Quddus and Tahirih.

Although at first Baháʼuʼlláh did not appear to have any special rank among the Bab's disciples, his role at the Conference was decisive. He rented the gardens in which the Conference was held, and for twenty-two days, all those who had gathered enjoyed his generous hospitality. Each day Baháʼuʼlláh revealed a Tablet to be read before the assembled believers. To each He gave a new name. To Tahirih and Quddus he gave the titles by which they will be known throughout history. The title Tahirih means The Pure One, and Quddus means Holy. He Himself was, from that time forward, to be known by the name of Baha. Later the Bab would reveal a special Tablet for each one of those who had attended the Conference, addressing them by the names they had received on that occasion.

The Conference of Badasht also marked the beginning of the most turbulent stage in the development of the Babi Faith. Soon the persecution of its followers would reach new levels of intensity, and many would be called to martyrdom. It was as if the Conference were a farewell gathering, from where they would go out to perform deeds of great heroism, only to be reunited in the Kingdom of God.

(Source: *Ruhi Book* 4)

Crisis and Victory

…The Message of the Bab continued to spread like wildfire throughout the district. Alarmed, the followers of the chief theologian began to put pressure on him to take some form of action, and finally he decided to send his two most outstanding pupils to visit Bahá'u'lláh and investigate the nature of the Message He was propagating. This is the story of what happened when those two representatives entered the presence of Bahá'u'lláh.

On being told, upon their arrival in Takur, that Bahá'u'lláh had left for His winter home, the representatives of the theologian decided to follow Him there. When they arrived they found Bahá'u'lláh engaged in revealing a commentary on one of the chapters of the Quran. As they sat and listened to Him, they were profoundly impressed by the eloquence of His presentation and the extraordinary manner in which He spoke. One of the representatives, unable to contain himself, arose from his seat and walked to the back of the room and, in an attitude of respect and submissiveness, stood still beside the door. Trembling and with eyes full of tears, he told his companion: "I am powerless to question Bahá'u'lláh. The questions I had planned to ask Him have vanished suddenly from my memory. You are free either to proceed with your inquiry or to return alone to our teacher and inform him of the state in which I find myself. Tell him from me that I can never again return to him. I can no longer forsake this threshold.

But the other representative was equally struck by Bahá'u'lláh's words and followed the example of his friend. 'I have ceased to recognize my teacher,' was his reply. 'This very moment, I have vowed to God to dedicate the remaining days of my life to the service of Bahá'u'lláh, my true and only Master.'

The news of the conversion of the theologian's pupils spread rapidly among the population of Nur. Dignitaries, state officials, religious leaders, traders and peasants crowded to the presence of Bahá'u'lláh. Hundreds were brought under the banner of the new Faith.

(Source: *Ruhi Book* 4, p. 84-85)

The Story of Two Martyrs

I wish to tell you the story of two martyrs; one was a Persian nobleman, a favorite at court, possessed of much wealth and known throughout all the country. When it was discovered that he was a follower of Bahá'u'lláh, this glorious man was taken into custody and in company with another thrown into prison without food or water. The third day one of them requested the jailer to give him a cup of tea. Struck with his attitude of humility, the jailer did as requested; thanking him the prisoner said: 'I am exceedingly sorry to trouble you, but pray have a little patience with our requests tonight, for tomorrow night we shall be the guests of God.'

On the fourth day they were taken out of prison and two bears were made to dance before them; also several monkeys were brought, in order to humiliate them. Solomon Kahn and his friend were taken into a room, their breasts lacerated and in the yawning apertures lighted candles were placed. In Persia this is considered the most degrading form of torture.

Then they started on parade through the town. Solomon Kahn looking about him said: 'There is no need for this commotion. Why such ado about our death? Verily, this is our wedding feast and we are very happy.' Accompanied by a band and followed by many people, they were paraded through the bazaars and streets of the city. People pricked them with long needles, saying, 'Dance for us!' With unflinching courage and exultant joy they walked along; from morn till eve walked they through the city. When the candles burned down, they were renewed by the jailers.

All the time our heroes were calm and happy and as they marched they smiled at the people on the right and left of them and looking heavenward murmured prayers. Finally they arrived at the outer gates of the city where each was cut into four pieces.

Teheran has four high gates and a section of their bodies adorned either side of the gates. Even while being dismembered, Solomon Kahn was praying and supplicating God. This story will be found in a history compiled by an enemy of this cause, for all has been recorded by the Shah's historians. At the end, the historian says of Solomon Kahn, 'This man was possessed by an evil spirit.' This account shows how readily the believers of God give their lives, how self-sacrificing they are, eternally firm and steadfast. These illumined souls are the result of the light of Bahá'u'lláh, who attracted them to the kingdom of God with such reflective power that like fixed stars these martyrs will ever shine from the horizon of El-Abhá.

(Source: Abdu'l-Baha, *Divine Philosophy*, p. 47-49)

The Divine Reason

Munirih Khanum, wife of Abdu'l-Bahá ... had this to say:

Five of my children died in the poisonous climate of Akkra. The bad air was, in truth, only the outside material reason. The inner spiritual reason was that no son of the Master should grow into manhood.

When my darling little son Husayn passed away, Bahá'u'lláh wrote the following: 'The knowledge of the reason why your sweet baby has been called back is in the mind of God, and will be manifested in His own good time. To the prophets of God the present and the future are as one.'

Therefore I understand how that wisdom has ordained the uniting of the two families, that of Bahá'u'lláh and of the Bab, in the person of Shoghi Effendi, eldest son of our daughter, Diyaiyyih Khanum, by her marriage with Aqa Mirza Hadi Afnan.

I have been writing to the friends in Persia; "You are longing to meet us, we are longing to meet you; what is the wisdom in our separation?"

Let us understand that if Bahá'u'lláh had not been exiled to Baghdad, Constantinople, Adrianople, and 'Akkra, the Divine Message could not have been so quickly spread, and the prophecies in the Holy Books would not have been fulfilled.

(Lady Blomfield, *The Chosen Highway*)

Forgive Thine Enemies

It is related of Shaykh Mahmud of Akka that he hated the Bahá'ís. While many of his fellow-townsmen had gradually come to realize how very wrong they had been and were speaking of the prisoners in terms of appreciation and praise, Shaykh Mahmud remained adamant in his hatred.

One day he was present at a gathering where people were talking of Abdu'l-Bahá as a good man, a remarkable man. The Shaykh could bear it no longer and stormed out, saying that he would show up this 'Abbas Effendi for what He was. In blazing anger he rushed to the mosque, where he knew Abdu'l-Bahá could be found at that hour, and laid violent hands upon Him.

The Master looked at the Shaykh with that serenity and dignity which only He could commend, and reminded him of what the Prophet Muhammad had said: "Be generous to the guests, even should he be an infidel." Shaykh Mahmud turned away. His wrath had left him. So had his hate. All that he was conscious of was a deep sense of shame and bitter compunction. He fled to his house and barred the door. Some days later he went straight into the presence of Abdu'l-Bahá, fell on his knees, and besought forgiveness: 'Which door but thine can I seek; whose bounty can I hope for but thine?' He became a devoted Bahá'í.

(Source: Honnold, Annamarie, *Vignettes from the Life of Abdu'l-Bah'a*, p. 50)

Thought for Reflection

Who is a true saint?

A true saint is he, who does not dwell apart from the people. A true saint is who mingles with the people, he who takes part in daily activities but who, does not for one moment, forget God. A true saint is he who lives the message – '*Each day, aspire to live in the love of God, in fellowship with broken ones, in kindness and in compassion, in love and in truth.*'

BUDDHISM

BRIEF INTRODUCTION

*B*UDDHISM IS ONE OF THE GREAT INDIC RELIGIONS, WHICH WAS initiated in North India around the fifth century BC by Gautama Buddha. It is based entirely on the teachings of the Buddha, and may be said to have been founded by the Buddha himself. But many Buddhists believe that there were countless Buddhas even before his time, just as there will be many after him.

A Buddha may be defined simply as 'an enlightened one' although some Pali scholars take the word to mean 'an awakened teacher'. Buddhism is a faith that encompasses a variety of traditions, beliefs and practises, largely based on teachings attributed to Gautama, the Buddha.

In a sense, Buddhism was one among numerous new ascetic religious and philosophical groups that broke with the Brahminic tradition and rejected the authority of the Vedas and the Brahmins. These groups, whose members were known as Shramanas, are now thought to belong to a non-vedic strand of Indian thought distinct from Indo-Aryan faith.

The history of Buddhism as a religion, begins with the life of Gautama Buddha, a historical figure whose life story is recorded in several early Buddhist texts. The foundation of Buddhism is indeed in the teachings of the Buddha, who lived the life of a wandering ascetic, spreading his message among the people as he moved among them. Starting in India, the cradle of all Indic faiths, Buddhism spread across Asia and is today established as a faith and a way of life, virtually in every continent of the globe.

Many Buddhists regard their faith as a philosophy rather than as a religion. But it is a definite system of beliefs and practises, and there are several sects or schools of Buddhism today, including the two major branches, Theravada (the school of the elders) and Mahayana (the great vehicle). Sub-sects include Pure Land, Zen, Nichiren Buddhism, Tibetan Buddhism, Shingon, Tendai and Shinnyoen. There is also a third branch, Vajrayana, which is recognized by many. In recent times, scholars have seen the birth of several new offshoots of the old faith, which they classify as Modern Buddhism.

If there is one thing that is common to all the sects, it is the basic adherence to a traditional formula in which the practitioner takes refuge in The Three Jewels: the Buddha, the Dhamma (the teachings of the Buddha) and the Sanga (the Buddhist community). Buddhism is also practised by adherents alongside many other religious traditions – including Taoism, Confucianism, Shinto, traditional religions, Shamanism and Animism – throughout East and Southeast Asia. Modern influences have led to many new forms of Buddhism that significantly depart from traditional beliefs and practises.

Sangam
Saranam
Gachhami:
The Blessed One and His Community of Monks

The sanga is the community of people who have the perfect right to cut through your trips and feed you with their wisdom, as well as the perfect right to demonstrate their own neurosis and be seen through by you. The companionship within the sanga is a kind of clean friendship – without expectation, without demand, but at the same time, fulfilling.

– Chögyam Trungpa Rinpoche

The Monastic order that the Buddha established was not some kind of a repressive community in which people lost their freedom to be themselves, and lived lives that were straitjacketed by rules and regulations. Rather, these aspirants chose the sanga to exercise the ultimate choice of taking refuge – becoming homeless and groundless and rootless to discover their own inner truths. Thus for many of them, taking refuge in the *sanga* became an expression of freedom: freedom from worldly bonds and desires and freedom to relate to the great truths and discover their own Buddha Nature.

There are many beautiful stories from the early *sanga* of the Master that tell us of this unfettered, aspirational life of inner quest.

The Power of Dhamma

One day, the Buddha and Ananda, his most trusted disciple, were walking towards a village when they saw an outcaste, Nidhi, walking out of the village, heading towards them on the road. They could see that Nidhi was carrying a large container of human excreta, which was his job to clean up and take away from the houses of the villagers. When Nidhi saw the Master approaching, he was both confused and embarrassed. Here was the Enlightened One about to cross his path, and he, a low-born outcaste, carrying defilement… No, no! It could not be!

The truth was that Nidhi was filled with deep devotion and reverence for the Master; and it was only matched by his deep sense of low self-respect and inborn loathing for himself. In short, he felt he was unworthy of even standing before the Buddha. To avoid what he felt would be a very disrespectful encounter, Nidhi suddenly left the road and turned into a narrow lane that led into the bushes.

The Buddha had seen Nidhi and had immediately sensed what was going on in his mind. He signalled to Ananda to walk on to the village, while he himself took another lane to approach Nidhi directly.

Coming face-to-face with the Master at a time when he thought he had just about managed to avoid meeting him, Nidhi was so upset that he dropped the container of excretion that he was carrying. The filth spread on the ground all around him. Overwhelmed by shame and delicacy, he sank to his feet, sobbing, 'Master, Master, forgive an unworthy one!'

Gently, the Buddha placed his hand on the man's shoulder and said, 'Nidhi, stand up!'

Nidhi could not believe his ears. The Blessed One had not only taken a special effort to go out of his way to meet him, but actually knew his name! 'How could he have known my name?' he wondered. 'How did he even know that I was trying to avoid him? And why has he taken the trouble to come here to meet me, an outcaste?'

And the tears flowed freely from his eyes.

The Buddha wiped his tears away and said to him, 'Nidhi, I would like you to join my *sanga* and become a monk.'

Nidhi could not contain himself any longer. 'Master, I am a low and unclean person. Your community is the sought after refuge of scholars, soldiers and aristocrats. I am not fit enough to be in such august company.'

The Buddha smiled. 'That is not the way we think, Nidhi,' he explained. 'Let me say to you, the Dhamma is like the cleanest and purest water; it can wash away the defilements and impurities of accumulated births. The Dhamma is like the most intense fire; it can burn away all forms of ignorance. The Dhamma is like the ocean, which can contain many things within itself. In the *sanga*, we do not entertain distinctions of caste and creed and birth and status, for we know that they are mere illusions.

'Even the bodies we wear, dear Nidhi, are mere illusions. I want you to rid yourself of these illusions of high and low, clean and unclean, and follow me from this minute.'

At that very moment, the veil of ignorance was lifted from Nidhi's mind and heart, and he decided to follow the Buddha as he had been told. His old life was cast away as he merged into the Master's community.

Sweep and Clean

One day, as the Buddha was passing near the monks' quarters, he heard someone sobbing loudly. The soul of compassion as he was, the Blessed One went in to investigate the matter.

It was a quiet and introverted young monk, Ksudrapanthaka, who was sobbing his heart out. He was surrounded by a group of monks who were not exactly sympathetic to his condition.

On enquiry, Buddha learnt that Ksudrapanthaka had followed his elder brother into the monastic life, as he had no one else to care for him. He was somewhat slow and dull; and though his brother had tried his best to teach him the Dhamma, he simply could not learn, he simply could not make any progress. Now, the elder brother had washed his hands of him and told him to leave the community.

'I don't want to go home! I have been so peaceful and happy, here in the *sanga*,' wept Ksudrapanthaka, 'but I just can't learn! I cannot remember what my brother teaches me; I cannot even repeat the teachings after him, and he has grown tired of me. He has asked me to leave the *sanga* and go back to the village, as I am incapable of learning anything. Blessed Master, please help me! Teach me how to learn, teach me to remember what I have been taught, because I cannot bear to leave your presence and go away from here.'

The Sakhya Muni said to everyone gathered around Ksudrapanthaka, 'Brother monks, to know that one is ignorant is also a form of wisdom; just as to imagine that one is very wise is a form of acute ignorance. How much you know and how much you have learnt is not as important as you think.' Turning to the sobbing monk Ksudrapanthaka, he said, 'From today, you will come to Ananda for your lessons every morning.'

The Master bade Ananda to take special care of the distraught Ksudrapanthaka. But a few days later, Ananda had to admit defeat. 'It is impossible to teach him, Master,' Ananda lamented. The Buddha then decided that he would himself take on the task of teaching Ksudrapanthaka.

The following day, the Buddha taught Ksudrapanthaka a simple sutra: 'Sweep and clean! Sweep and clean!' He made the monk repeat the sutra several times before him, and told him to keep on repeating it throughout the day, no matter what he was doing.

Unfortunately for him, Ksudrapanthaka could not remember even this simple sutra. The Buddha was patience personified; day after day, he spent a great deal of time with the dull monk, repeating the words, and urging him to remember them of his own accord. When this did not work, the Blessed One thought of a different method. He took Ksudrapanthaka out into the courtyard, gave him a broom and bade him clean the whole courtyard, repeating with each stroke of the broom, the sutra, 'Sweep and clean! Sweep and clean!'

Alas, some of his brother monks were not so patient and forbearing as the Master. They came and complained to the Buddha that Ksudrapanthaka disturbed their morning meditations and chanting, by constantly crossing their paths with his broom, muttering the sutra which he was desperately trying to memorize; hitting their legs with his broom, when they were out walking in the courtyard, as he looked heavenward, trying to remember the simple words; and constantly mumbling the words, as they observed silence.

'Let us send him away,' they said in one voice. 'He cannot learn anything.' But there were other members of the *sanga*, who were inspired by the Master's example to help him. With their support and the Buddha's grace, Ksudrapanthaka was able to master the sutra. But he did not stop there; he began to think about the words as he suited the action to the words and swept the courtyard clean. 'Sweeping and cleaning clears all the dirt and dust that has gathered in the yard,' he thought to himself. 'But there are two things that must be swept and cleaned: one is the outside and the other is inside. Therefore, I must also sweep my mind clean of all its impurities.' And as he began to think on these lines, he grew in wisdom and reflection.

He reflected on the words of the Buddha, as his capacity to remember and retain all that he was taught, improved gradually. He reasoned to himself, 'The blessed Master tells us that anger, hatred and greed are the inner impurities which we must clean up. And this requires great wisdom, which I can only get from the Blessed One.'

Ksudrapanthaka continued to think, even as he swept and cleaned the yard diligently. His constant practise of reflection on the Master's teachings transformed his thinking, and he became wiser and wiser. 'Wisdom is the remedy for suffering,' he reflected. 'It takes wisdom to realize that desire is the root of all suffering. It takes wisdom to conquer desire and annihilate all suffering.'

The more he thought and reflected, the more radiant and bright his eyes and face became. He glowed with the light of hard-earned wisdom. Soon he reached a state of utter equanimity, free from desire, untouched by joy or sorrow, and was always in a constant state of mindful awareness. It was not long before the dull, slow and 'stupid' monk became enlightened.

He went and bowed before the Master. 'You taught me the sutra, "Sweep and clean". It has helped me clean myself from the inside. I have perceived, and have swept my mind clear of dust and dirt. I thank you for this great gift of awareness.'

The Master smiled and said to Ananda and the other monks, 'It is not enough to learn from discourses and learn the sutras. How can anyone benefit if he does not perceive the meaning of the many sutras he recites? Of what avail are the sutras if one does not practise what they teach? It is better that each of us learns just one sutra and practises it really well to be assured of attaining the way. Ksudrapanthaka is indeed a shining example to us all!'

From then onwards, Ksudrapanthaka became one of the most respected monks in the community.

Two Alms Bowls

It was dusk. The simple meal of the sanga was over, the monks began their walking meditation. But the Master noticed that one promising young monk seemed to be somewhat perturbed.

Calling the monk over to him, the Master enquired gently, 'Is there something that is troubling you?'

'I would be the last person to break the rules laid down for the monks, Blessed One,' the young monk blurted out. 'But I am in a dilemma...'

'Perhaps you would like to tell me what it is.'

'Yesterday, while I was out begging for alms, a kind householder gave me a beautifully decorated wooden begging bowl. In my mind I decided that Ananda was the one person who should have that bowl.'

'That was really kind of you! Do go on.'

'The trouble is that Ananda is away on a teaching yatra now, and he will not be back with us for a week. The rules of the sanga stipulate that no monk shall be permitted to have more than one alms bowl for longer than twenty-four hours. I just don't know what to do.'

The Buddha was exceptionally sensitive to people's feelings and sentiments. He called the monks around him and announced, 'Hereafter, every monk will be permitted to keep two alms bowls with him for the period of a week at a time.'

By changing his own rule to help the young monk, the Buddha expressed his appreciation for Ananda as well as the devotion of the monk. The Master could always find a solution that made everyone happy!

———◇◆◇———

Thought for Reflection

Our ancient scriptures taught sankhya and yoga. Sankhya is knowledge; yoga is action. Ignorant men tend to separate the two: but in reality, they are inseparable.

Gnana and karma – wisdom and action – should be in harmony, for there is no conflict between the two. There is only a question of discipline.

May I also add that according to our sages, gnana does not mean book of knowledge. A *gnani*, Gurudev Sadhu Vaswani often told us, is not a bookworm. A man may quote from many books – but he may not have true wisdom. Therefore, Gurudev Sadhu Vaswani taught us, that gnana is direct perception. A true gnani seeks truth. He is not a mere reporter. He does not talk by hearsay. He speaks because he sees and feels. He has *sakshatkara* or direct perception.

Gnana is not gathered from books, but from inner life. This, our ancient rishis cultivated, and the Guru is one who can impart to us – not merely the text, not merely the 'sayings' and words – but the distilled essence of that wisdom.

The Story of Queen Mallika

*Some women are better than men, O king. There are women
who are wise and good, who regard their mothers-in-law as
goddesses, and who are pure in word, thought and deed. They
may one day give birth to brave sons who would rule a country.*

– The Buddha's words to King Pasenadi

*D*URING THE TIME OF THE BUDDHA, A DAUGHTER WAS BORN TO THE
foreman of gardeners and garland makers in the city of Sravasti, capital
of the Kosala kingdom. She was called Mallika and she grew up to be
a beautiful, virtuous and well-behaved young lady who was indeed a
source of great joy to her parents.

When she was in the full bloom of youth, she set out on a picnic
with her friends. She took three steamed rice cakes with her, for lunch.
As the girls were playing in a shady grove, the Blessed One and his
brother monks came by, begging for alms as was their custom. Mallika
did not know who the radiant ascetic was; but she was so deeply struck
by her first darshan of the Buddha, that she put all the food she had into
his alms bowl, and prostrated at his feet asking him to bless her. The
Master smiled his radiant smile, and Mallika went away, touched by an
inexplicable joy that filled her whole being. The Buddha watched her
with the smile that lit up both his eyes and his countenance.

Ananda, who was accompanying him, knew that the Master's smile
carried a special significance. 'I know you do not smile without reason,

Blessed One,' he said. 'May I know what has brought this radiant smile on you?'

'That young lady has given away all the food she had to me,' said the Buddha. 'Before the night is out, she will have become the Queen of Kosala.'

'How is that possible?' asked Ananda, amazed. 'She is from a poor family, and the King of Kosala is a proud man who can choose his bride from the wealthiest family in the land…'

'And yet, Mallika, the garland maker's daughter, will soon be his queen,' said the Buddha. 'She will surely reap the good karma for her act of compassion and charity to an ascetic today.'

It seemed incredible at that time; how could a poor, low caste girl be elevated to the position of queen of the land?

As for Mallika, she spent the rest of the day in a state of elevated consciousness. Her heart overflowed with joy, and as night fell, she walked about the public garden, singing her heart out in a beautiful melody.

Now, King Pasenadi of Kosala happened to be returning to his capital after an unsuccessful encounter with his rival, the King of Magadha. Battle-weary and disheartened, the melodious song of the maiden brought great comfort to his heart. He called out to the maid, and enquired who she was, and whether she was married. Mallika who was unaware of his identity, readily came forward and looked into his eyes as she answered, 'My name is Mallika and I am unmarried.' Such was her radiant beauty, such was her love-filled gaze, that the king lost his heart to her. He asked her to lead him to her parents; at the cottage of the humble gardener, he asked for their daughter's hand in marriage. The gardener, who knew his royal visitor by sight, was speechless with joy. Then and there, he sent for his royal entourage and took Mallika to his palace to become his chief queen.

The whole of Sravasti rejoiced in the good fortune that had befallen the garland maker's virtuous daughter. She was beautiful like a goddess and her selfless act of giving her food away to the Buddha was the talk of the town. 'She is the young lady who gave alms to the Buddha,' they said. 'Look where her good karma has taken her.' Such was the impact of this event, that people became more generous and charitable, inspired by her example.

Mallika was dearly beloved of the king, who lavished her with love and generosity. In those days, it was the custom of the Buddha to spend the rainy months in Sravasti. The young queen became his most ardent disciple, and benefitted from his teachings.

Once she asked the Buddha why some girls were beautiful, but poor and talented, while some were wealthy, beautiful and unskilled; and then again, some were rich and ugly but highly skilled, while a few unfortunate ones were poor and ugly and without any talents. It is not as if she was the first to notice these things; but she was convinced that there must be an underlying cause to this, which she was keen to learn.

The Buddha explained to her that beauty, wealth, skill and talents were all the result of one's karma; those who were gentle and forgiving, would be blessed with great beauty in their next birth; those who were generous and kind would be blessed with great wealth; those who were never envious of others' good fortune, would be blessed with special skills and talents. Whichever of these virtues one cultivated, they would show up in their destiny; and at times, as a combination of one or more of these graces.

When Mallika heard this, she decided that she would always be kind and generous to the poor, and to be gentle and sweet to all her subjects. Very soon, she surrendered to the Master and his Dhamma, becoming his lifelong disciple. She had a long ebony-lined hall built for the sanga, where discussions and discourses could be held for the benefit of the public.

She was also a loving and loyal wife to King Pasenadi. She was always obedient; she uttered only the gentlest and kindest words; she was generous to her subjects; all the monks of the sanga held her in great esteem as the epitome of gentleness and kindness.

She was soon to prove that she was singularly free from jealousy; for very soon, the king married a princess who belonged to the Sakhya clan, and was related to the family of the Buddha. In his infatuation, he also made her the principal queen; but Mallika loved the new queen like her own sister, and readily allowed her to take the lead in the royal household. It came to pass that the new queen gave birth to a son, who became the crown prince; while Mallika gave birth to a baby girl.

The king was bitterly disappointed and asked the Buddha why Mallika was not able to bear a son for him. Smiling, the Buddha replied that a woman was far superior to a man, if she were blessed with beauty, intelligence and good grace. 'Your son will of course become a king,' he said to Pasenadi. 'But your daughter can become the mother of an almighty ruler,' he explained.

The words of the Blessed One were never ever proved false; Princess Vajira, Mallika's daughter grew up to marry the King of Magadha and in her lineage was born the great Emperor Asoka.

King Pasenadi was also drawn to the Buddha by Mallika's influence. It happened this way:

One night, King Pasenadi had a fearful dream in which terrible demon-like creatures in gruesome form yelled 'Du, Sa, Na, So' in blood-curdling fashion. The king woke up in a cold sweat, and ordered the Brahmins to be consulted on what he feared to be an ill-omen.

The greedy priests of the royal circle saw an opportunity to make money out of the king's inordinate fear. They said to him that the omens were indeed terrible, and that a great sacrifice had to be performed to ward off the impending evil to the kingdom. Forthwith a huge yagyashala was constructed and dozens of dumb, defenceless animals brought for sacrifice. The greedy Brahmins were rubbing their hands in glee at the thought of the gold and the gifts that they would collect very soon; and the king was still reeling from the fear of the nameless.

Mallika, who spent most of the time in reflection and meditation, was quite unaware of the hectic preparations going on in the main palace. One morning, when she went to greet her sister-queen, she saw the great sacrificial altar being built and the scores of wailing animals tethered to the poles for the forthcoming sacrifice. Upon enquiry, she learnt that a great sacrifice was about to be conducted to ward off evil spirits that had gathered around the king.

Distressed at the himsa that was about to take place in the palace, Mallika confronted the king to ask him how he could allow such a sacrifice to take place in his palace. The king, who was selfish and superstitious, grumbled that she never ever took an interest in his welfare; else, how could she be indifferent to his problems? The sacrifice was being planned for his benefit; surely she could not question its necessity.

'But of course I care for your welfare, Your Majesty,' Mallika said to him. 'My only concern is that you must consult the best Brahmin in the kingdom for this purpose.'

'And who could be a better Brahmin in Kosala than my head priest?' asked the king suspiciously.

'The Sakhya Muni, of course,' replied Mallika.

'But my dear, he is not a Brahmin by birth,' the king protested.

'Dear lord, one is not a Brahmin by virtue of his birth alone,' Mallika explained. 'The Awakened One is first and foremost in the world of Gods and men, the first of all Brahmins. Let us take our troubles to him.'

The king went directly to the grove where Buddha was staying and narrated his fearful nightmare to him. 'What will become of me?' he asked the Buddha in deep distress.

The Buddha assured him that no harm would visit him under these circumstances. The dreams he had seen were a warning that were delivered to him. 'They are meant to tell you that the world will face a gradual deterioration in moral standards,' the Master explained. The four voices he had heard were of four great sinners who had once lived in Sravasti. They had been trapped in hell for millions of years, and the words 'du', 'sa', 'na', 'so', were explained by the Blessed One as follows:

Du: Dung-like life we lived,
No willingness to give,
Although we could have given much,
We did not make our refuge thus.

Sa: Say, the end is near?
Already 60,000 years have gone
Without respite the torture is
In this hell realm.

Na: Naught, no end near, Oh, would it end!
No end in sight for us.
Who once did misdeeds here
For me, for you, for both of us.

So: So, could I only leave this place
And raise myself to human realm,
I would be kind and moral too,
And do good deeds abundantly.

The king heard these explanations with great attention, and was convinced by the Buddha's words. He agreed to the request of his compassionate queen to free all the animals and destroy the sacrificial altar. Instead, alms would be given to the poor and medical care extended to the infirm and disabled.

The king then requested the Buddha to send someone who could offer instructions and teachings to his queens. The Buddha appointed Ananda for this purpose, and Mallika's delight knew no bounds. So greatly did she benefit from the teachings that she attained liberation when she passed away.

———⬥✦⬥———

THOUGHT FOR REFLECTION

Swami Vivekananda, at the state of highest realization, said that he saw the presence of the Divine Mother in all women. He worked tirelessly for the upliftment of women, saying: 'The best thermometer to the progress of a nation is its treatment of its women,' and again, 'There is no chance for the welfare of the world unless the condition of women is improved.'

It is truly inspiring to hear his impassioned defence of the equality of the sexes, citing nothing less than the Vedas as the ultimate authority: 'It is very difficult to understand why in this country [India] so much difference is made between men and women, whereas the Vedanta declares that one and the same conscious self is present in all beings. You always criticize the women, but say what have you done for their uplift? Writing down smritis etc., and binding them by hard rules, the men have turned the women into manufacturing machines! If you do not raise the women, who are living embodiment of the Divine Mother, don't think that you have any other way to rise!'

Mahatma Gandhi was not only the father of our nation, the architect of our independence; he was also a great social reformer. He fought spiritedly to eradicate the wrongs committed against the women of the country through ages. His political ideology was strongly anchored in humanitarian values, and reflected his deeply spiritual nature.

Not only did Gandhi bring about a general awakening among the women, but brought them boldly out into the national mainstream, standing shoulder to shoulder with their fellow Indians in the Satyagraha and Quit India Movements. Gandhi asserted: 'To call women the weaker sex is a libel; it is man's injustice to women.' Indeed, he played a stellar role in uplifting the status of women in India.

Sadhu Vaswani brought about a quiet and meaningful revolution in his homeland. He pointed out to the women, whom he regarded as his own sisters, that they were not weaklings, but symbols of true shakti, the inner strength of the spirit. He did not stop with words: he offered the purdah clad, kitchen-bound women of Sind, spiritual liberation in the true sense of the term. The Sakhi Satsang started under his benign guidance, enabled many women to become decision-makers for the first time in their personal lives – by the very act of voluntarily joining his satsang. He did everything he could to break the shackles of superstition and hidebound 'customs' that had kept Sindhi women restricted and confined for centuries. He spoke out against the purdah as also against the deadly custom of *deti-leti* (dowry). At the same time, he was also aware of the dangers of excessive 'modernism', warning women against aping western fashions blindly. He encouraged them to cultivate the virtue of simplicity in their dress and in their daily life.

It is the moral obligation of all of us to ponder the question: What has become of the values and ideals that Swami Vivekananda, Mahatma Gandhi and Sadhu Vaswani left behind as their legacy to us? Why have we become so degraded as to descend to a society that fails to respect its women and treat them well?

Let us search our own conscience for the answers.

HE CONQUERED BY LOVE:
THE BUDDHA'S EARLY DISCIPLES

However many holy words you read, however many you speak,
what good will they do you if you do not act upon them?

– Gautama, the Buddha

$\prec\!\succ$

*T*HE BUDDHA'S FIRST IMPULSE, ON ATTAINING ILLUMINATION, WAS TO
withdraw from the world. But, the compassionate one that he was, he
saw that the world needed his ministration and his message. He was
filled with compassion for the people. And, filled with compassion, he
went out among them to give his message.

As history tells us, his task was by no means easy! It was no path of
roses that lay before him. In the early days of his mission, he met every
form of abuse, opposition, and persecution. But he chose the way of
love! He conquered by love.

Buddha was once threatened with death by a bandit.

'By all means take my life, but do be kind enough to fulfil my dying
wish,' said the Buddha.

'And what is that?' asked the bandit.

'Cut off the branch of that tree.'

One slash of the sword, and the branch was severed! 'What now?'
asked the bandit.

'I request you to put it back again,' said the Buddha.

The bandit laughed scornfully, 'You must be crazy to think that
anyone can do that.'

'On the contrary, it is you who are crazy to think that you are powerful just because you can hurt and wound, and even kill people. Any man with brawn could do that. The truth is: they are truly great who can restore and heal.'

The bandit gave up his life of violence and became a disciple of the Master.

***

During the lifetime of the Buddha there lived a terrible murderer by the name of Angulimala, which means 'Necklace of Thumbs'. He was given this nomenclature because he would cut off the thumb of each of his victims, put it on a string and wear it around his neck.

The Buddha heard of Angulimala; in his infinite compassion, the Master decided to bring him unto the path of righteousness. At that moment in time, it had been rumoured that Angulimala had attacked, robbed and killed almost one thousand people. Hence, his necklace was made up of 999 human thumbs. It was no longer worn around his neck, but hung on the branch of a huge tree in the forest. It was said that Angulimala was roaming the forests eagerly in search of his thousandth victim.

In order to meet Angulimala face-to-face, the Buddha set off in search of him, alone and on foot, to the forest, where he was believed to be in hiding. Angulimala, on seeing the Buddha, started running towards him. To his amazement, the saffron clad ascetic seemed to be running faster than him!

Now the Sutta tells us:

...Then the Blessed One performed such a feat of supernormal power that the bandit Angulimala, going as fast as he could, was unable to catch up with the Blessed One, who was walking at his normal pace. Then he thought: 'It is marvellous! Formerly I caught up with even a galloping elephant and seized it; I caught up with even a galloping horse and seized it; I caught up with even a galloping chariot and seized it; I caught up with even a galloping deer and seized it. But yet, though I am going as fast as I can, I am unable to catch up with this monk who is walking at his normal pace.' He stopped and called, 'Stand still, monk! Stand still, monk!'

'I stand still, Angulimala. Do you stand still, too.'

Then the bandit Angulimala thought: 'These monks, followers of the Sakya scion, speak truth, assert truth; but though this monk is running, yet he says "I have stopped, Angulimala; do you stop, too." Suppose I question the monk?'

Angulimala addressed the Sakhya Muni thus:

'While you are walking monk, you tell me you have stopped;
But now, when I have stopped, you say I have not stopped.
I ask you now, O monk what is the meaning of it;
How is it that you have stopped and I have not?'

The Blessed One replied:

'Angulimala, I have stopped for ever,
Foreswearing violence to every living being;
But you have no restraint towards things that breathe;
So that is why I have stopped and you have not.'

These words, the loving compassion in the Buddha's eyes and the face-to-face meeting with the Blessed One bring about a tremendous transformation in Angulimala's life. He requests the Buddha to ordain him as a monk and permit him to live among the Sanga community.

The story goes on to tell us that Angulimala became Ahinsaka, a monk belonging to the sanga. He took on the severest form of asceticism, begged for alms. The people of the land who still hated him and feared him, refused to offer alms to him, and many were the days he was forced to go without even a grain of food or a drop of gruel. Some people even pelted him with stones, notwithstanding the fact that he was a monk. He bore it all patiently, eventually attaining sainthood.

These are the verses as recorded in the 'Songs of the Elders' (Theragatha; Thag 16.8):

Who once did live in recklessness
And then is reckless nevermore,
He shall illuminate the world
Like the full moon unveiled by cloud. (v. 871; Dhp 172)

The story of this remarkable transformation is mentioned in the Angulimala Sutta of the Majjhima Nikaya.

Buddha's opponents called him a thief, because he had destroyed faith in animal sacrifices. 'Do not even see his face,' they said to the people. Once, he went hungry, as no one in the village was prepared to give him even a morsel of food as alms.

Sonadanda was a learned Brahmin. People advised this scholar not to see the Buddha, for it would affect his reputation adversely.

Sundari was a nun. The Buddha's opponents arranged for hired killers to murder her and throw her body in the woods near the Buddha's monastery.

'It is Gautama who perpetrated this heinous crime!' cried his opponents. Gautama was quiet, patient, and forgiving. One day, the hired assassins, got drunk and, in their intoxicated condition, revealed the conspiracy. Thus, the real culprits were brought to book, and the Buddha's enemies were put to shame.

Cinca was a beautiful young woman. The Buddha's enemies bribed her to accuse the Master of having an illicit relationship with her. Misguided and misled by these men, she took up a wooden globe and made herself appear like a pregnant woman. Her false accusations made the Buddha's enemies revile him in public. The Buddha remained unaffected by the slander and malice. He was calm, silent and serene. However, this plan was also foiled by Divine Will. In the ninth month, the young woman appeared at the Buddha's evening satsang, to make a public accusation against the Buddha in the presence of the people. She accused the Master of having lived with her and demanded that he should provide her with a place for her approaching confinement.

The Buddha remained calm. In gentle words, he said to her, 'Sister! Whether your words be true or not, nobody knows but you and I.' At these words, the woman's wooden globe fell down in public! The people saw the truth, and they hooted her out and pursued her till she confessed the truth and begged for forgiveness.

Then came the days when countless men flocked to him and began to follow him. The rich, the powerful and the nobly born, renounced their lives of comfort and ease to embrace his order and become bhikkhus, cheerfully accepting the rigours of a homeless life.

Gautama's cousin Devadatta was jealous of the Buddha's growing eminence. Infatuated with the lust for power, he even schemed to put an end to his cousin's life. He had joined the sanga, but his heart was inflamed with jealousy of the Master. He felt that it was he who should be the Head of the Order and not the Buddha.

He tried to kill the Buddha by pushing a huge boulder from the mountaintop on to the path of the Master. The boulder broke into smithereens, but the Master was unharmed.

Devadatta conspired with King Ajatasatru to assassinate the Buddha. When the fierce mercenaries hired by the king and Devadatta beheld the Buddha face-to-face, they dropped their weapons and fell at his feet.

Devadatta would not give up. He set Nalagiri, a fierce and wild elephant lose on the Buddha's path. To make matters worse, the elephant had been forcefully intoxicated with drugs.

As the raging elephant rushed into the unsuspecting crowd which had gathered to listen to the Buddha, people panicked and fled in all directions; but the Buddha stood still and calm. There was a heavenly loveliness in his face; a divine light in his eyes. With infinite compassion he said to his terrified disciples, 'Fear not, my brethren! He who harmeth none, will be harmed by no one!'

The magic of the Master's presence tamed the raging elephant and made it docile!

Next, Devadatta tried to 'take over' the sanga, in an attempt to show that he was higher in moral rectitude than the Buddha himself. He persuaded five hundred monks to join him in a rival order. But on hearing Buddha's disciple, Sariputra, preach the Dhamma to them, the wayward monks returned to the Master's fold.

There is a legend which tells us that Devadatta was trapped in quicksand, and began to sink rapidly. He cried out for help and nobody came to save him. Ultimately, it was the Master who happened to be passing by, who took pity on his wayward cousin and helped him out in the nick of time. Perhaps this is a symbolic reference to the quagmire of sin and evil into which Devadatta had sunk.

It is said that when Devadatta was on his deathbed, he repented of his sins and wished to seek the Buddha's forgiveness. But he died when he was being carried to the Master.

To turn to others, there were men who spread malicious slanders against the Buddha and even hired men to murder the Master. These men went to kill the Buddha but, they remained to revere him! In his sacred presence their hearts were conquered, and they were converted.

They fell at the Master's feet; they confessed their sin; they repented and asked him to accept them as his disciples.

***

Purna was one of Buddha's devoted disciples. He was inspired to spread his Master's message among the people of Sonapranta. Now, it was well-known that the people of Sonapranta were wild and ferocious. No preacher's life was safe in their country. Purna's plan appeared preposterous to many of his fellow bhikkhus, who feared for his life.

But Purna was a man of faith: there was no fear in his heart, for it was filled through and through with love for all living creatures, and profound compassion for those who live in the darkness of ignorance.

He went to the Buddha for his blessings. The Master said to him, 'Purna, you know so well that the people of Sonapranta are wild and ferocious, they insult and slander one another, and are given to uncontrollable fits of anger. If they insult you and abuse you and vent their wrath on you, what will you do?'

'If they abuse me and insult me, Master,' said Purna, 'I shall still think them to be kind and friendly, since they do not beat me or stone me.'

'And what if they beat you or stone you?'

'I would still regard them as being kind, since they do not attack me with weapons!'

'And if,' said the Buddha, 'they should attack you with weapons?'

'Then, too,' answered Purna, 'I would regard them as kind and friendly, since they do not kill me.'

'And what if they kill you, Purna?'

'Even if they kill me, Master,' said Purna, 'I shall thank them at the moment of my death, for they will liberate me from the limitations of the body and the bonds of human life!'

The Blessed One was well pleased with Purna. 'You are gifted with the greatest gentleness and patience,' he said. 'You may go and dwell among the people of Sonapranta. Show them the way to be free, even as you are free!

Blessed was Purna! He was free, he was fearless. He also showed the people of Sonapranta the way to be free and fearless.

The Buddha's way was the way of quenching sorrow. On one occasion, he gave his teaching in a few significant words: 'Quench the flames!'

He pointed out the three 'flames' threatened to destroy man:

(1) The flame of greed,

(2) The flame of the ego: the 'I', and

(3) The flame of hate.

'Quench the flames,' he urged people, again and yet again. Now kings left their kingdoms and sought to follow him. Buddha was the unique Master in history whose father, son and wife were initiated into the order by himself.

, ***

Once, Gautama Buddha was sitting among his disciples and devotees. Someone in the crowd said, 'Lord, many of us have come from afar to hear you. Pray, give us a teaching which we can carry with ourselves as we leave.'

The Buddha picked up a ripe mango placed beside him, showed it to everyone present and then put it back in its place. A few minutes passed. The devotees could not understand what this gesture meant. Once again, they requested him for a message, a teaching which they could imbibe in their daily life. 'Pray, give us a teaching, which we can inscribe on our hearts,' they begged the Master.

The Buddha repeated his gesture. Once again, he picked up the mango, showed it to all and then kept it back in its place. This was repeated for the third time. The fourth time, the crowd asked for a message, the Buddha said to them, 'My dear ones, three times did I give you my teaching, but you did not understand it.'

People were surprised. Bewildered, they asked; 'Master, pray tell us what is your message to us?'

'I showed you the mango,' replied the Enlightened One. 'The mango is sweet. You too, must be like a mango, sweet to the core. That is my message to you.'

This is the Blessed One's advice that all of us should heed: Speak sweetly to all. Speak words which will erase the ego. Speak words which will soothe others and will bring serenity to you.

The *Mahaparinirvana Sutta* of the Pali canon tells us that just before the Buddha left his earthly form, he gathered all his monks around him and offered to answer any questions, clear any doubts they had about his teachings. They had none. The Buddha's final words are reported to have been:

'All composite things [Sakhāra] are perishable. Strive for your own liberation with diligence.'

(Pali: 'vayadhammāsakhārāappamādenasampādethā'.)

Later that day, followers tried to portray the Buddha as a god, as an avatar. But the fact of the matter was that the Buddha lived and died a teacher.

The Buddha lived to the age of eighty years. Forty-five of these years he spent in teaching. In fact, he preached to the very last day of his earth-life. He preached and he healed the lame, the deaf and the blind. He conquered hearts and souls by his love and healing.

THOUGHT FOR REFLECTION

The Guru, Gurudev Sadhu Vaswani taught us, is much more than an 'instructor' or 'adviser'. He is a dynamic person with a transforming power – for spirituality is a tremendous shakti; and the true Guru is a man of shakti. By the method of evocation, the Guru draws out the disciple's spiritual energy. Therefore we read in the ancient texts: 'The Guru leads forth the pupil to Himself.' It is in this process of 'leading forth', drawing the disciple to Himself – not in merely communicating information – lies the secret of the Guru's shakti.

The word Guru, as we all know, is derived from two Sanskrit root words: Gu means darkness; ru means light. Thus, the Guru leads us from darkness to light.

The Jignasus of ancient India constantly prayed: '*Tamaso ma jyotirgamaya!*' ('From darkness, lead me into the Light!') This light indeed is the light of the spirit. The Guru can kindle this light in the heart of the receptive disciple. Therefore, is the Guru revered as a 'light bringer'.

Upali: The Patriarch of the Vinaya

Then the Buddha said to his monks, walk over the earth for the blessing of many, the happiness of many, out of compassion for the world, for the welfare and the blessing and the happiness of gods and men.

– Vinaya Pitaka

⟨✦⟩

WHEN WE STUDY THE HISTORY OF BUDDHISM, WE READ THAT THE most sacred texts of the faith, namely the Suttapitaka (basket of threads) and Vinaya Pitaka (basket of rules) were first recited in their entirety at the council of the sanga held after the Buddha passed away. The entire community of monks heard the leading disciples of the Buddha recite the Master's teachings (Buddha vachana) from memory and gave the recital their seal of approval, before the teachings were finalized as oral traditions in the canon. We also know that it was the Buddha's chief disciples, Ananda and Upali, who recited from their memory, the two sacred texts mentioned above. This shows how diligent and faithful they were in memorizing and preserving the sacred teachings; and also the integrity and trust that the entire community attributed to them.

Of these two chief disciples, we know very little of the life of Ananda, whose name is frequently mentioned by the Buddha in the course of his conversations or questions and answers. But quite a few details have come down to us of the amazing monk called Upali, who excelled in knowing the rules of the Order and was the foremost in keeping the precepts of the Master.

Tradition tells us that Upali was born in a clan of barbers, and by dint of his skill and expertise, became the royal barber of Kapilavastu, whose service extended to both Prince Siddhartha as well as his royal cousins like Prince Aniruddha and Prince Bhaddiya.

It is said that when the Buddha returned to Kapilavastu after his enlightenment, Upali was ordered to give him a tonsure. Legends say that Upali was so overwhelmed by this rare opportunity, that he sought the advice of his mother. His mother assured him that the Buddha was the very soul of compassion and instilled courage into him and actually accompanied him to the Buddha's presence. We are told that during the course of this tonsure that he performed for the Blessed One, Upali mastered the four forms of meditation. It came to pass in the following manner:

As we saw, Upali was an expert at his job and the tonsure of the Blessed One was happening smoothly, when the mother, who sat at a little distance, enquired of the Buddha, 'Lord, what do you think of Upali's skill?'

The Buddha replied, 'He bows too low.'

Immediately, Upali straightened his spine, attaining the first stage of meditation. After a little while, the mother bowed and asked the Master, 'Lord, what do you think now?'

'His body seems to be too straight,' replied the Buddha.

At once, Upali concentrated his attention on his breathing, achieving the second stage of meditation.

The mother repeated her question, 'Lord, pray tell me what you think of his skill now.'

'He breathes in too fast,' the Buddha replied.

Upali held his breath and began to control his breathing, attaining the third stage.

The mother repeated her earnest question and the Buddha replied, for the fourth time, 'He breathes out too fast now.'

Upali watched his exhalation and attained to the fourth stage.

The experience left a deep impression on Upali.

Now it came to pass that the visit of the Buddha to his father's kingdom had a powerful impact on his royal kinsmen. Many of the young Sakhya princes decided to follow the Blessed One and embraced the monastic life. The Princes Ananda, Aniruddha, Bhaddiya, Bhagu, Devadatta and Kimbila decided to renounce the world and become the

Buddha's chief disciples. They left Kapilavastu with a great train of carts and horses and elephants as well as a number of attendants, so that their families were under the impression that they were taking a royal excursion. But at the border of Magadha, they sent all their escorts back to Kapilavastu, only retaining Upali with them for the final ritual of shaving their heads.

As Upali tonsured his royal masters, he thought of the enormous transformation that was to come upon them, and the moment-ous decision they had made to join the Enlightened One, and he shed tears. Prince Aniruddha noticed this.

When the tonsure was over, Aniruddha spread his velvet mantle on the ground. He dropped on it his coronet and all the rich jewels that he wore on his person. His fellow princes followed his example. Aniruddha wrapped up all the precious jewels in the mantle and handed them over to the faithful barber. 'You have served us well, Upali, and we offer these ornaments to you as a mark of our appreciation. We are travelling now to join the Blessed One. When you go back to Kapilavastu, please inform our families of our decision.'

Upali found himself handed a veritable fortune, even as he saw the high-born princes shed their rich clothes and put on the ochre robes of sannyasis and walk the dusty road that led out of the kingdom. He sat down to reflect on the events of the last few days: the unforgettable experience of offering his services to the Buddha and his mother's questions to the Lord; the tonsure of the royal princes and their generous gifts to him; the decision they had made to give up their wealth and power and luxury and follow the Buddha; and the tears flowed freely from his eyes. He wept for the princes who were embracing a life of penance and austerity; he wept as he imagined the Buddha blessing them and embracing them as brothers in the sanga; he wept as he wished he too, could follow them; and finally, he wept as he felt that nobody would accept him, a poor barber, if he went and offered to join the sanga.

It was in this condition that Sariputra, one of the trusted disciples of the Buddha, found him on the roadside.

'Brother, why do you weep so bitterly?' Sariputra asked him.

'The princes whom I have served faithfully, have renounced the world to follow the Blessed One,' Upali replied. 'They have left me with a fortune which is enough to support me comfortably for the rest of my life. But having seen the Blessed One, I know this fortune is nothing compared to the grace and peace that he can offer me. I wish to follow the princes into the sanga. But will the sanga accept me, a poor, low-born barber? How can I presume to be in the company of princes and scholars, who have chosen to make the Blessed One their teacher?'

Sariputra said to Upali, 'The sanga does not subscribe to the distinctions of caste and class. Anyone who is ready to observe the precepts can become Buddha's disciple. Come with me, brother. I am sure the Buddha will be very glad to have you ordained.'

And so it came to pass that a succession of new entrants entered the Buddha's presence the following day; the six princes who were his royal kinsmen followed by Upali, the barber. Together, they bowed at the Master's feet.

The Buddha's eyes fell on Upali first. He asked Upali to come forward. 'Have you come to seek the way?' the Buddha asked. 'Yes, noble sir,' replied Upali humbly, 'if a person of low birth might be permitted to enter the order.'

The Buddha told Upali that in the sanga, caste or former occupation were irrelevant. The only rank that mattered was seniority. And then he said, 'Upali, you may receive your ordination now. For you have attained the four stages of meditation and you are ready to enter the order.'

Then and there, the Buddha ordained the astonished Upali. As for the Sakya princes, they had to go through a week of meditation training before they could be ordained. Upali was now their senior and he was to be accorded due obeisance from them. The Buddha told the princes, 'If you leave the world to follow me, you must also leave behind the social distinctions and privileges that the world follows.'

And so it came to pass that the barber became one of the Buddha's foremost disciples, and the keeper of the rules for the whole community. And when the Buddha passed away, it was Upali who recited the precepts of the Order as laid down by the Master. The entire community ratified his recital; and thus was born the Vinaya (discipline), which sustained the sanga for centuries to come.

Thought for Reflection

Gurudev Sadhu Vaswani who has been the inspiration, the guide, the guardian and the leading light of my life, offered us a simple, straightforward sadhana which each and every one could practise effortlessly: the three S – sadhana of Silence, Sanga and Service. He urged us to practise silence every day; he emphasized the spiritual fellowship that was available to us at the satsang; and, above all, he urged that our life, our wealth, our talent and our time were all but a loan given to us by the Almighty, to be poured out in selfless service to those less fortunate than ourselves.

Silence, sanga (fellowship) and service! If only we could follow these simple techniques of sadhana we would, indeed, find our lives transformed.

Why should we practise such a sadhana? What will it achieve for us? What will we get out of it? These are questions that many people ask themselves when they hear about sadhana, and its necessity for the seeker.

If these questions arise in your mind too, I can offer you a simple answer: there is a simple input-output ratio that operates in sadhana; you will get as much out of it as you put into it! Put in sincerity, dedication, commitment, faith and perseverance: and you will achieve your goal – indeed, you will achieve much more than you expect, with the grace of God.

ANGER BEGETS ANGER

Holding on to anger is like grasping a hot coal with the intent of throwing it at someone else; you are the one who gets burned... For hatred does not cease by hatred at any time: hatred ceases by love. This is an old rule.

– Gautama, the Buddha

ONCE, THE BUDDHA SAW THAT A QUARREL HAD ERUPTED AMONG two factions of his students. The animosity grew until they became virtually irreconcilable. The Buddha brought them to their senses with the following story.

Brahmadatta was the King of Banaras. When he conquered his neighbouring kingdom Kaushala, he sought to kill Dirgheti, the king of that country, and his queen, so that his rule would be secure. However, Dirgheti and his wife made their escape by going into hiding and living in disguise at the humble dwelling of a potter, who was their loyal and devout follower.

In time, they had a son called Dirghayu whom they brought up with loving care. When he was sixteen, he was sent to a gurukul to complete his education.

When the son was away, Dirgheti and his queen were spotted by a barber who recognized them and betrayed the secret of their presence to Brahmadutta. Determined to destroy his old enemy, Brahmadutta ordered them to be executed.

A large crowd had gathered to witness the execution in Banaras. Among the crowd was Dirghayu, who was shocked and grieved to find that his parents were about to be killed. However, Dirgheti saw him pushing his way through the crowds and gave him a warning shout: 'Oh my son, do not look long, do not look short. Hatred is not appeased by hatred, but by non-hatred alone.'

That stopped Dirghayu in his tracks, for he realized the wisdom of his father's words. Brahmadutta realized that there was a son somewhere in the crowd, but there was no way he could be spotted. Before the eyes of their son, King Dirgheti and his wife were executed. Dirghayu was devastated, left with a terrible sense of loss and pain.

Years rolled by. The orphaned prince, Dirghayu, became an expert elephant handler and obtained employment in the royal elephant stables. Here he would play the flute in his leisure hours. The king heard the melodious music of the flute and was enchanted by it. He asked to see the young man, and found him to be handsome, virtuous and courteous. He was forthwith appointed as the king's chosen companion and confidant, to accompany him wherever he went.

Little did Brahmadatta realize that the young man whom he held in such affection and trust was the son of the king whom he had executed so ruthlessly. Nor did he know that Dirghayu was just biding time to find the right opportunity of killing him in revenge.

One day, the long-awaited opportunity came. Hunting in the forests, Brahmadatta and Dirghayu were separated from the rest of the king's party, as they pursued their quarry. Dirghayu was driving the king's chariot, and they stopped when they realized they had lost the others. So, they got down from the chariot. It was a hot day and the king was tired. Dirghayu asked him to lay his head on his lap and go to sleep. The king did so without hesitation, for he trusted the young man absolutely.

Soon he was fast asleep. Dirghayu saw that this was the opportunity he had been waiting for all along. There was no one around, and the king was utterly in his power. Quietly, the young man unsheathed his sword and then, the words of his father flashed across his mind, and he put the sword away.

At the same time, the king was awakened by a terrible dream. He dreamt that the son of the royal couple executed by him, had managed to reach him, and was standing over him with a drawn sword, ready to kill him in vengeance.

As the king narrated this frightening dream, Dirghayu drew his sword again and said, 'That was no ordinary dream. It was a warning to you. I am the son you dreamt of, and I am about to kill you in revenge for the death of my parents.'

'Please spare my life!' begged the king, holding the young man's hands in despair. 'Do not kill me, I beg of you.'

'Surely oh king, you will have me executed if I spare your life,' said Dirghayu. 'For you know my identity now, and you will not have me around, as I am the royal heir to the throne of Kaushala. If I don't kill you, I must get killed!'

'Let us then make a pact not to kill each other,' said the king. 'Let this vicious cycle of fear, hatred and vindictiveness be broken forever!'

The two pledged lifelong loyalty and friendship. The king, recovering from his traumatizing experience, asked Dirghayu to tell him the meaning of his father's intriguing final message.

Dirghayu explained to him, 'Do not look long – it means do not nurse your hatred for a long time. Do not look short – this means do not act hastily. If I had acted hastily I would have killed you – only to be killed by your guards when they found us. Then my friends and followers would have pursued your people in vengeance and the hatred would have continued. However, you and I have extended mutual forgiveness, and therefore both of us can be free of fear. The cycle of violence is now broken.'

Concluding the story, Buddha reminded his disciples that hatred only leads to further hatred, while love and forgiveness can conquer hatred and promote peace.

THOUGHT FOR REFLECTION

Resentment and anger are destructive emotions. They damage us from within; and the damage is manifested in symptoms that are almost unbearable: the inability to go to sleep in peace; the gnawing feeling in the pit of the stomach; the heavy burden of sorrow on the heart; the throbbing headache; the blinding pain....

No wonder Emerson wrote, 'For every minute you remain angry, you give up sixty seconds of peace of mind.'

Forgiveness holds the promise of freedom and relief from such anguish.

Forgiveness offers the chance for reparation, reconciliation and atonement – in some cases, after years of hostility and estrangement.

Forgiveness brings peace and joy into our life. Forgiveness puts an end to the inner struggle that rages in the soul within, and teaches us to face life with tolerance, understanding and equanimity.

CHRISTIANITY

BRIEF INTRODUCTION

CHRISTIANITY IS THE WORLD'S MOST POPULAR RELIGION, IN TERMS OF sheer numbers. Over 30 per cent of the world's population is Christian by faith; as many as 75 per cent of Americans, Canadians and Europeans identify themselves as Christian, although these people belong to 1,500 different denominations of Christianity; from the grandeur and ritual splendour of St Peter's Basilica in Rome to the makeshift shacks on the wayside where newly converted Christians congregate in rural India, from the intellectual complexity of St Thomas Aquinas to the simple and selfless service of the Little Sisters of the Poor, from idealistic reformers like Martin Luther to twenty-first century saints like Mother Teresa, from Quakers and Unitarians, to Anglicans and Christian Scientists, from Seventh Day Adventists to the Syrian Orthodox Church, there are over two billion people who share the basic tenets of Christianity – i.e., belief in Jesus Christ as the Saviour, belief in the Bible as the word of God, and the firm belief that theirs is the true Christian faith, among all others.

Given this kind of diversity in belief and practise, it is not easy to give a brief introduction to Christianity. Mainstream Christians tend to be inclusive; they regard everyone, who believes in Christ, as a true Christian. Liberal Christians are engaged in reinterpreting their religion for the third millennium, and encourage serious dialogue with other faiths in an attempt to understand and appreciate the value of non-Christian religions. At the other end of the scale, we have more fundamentalist and evangelical denominations who dismiss other religions and other notions of God as being false, and indeed 'damned' in Christian terms. Protestants believe in a unique personal and individual approach to their God and their faith; Roman Catholics insist on the intermediation of the Church as their approach and access to God. This wide diversity of beliefs and practises is a characteristic of the larger Christian umbrella of sects and churches in the world today.

Who is a Christian? There are many answers to this question: to some believers, one has to be 'born again' to be a true Christian; to others, one has to be baptized to take such a description; there is no consensus on who is a true Christian among the various Christian denominations. But, in a broad world view, we must accept as a Christian, any individual who seriously regards himself to be Christian, and honestly follows the teachings of Jesus Christ. The Christian concept of salvation tells us that God sent His son among men to be a guide and saviour. It is from Jesus Christ that Christianity derives its origin and its name.

My Favourite
New Testament Stories

*So I say to you, ask and it will be given to you; search, and you
will find; knock, and the door will be opened for you.*

– Jesus Christ

$$\rightleftharpoons$$

𝒪N THE GOSPEL ACCORDING TO ST LUKE[1], JESUS VISITS THE HOUSE
of the sisters Martha and Mary. Martha gets busy attending to various
household chores to make Jesus and his disciples comfortable. As
for Mary, she sits at the feet of Jesus, listening eagerly to his words
of wisdom. Martha complains about her sister, 'Shouldn't she do
something to help?' Jesus tells Martha, 'You are worried and anxious
about many things, but only one thing is needed. Mary has chosen
what is better, and it will not be taken away from her.'

What was it that freed Mary from the anxiety and fretful activity
that kept her sister so 'busy'? Mary chose to focus on Jesus, and on
Jesus alone; to listen to his every word. In the process, she ignored the
demands of hospitality. She was not being irresponsible; she was not
trying to shirk her duties; she had her own priorities. She would listen
to Jesus first – everything else could be done later.

How many of us can be certain about our priorities?

'No one can serve two masters,' Jesus once said to his disciples, who
were worried about their life and their livelihood.[2] He wanted them

[1] Ch.10, verses 38-4.
[2] Matthew 6: 25-30.

to realize that love for God should override all our material concerns, especially the desire for more and more money. We have to choose between God and Mammon (the 'god' of money). 'Either you will hate the one and love the other, or you will be devoted to the one and despise the other. You cannot serve both, God and money.'

The disciples probably looked doubtful; so Jesus continued: 'Therefore I tell you, do not worry about your life, what you will eat or drink; or about your body, what you will wear. Is not life more than food, and the body more than clothes?'

'Look at the birds of the air; they do not sow or reap or store away in barns, and yet your heavenly Father feeds them. Are you not much more valuable than they?'

'And why are you worried about clothing? Observe how the lilies of the field grow; they do not toil nor do they spin; yet I say to you that not even Solomon in all his glory clothed himself like one of these.'

'But if God so clothes the grass of the field, which is alive today and tomorrow is thrown into the furnace, will He not much more clothe you? You of little faith! Do not worry then, saying, "What will we eat?" or "What will we drink?" or "What will we wear for clothing?"'

When you feel that He is taking care of your needs, you cease to worry! You do not have to plan in advance for unforeseen eventualities. You do not have to worry about calamities. You simply allow the Divine Plan to unfold. You claim nothing; you ask nothing; you seek nothing; you plan nothing. You simply become a channel for the Divine Plan to flow through.

How many of us are capable of such faith and trust?

***

Once, Jesus was on his way to Jerusalem.[3] On the long, narrow, dusty road between Samaria and Galilee, he came across a row of lepers who were standing at some distance from the road, huddled together in a group.

You see, in those days leprosy was regarded as a deadly, infectious disease. Lepers were not allowed to mix with the people. In fact they were not even allowed to present themselves before the eyes of their

---

[3.] Luke 17: 12-19.

'clean' and 'healthy' brothers. They were condemned to live in caves and catacombs outside human settlements. Food and clothes in the form of pitiful alms were dumped near their site, so that they would not venture out to seek food or other forms of relief.

When the group of lepers saw Jesus approaching, they cried out in desperation and misery, 'Master! Heal us! For only you can help us in our affliction. We pray you Master, heal us!'

Jesus looked at them with compassion. Nine of them were Jews, and one of them was a Samaritan. In those days, the Jews regarded themselves as superior, while the Samaritans were treated as outcastes. However, the common bond of suffering and affliction had united these men together in a brotherhood of despair. Together, they cried out again and again, 'Master! Heal us!'

Jesus looked at them with loving compassion and said to them, 'Go to the priest!'

Now, the lepers were puzzled. They had put all their faith in Jesus. Why did he want them to go to the priest? However, the Master had spoken, and they obeyed him implicitly. They turned to walk in the direction of the Temple.

Hardly had they walked a few halting paces, when they became aware of a strange sensation. They felt their spirits lifting; their hearts became light; vigour returned to their limbs; at the same time, the hideous sores on their body began to disappear and melt away, and their very skin became smooth as that of a new born baby. They saw each other's faces becoming radiant and beautiful! It was a miracle!

'We are healed!' they exclaimed, jubilant and elated. 'We are healed! We are healed!'

Amidst their ecstasy and self-congratulations, they remembered their families who had been bereft with grief. 'Let us rush to our loved ones,' they said to each other. 'Let us give them the good news that we are now healed and whole again! Let us share this wonderful moment with our near and dear ones!'

In a moment, the nine Jews had rushed off in the direction of their homes. But the Samaritan lingered.

'Yes,' he mused, 'I must go back to my family … but before I do, I must return to the Master and thank Him for the miraculous gift that He has bestowed upon me!'

The Samaritan rushed to catch up with Jesus. He fell at Jesus's feet and said to the Lord with tears in his eyes, 'Master! My gratitude to you. You have healed me and given me a new lease of life! Thank you, thank you, thank you!'

Jesus blessed the Samaritan and said: 'Ten were cleansed. But only one has come. Where are the other nine?'

Even God misses something when you don't express your gratitude!

***

Once, Jesus sat outside the Temple, talking to his disciples.[4] The Scribes and Pharisees i.e., the religious teachers and law-makers brought to him a woman who had sinned, and made her stand in the middle of the crowd. 'She has sinned. We have decided to punish her. Now in the law, Moses commanded us to stone such women; what then do you say?'

These men were obviously hoping to trap Jesus, so that they might have grounds for accusing Him. But Jesus stooped down and with His finger wrote on the ground.

But when they persisted in asking Him, He straightened up, and said to them, 'He who is without sin among you, let him be the first to throw a stone at her.' And he continued to stoop down and write on the ground.

When the accusers heard this, they slipped away one by one, beginning with the oldest, until only Jesus was left in the middle of the crowd with the woman.

Straightening up, Jesus said to her, 'Woman, where are they? Did no one condemn you?' She said, 'No one, Lord.' And Jesus said, 'I do not condemn you, either. Go. From now on sin no more.'

***

The great German poet Goethe was particularly fond of a story relating to Jesus and his disciples. Peter, the fisherman, the foremost among the disciples, once said to Christ, 'Master, how is it that you can walk on the waters, and we cannot?'

Jesus answered, 'Because I have faith!'

Peter protested, 'But we have faith in you too!'

'Then follow me,' said Jesus, and stepped on the water. Peter followed him – he actually walked upon the waters behind his Master!

[4]. John 8: 3-10.

They had not gone very far when a huge wave arose before them. Peter cried out, 'Master, save me! I am about to drown!'

'Why are you afraid?' asked Jesus.

'I saw the huge wave Master,' Peter replied, 'and fear entered my heart!'

Jesus said to him, 'You feared the wave: you did not fear the Lord of the waves!'

***

It is said that one day, early in the morning, as he was on his way to a city, Jesus became hungry. Seeing a fig tree by the road, he went up to it but found nothing on it except leaves. Then he said to it, 'May you never bear fruit again!' Immediately the tree withered.

When the disciples saw this, they were amazed. 'How did the fig tree wither so quickly?' they asked.

Jesus replied, 'I tell you the truth, if you have faith and do not doubt, not only can you do what was done to the fig tree, but also you can say to this mountain, "Go, throw yourself into the sea", and it will be done. If you believe, you will receive whatever you ask for in prayer.'

Christian scholars explain this incident by saying that it teaches us the principle that religious 'profession' and observances are not enough to guarantee salvation, unless there is the fruit of genuine salvation evident in the life of the person. As the Apostle James would put it later: 'Faith without works is dead.'[5]

***

The Parable of the Prodigal Son

There lived a rich man who had two sons. One day the elder son said to his father, 'Father I am grown up now; I wish to live separately. I want to be independent and lead my own life. Therefore I ask you, kindly give me my share of your wealth.'

The son wanted to break away from his father. But the father was reluctant, 'My son, you are still inexperienced in life,' he said in all earnestness, 'you have not seen the world, you do not know the ways of this world; wait a while, when you are mature enough, I myself will

[5] James 2:26.

give you your share of wealth and send you out into the world to live on your own.'

However, the son was not convinced. He was unhappy with his father's attitude. 'Father, you have been saying this for a long time,' he said impatiently, 'but now the time has come when you should let me go gracefully with my share of property and wealth, which is mine by right.'

Deeply saddened, his father gave him one-third of his wealth – a considerable deal of money in those days. The son, loaded with money, started off on a journey to a far off place, where he could live the life of his choice. He wanted to be as far away as possible from his father and his family.

The Sufi masters tell us that there are three journeys on the road to self-realization. During the first journey man wanders endlessly and moves away from reality. The restless mind pushes man to the pleasures of the world and man gets caught in the worldly affairs, forgetting the purpose of his journey. On the first journey, man wanders away from his home and idles away his time and money.

He made new friends instantly; in fact, friends flocked to him, for they had heard of his wealth and the way he had acquired it. He was a good catch for them. They allured him with all kinds of pleasures and entertainments. Money flowed like water from the young man's purse. And wealth, as you know, is not inexhaustible! In due course he wasted away all his wealth and became penniless. Now his new friends abandoned him. The others refused to help him out. He began to starve due to poverty, and there was no one to give him even a morsel of bread, no one to give him a job or lend him money. At long last, after much endeavour, he managed to get a job on a pig farm, where he lived in filth and dirt along with the pigs in the sty. In fact, he ate the food of the pigs when he was hungry!

One night, as he lay exhausted on the straw in the pig sty, he was overcome with self-pity. 'Why should I live in this miserable condition,' he thought. 'Why should I not go back to my own father?' Then and there he decided to return home. 'Back to my father's house I shall return,' he resolved.

The second journey begins from here. And when his life becomes miserable and unbearable, the thought of returning to his heavenly Father awakens in his soul – and this is when the second journey, the journey that takes us back to our true homeland begins.

The second journey begins with the awakening of the soul. It begins with the awareness that we have to return home. For long have we floundered. It is time to go back. A voice within us urges us, 'Awake. Awake. Return to your original home.' The wheel of time has hit us hard. Now, we realize, it is time to return.

But, returning to our story of the prodigal son, when the prodigal son reaches home, his father's joy is boundless. Overwhelmed by the sight of his son, he rushes to him and embraces him. The return of his wayward son is an occasion of celebration. So the father, in his abundant kindness and love, decides to celebrate the return of his prodigal son. He orders his servants to prepare a sumptuous feast for him. He orders for a variety of food including his son's favourite dishes. His joy is boundless. He rejoices for his prodigal son has returned home! As for the son, he is overcome by shame and guilt. He begs for forgiveness. 'Forgive me father, for I have behaved abominably,' he says. 'I fought with you for my share of wealth. I forcibly took away my share of money and material possessions. I misbehaved. Please forgive me father! I have no right to stay in your house. I have no claim over the luxuries in your home. But I beseech you; keep me here even as a servant and I shall feel grateful to you!'

The father replies, 'You are not my servant. You are my lost son who has returned safely. You are my prodigal son, who went astray but had the good sense to return home! I am overwhelmed with joy at your safe return. You are precious to me. You were lost and you are now found.'

***

The Parable of the Rich Man

Jesus said: There was a rich man who had much money. He said, 'I shall put my money to use so that I may sow, reap, plant and fill my storehouse with produce so that I lack nothing.' Such were his intentions, but that very night, he passed away.[6]

The Parable of the Wise Merchant

Jesus said: The kingdom of Heaven is like a merchant who had a consignment of merchandise and who discovered a pearl. He sold all his

6. Luke 12: 16-20.

merchandise and bought the pearl alone for himself. You, too, seek this enduring and unfailing treasure where no moth comes near to devour and no worm destroys.

The pearl referred to above is the ever-lasting wealth of the spirit.[7]

THOUGHT FOR REFLECTION

Anyone who reads the gospel, including non-Christians, is profoundly moved by the depth, profundity and the intense conviction with which Jesus taught his followers. He did not refer to external powers, but spoke with the quiet conviction of his own authority. He often preached through the form of parables – disarmingly simple stories from nature, agriculture and the life of the common people, which nevertheless carried profound and difficult teachings. It is said that his teachings left people baffled and tongue-tied, shaken out of their complacency and self-righteousness. He spoke of loving God above all other things, caring about all other people as much as we care about ourselves, the coming kingdom of God and eternal life.

Jesus taught that God was like a loving father to all of us: God knows and loves each of us personally, as parents know and love their children. God will give good things to those who ask: 'For everyone who asks receives, and he who seeks finds, and to him who knocks it shall be opened.' God is loving and merciful, and always ready to forgive repentant sinners. In a conversation with the skeptical Pharisee, Nicodemus, Jesus revealed his own divinity: God loved the people He had created, so much so that He sent Jesus, His own son, to save them from the forces of evil and their sinful ways. Those who put their trust in Jesus and His teachings could be saved and reach God's spiritual kingdom: 'For God so loved the world that He gave His only begotten son, that whoever believes in Him should not perish, but have eternal life. God did not send the Son into the world to judge the world, but that the world should be saved through Him.'[8]

[7.] Matthew 13: 45-46.
[8.] John 3:16-17.

MARY, MOTHER OF JESUS

Then God's temple in heaven was opened, and the ark of His covenant was seen within His temple; and there were flashes of lightning, voices, peals of thunder, an earthquake, and heavy hail. And a great portent appeared in heaven, a woman clothed with the sun, with the moon under her feet, and on her head a crown of twelve stars...

– Vision of Mother Mary in Revelation 11:19-12:1

CATHOLICS AND PROTESTANTS ALIKE VENERATE VIRGIN MARY AS THE Mother of Jesus Christ. For many of them she is Theotokos (Greek, 'God-bearer').

As far as Biblical references to Mary are concerned, probably the first is to be found in Isiah, 7:14: Here we have the prophesy that Christ will be born of a Virgin:

'Therefore the Lord Himself will give you a sign. Behold, a virgin shall conceive and bear a son, and shall call his name Immanuel.' (where Immanuel means, 'God with us'.)

The story of the Immaculate Conception is related in Luke 1:26-28: 'In the sixth month the angel Gabriel was sent from God to a city of Galilee named Nazareth, to a virgin betrothed to a man whose name was Joseph, of the house of David; and the virgin's name was Mary. And he came to her and said, 'Hail, full of grace, the Lord is with you!'

But Mary was much perplexed by his words and pondered what sort of greeting this might be.

The angel said to her, 'Do not be afraid, Mary, for you have found favour with God. And now, you will conceive in your womb and bear a son, and you will name him Jesus. He will be great, and will be called the Son of the Most High, and the Lord God will give to him the throne of his ancestor David. He will reign over the house of Jacob forever, and of his kingdom there will be no end.'

Mary is confused and said to the angel, 'How can this be, since I am a virgin?'

The angel said to her, 'The Holy Spirit will come upon you, and the power of the Most High will overshadow you; therefore, the child to be born will be holy; he will be called Son of God. And now, your relative Elizabeth in her old age has also conceived a son; and this is the sixth month for her who is said to be barren. For nothing will be impossible with God.'

Then Mary was convinced and said, 'Here am I, the servant of the Lord; let it be with me according to your word.' Then the angel departed from her.

Mary then goes out to visit her relative, Elizabeth, who recognizes the miracle that has happened to Mary and greets her with joy as the Mother of the Saviour.

From Matthew 1:18-25, we learn how the birth of Jesus the Messiah came about: His mother Mary was pledged to be married to Joseph, but before they came together, she was found to be pregnant through the Holy Spirit. Now Joseph her husband-to-be, was a pious and faithful man, obedient to the law. He did not want to expose her to public disgrace, and therefore, he had in mind to divorce her quietly.

But even as he was considering this, an angel of the Lord appeared to him in a dream and said, 'Joseph son of David, do not be afraid to take Mary home as your wife, because what is conceived in her is from the Holy Spirit. She will give birth to a son, and you are to give him the name Jesus (in the original meaning, 'God Saves') because he will save his people from their sins.'

All this took place to fulfill what the Lord had said through the prophet: 'The virgin will conceive and give birth to a son, and they will call him Immanuel.'

When Joseph woke up from the dream, he did what the angel of the Lord had commanded him to do; he took Mary home as his wife. But he did not consummate their marriage until she gave birth to a son. And he gave him the name Jesus.

Part of the catholic Rosary is the beautiful and pious 'Hail Mary', which is actually a prayer of intercession; it is also called the Ave Maria (Latin) or Angelic Salutation, which refers to the immaculate conception in lyrical and poetic terms:

Hail Mary, full of grace, the Lord is with thee; blessed art thou amongst women, and blessed is the fruit of thy womb, Jesus. Holy Mary, Mother of God, pray for us sinners, now and at the hour of our death. Amen.

The prayer incorporates two passages from Saint Luke's Gospel: 'Hail, full of grace, the Lord is with thee,' and 'Blessed art thou amongst women and blessed is the fruit of thy womb.'

The beautiful prayer has been set to music by Charles-François Gounod and Franz Schubert as the famous Ave Maria.

Luke 2:1-7 narrates the events prior to the Birth of Jesus. We are told that in those days a decree went out from Emperor Augustus that all the people should be registered in a census being made of the Roman Empire and all its provinces. Everyone was to return to their hometowns to be registered. Therefore, Joseph also went from the town of Nazareth in Galilee to Judaea, to the city of David called Bethlehem, because he was descended from the house and family of David. He went to be registered with Mary to whom he was engaged and who was expecting a child. While they were there, the time came for her to deliver her child. 'And she gave birth to her firstborn son and wrapped him in bands of cloth, and laid him in a manger, because there was no place for him in the inn.'

Luke 2:8-20 narrates the beautiful story of The Shepherds and the Angels who came to visit baby Jesus. The shepherds living in the fields, keeping watch over their flock by night, are visited by an angel of the Lord who said to them, 'Do not be afraid; for see, I am bringing you good news of great joy for all the people: to you is born this day in the city of David a Saviour, who is the Messiah, the Lord. This will be a sign for you: you will find a child wrapped in bands of cloth and lying in a manger. And they heard the heavenly choir sing: "Glory to God in the highest heaven, and on earth peace among those whom He favours!"'

The shepherds said to one another, 'Let us now go to Bethlehem and see this thing that has taken place, which the Lord has made known to us.' So they went with haste and found Mary and Joseph, and the child lying in the manger. When they saw this, they made known what had been told to them about this child; and all who heard it were amazed at what the shepherds told them. But Mary treasured all these words and pondered them in her heart. The shepherds returned, glorifying and praising God for all they had heard and seen, as it had been told to them.

The next event in Jesus's infancy is narrated to us in Matthew 2:1-12: namely, The Visit of the Magi. These three wise men from the East, we are told, followed a star to find the new King of the Jews; unaware of the Roman's animosity to this idea, they seek Herod and tell him of their mission. Herod requests them to come back and report to him of the new leader. The star leads them on to Bethlehem, where they see the child with his mother Mary, and falling to their knees they do him homage. Then, opening their treasures, they offer him gifts of gold, frankincense and myrrh. They are warned in a dream to go back home without meeting Herod.

Luke 2:21-40 chronicles The Naming of Jesus and the Presentation in the Temple. Eight days after his birth, his parents take him to the temple; he is circumcised and a sacrifice is offered on his behalf. Here they are met by Simeon, a just and righteous man, who takes the infant in his arms and proclaims, 'This child is destined for the falling and the rising of many in Israel, and to be a sign that will be opposed so that the inner thoughts of many will be revealed.' He adds, prophetically, a warning to the Virgin Mother, 'And a sword will pierce your own soul too.'

Matthew 2:13-18 chronicles the subsequent events: The Flight to Egypt and The Massacre of the Innocents. After the wise men had left, the angel of the Lord appeared to Joseph in a dream and said, 'Get up, take the child and his mother with you, and escape into Egypt, and stay there until I tell you, because Herod intends to search for the child and do away with him.'

Joseph obeys the angel; taking the child and his mother with him, he left that night for Egypt, where he stayed until Herod was dead. This too fulfills what the Lord had spoken through the prophet: 'I called my son out of Egypt!'

Herod was furious when he realized that he had been outwitted by the wise men, and in Bethlehem and its surrounding district orders the killing of all the male children who were two years old or under, reckoning by the date of the birth which he had been careful to ask the wise men.

The birth of Christ in the manger, the Visit of the Magi, the Flight to Egypt and the Massacre of the Innocents are all subjects of masterpieces in painting rendered by the most famous artists of the Italian Renaissance.

Matthew 2:19-23 records the Holy Family's Return to Nazareth. Once again, the angel of the Lord appeared in a dream to Joseph in Egypt and asks him to return to the land of Israel with Mary and Jesus, as those who wanted to kill the child are dead. Once again, Joseph obeys implicitly returning to settle in Nazareth, a village in Galilee.

Luke 2:41-52 tells us the significant story of the boy Jesus in the Temple. When Jesus was twelve years old, his parents take him to Jerusalem for the Passover festival. When they return to Nazareth, Jesus is left behind. After a day, they go back to the temple and find him there. When they reproach him for causing so much anxiety to them, he only replies, 'Why were you searching for me? Did you not know that I must be in my Father's house?'

John 2:1-12 gives us an account of the wedding at Cana. Mary and Jesus have both been invited to the wedding. The hosts run out of wine to serve the wedding guests, and on Mary's request, Jesus turns water to wine. Luke adds, 'Jesus did this, the first of his signs, in Cana of Galilee, and revealed his glory; and his disciples believed in him.' The first of his miracles is thus performed at the request of his mother.

Matthew 13:54-58 narrates the story of Jesus returning to his hometown. But he is greeted with skepticism and disbelief when he begins teaching at the local synagogue. Hearing him preach, we are told that his townsmen were quite astounded and said, 'Where did this man get this wisdom and these deeds of power? Is not this the carpenter's son? Is not his mother called Mary? And are not his brothers James and Joseph and Simon and Judas? And are not all his sisters with us? Where then did this man get all this?'

We are also told that they took offense at him. But significantly, Jesus tells them: 'Prophets are not without honour except in their own country and in their own house.'

It is from John 19:25-28a that we get the final view of Mary in the Gospel. Mary, the beloved disciple John, and Mary Magdalene are seen at the foot of the Cross on which Christ is crucified. When Jesus saw his mother and the disciple whom he loved standing beside her, he said to his mother, 'Woman, here is your son.' Then he said to the disciple, 'Here is your mother.' And from that hour the disciple (John) took her into his own home.

Once again, it is the great artists and painters who have captured for us the lasting image of the grief and sorrow of the Mother of God in immortal works like the Pieta.

Thus, the Gospels give us a living tradition which venerates the Mother of the Lord unencumbered by exaggerations. Hers is a story of Divine Revelation and a 'maternal presence' always operative in the life of the Church.

Unforgettable Women Named 'Mary' in the Gospels

But Martha was cumbered about much serving, and came to him, and said, Lord, dost thou not care that my sister hath left me to serve alone? Bid her therefore that she help me. And Jesus answered and said unto her, Martha, Martha, thou art careful and troubled about many things: But one thing is needful: and Mary hath chosen that good part, which shall not be taken away from her.

— St Luke10:40-2

$\bowtie$

Rachel Evans, an American feminist historian writes of the women in the Gospels:

'When referring to the earliest followers of Jesus, the Gospel writers often speak of two groups of disciples: the Twelve and the Women. The Twelve refer to the twelve Jewish men chosen by Jesus to be his closest companions and first apostles, symbolic of the twelve tribes of Israel. The Women refer to an unspecified number of female disciples who also followed Jesus, welcoming him into their homes, financing his ministry, and often teaching the Twelve through their acts of faithfulness and love. Just as Jesus predicted, most of the Twelve abandoned him at his death (John 16:32). But the women remained by his side through his death, burial, and resurrection…'

The amazing fact is that several of them shared the blessed name Mary!

There are several Marys in the Gospel, quite apart from the Mother of Jesus.

1. There is Mary of Bethany. John identifies her as the sister of Martha and Lazarus, who bathes Jesus' feet in perfume and wipes them with her hair. In John's account, it is Judas who chastises Mary for her waste.

Here is what Luke[9] says of her:

As Jesus and his disciples were on their way, he came to a village where a woman named Martha opened her home to him. She had a sister called Mary, who sat at the Lord's feet listening to what he said. But Martha was distracted by all the preparations that had to be made. She came to him and asked, 'Lord, don't you care that my sister has left me to do the work by myself? Tell her to help me!'

'Martha, Martha,' the Lord answered, 'you are worried and upset about many things, but few things are needed or indeed only one. Mary has chosen what is better, and it will not be taken away from her.'

Matthew, Mark and John tell us of another lady of the same name: Just days before his betrayal and death, Jesus and his disciples were eating at the home of Simon the Leper in Bethany. While they were reclining at the table, a woman, who John identifies as Mary of Bethany, approached Jesus with an alabaster jar of expensive perfume, worth about a year's wages. Mary broke the jar, pouring the perfume on Jesus's body.

While John writes that Mary anointed Jesus's feet, wiping them with her hair, Matthew and Mark report that the woman of Bethany anointed Jesus's head. Both actions carry important symbolic meaning. Only kings and great leaders were ever anointed with oil as part of their coronation. Thus by anointing Jesus, Mary of Bethany becomes a prophet who has identified Jesus as the Messiah.

She is chastised by the other disciples for wasting expensive perfumed oil on such an act. But Jesus comes to her defence in a wholly unexpected manner: 'Leave her alone,' Jesus replied. 'It was intended that she should save this perfume for the day of my burial. You will always have the poor among you, but you will not always have me.'

Whenever Jesus had spoken of his impending death, the Disciples had always been in denial of the same. There is undeniable sadness in

9. 10:38-42.

Jesus' words which refer to his forthcoming death. Whether Mary was aware of the truth is not specified to us; but certainly, she seems to have sensed it instinctively.

2. There is Mary, the Mother of James and Joseph. Along with Mary Magdalene and Mary of Clopas, Mary the mother of James is known as one of the Three Marys who was present at the cross during Jesus's last hours. It is ironic that it is these women who are unafraid to be noted as the disciples of the condemned teacher.

She also visits his tomb after his burial and is identified as one of the 'myrrh bearers' – that is, ones who carried herbs and spices for the burial according to Jewish rites. She is thought to be the Mother of the Apostle known as James, the Less. Very little is revealed about her in the Gospels.

3. There is Mary, the wife of Clopas. Mary of Clopas is explicitly mentioned only in John 19:25, where she is among the women present at the Crucifixion of Jesus:

'Now there stood by the cross of Jesus His mother and His mother's sister, Mary [the wife] of Clopas and Mary Magdalene...'

Some scholars say that this Mary was the wife of Clopas, who was actually the brother of St. Joseph, the father of Jesus. Matthew (28:1) calls her 'the other Mary' to distinguish her from Mary Magdalene.

4. Last but not the least there is Mary Magdalene.

The name of Mary Magdalene is mentioned in the New Testament Versions of Mark, Matthew and Luke, as one of the foremost female disciples of Jesus Christ. Her role in this canonical gospel may be small – but it is of special interest to all scholars who seek to learn about the role of women in early Christianity, as well as in Jesus's ministry during his lifetime.

We read in Luke 8: 1-3:

Now after this [Jesus] made his way through towns and villages preaching, and proclaiming the Good News of the Kingdom of God. With him went the Twelve, as well as certain women who had been cured of evil spirits and ailments: Mary surnamed the Magdalene, from whom seven demons had gone out, Joanna the wife of Herod's steward Chuza, Susanna, and several others who provided for them out of their own resources.

What exactly is implied by the reference that seven demons (NOT seven devils!) had been driven out of her? This is the extent of her 'sin' that she was probably given to extreme nervousness and so suffered from epileptic fits; and that the blessed sight of Christ and his peace-filled gaze cured her forever! It is not wickedness of character that is implied, but only mental derangement which continued to be associated with 'demonic possession' until very recent times. As one Biblical scholar remarks, 'When Christ saved her, He liberated the highest virtues of sacrifice, fortitude and courage in her. Having been delivered from her demons, Mary Magdalene became a devout Disciple.'

This particular Mary is distinguished from all others of the same name as 'The Magdalene', which, scholars point out, identifies her with her place of birth, Magdala (just as Jesus was called 'The Nazarene' because of His association with Nazareth). Magdala means 'tower' or 'castle', and in those times, was a thriving, well-populated town on the coast of Galilee, about three miles from Capernaum. It is said that Magdala housed dye works and primitive textile factories, which added to the wealth of the community. Scholars feel that 'The Magdalene' was connected with the industry of the town, for she seems to have been a lady of means; the passage mentions that she had her own resources which enabled her to accompany her Divine teacher and to serve the Lord with her substance. We can also assume that as she was free to follow Lord Jesus with his disciples, she must have been of a mature age and was independent of family obligations that would have constrained her moving out from home.

After the crucifixion, John tells us:[10] 'But standing by the cross of Jesus were His mother and His mother's sister, Mary the wife of Clopas and Mary Magdalene.'

Matthew also tells us that Mary Magdalene was found sitting by the side of the grave where Jesus was buried.[11] Mark adds[12] 'When the

---

[10.] 19:25.

[11]. 27: 61.

[12.] 16:1.

Sabbath was over, Mary Magdalene, and Mary the mother of James, and Salome, bought spices, so that they might come and anoint Him.'

It is she who first discovers that Jesus' tomb was empty.[13]: 'Now on the first day of the week Mary Magdalene came early to the tomb, while it was still dark, and saw the stone already taken away from the tomb.'

Among the few disciples who lingered at the Cross on which Jesus died, she was also the first at the garden tomb to witness the most important event in Christian history and the pivotal truth of Christianity, namely the Resurrection of Jesus Christ. What a singular and great honour God conferred upon the faithful Mary Magdalene, in choosing her to be the first witness of that Resurrection! As we know from John (cited above) she was at the tomb early on that first Easter morning, and as the light of earliest day filtered across Jerusalem, she peered into the cave. Seeing it was empty, she wept. Finding the grave empty (John tells us) Mary rushed to Peter and John, and cried out, 'They have taken away the Lord out of the sepulchre and we know not where they have laid him.'

Peter and John go back to the grave with Mary Magdalene and find that she has indeed spoken the truth. They then departed 'to their own homes' but not Mary! She stood at the door of the sepulchre weeping, and as she wept, we are told, two angels appeared, one at the head and the other at the feet, where the body of Jesus had lain. Seeing her distressed and afraid, they tenderly ask her, 'Woman, why weepest thou?' Tremblingly she replies, 'Because they have taken away my Lord, and I know not where they have laid him.'

We must return to John's Gospel for the amazing narration.[14]

At this, she turned around and saw Jesus standing there, but she did not realize that it was Jesus. He asked her, 'Woman, why are you crying? Who is it you are looking for?'

Thinking he was the gardener, she said, 'Sir, if you have carried him away, tell me where you have put him, and I will get him.' Jesus said to her, 'Mary'.

She turned toward him and cried out in Aramaic, 'Rabboni!' (which means 'teacher').

---

13. John 20:1.
14. John 20.

Jesus said, 'Do not touch me, for I have not yet ascended to the Father. Go instead to my brothers and tell them, "I am ascending to my Father and your Father, to my God and your God."'

Mark corroborates this decisively:[15] 'Now after He had risen early on the first day of the week, He first appeared to Mary Magdalene, from whom He had cast out seven demons.'

John corroborates this in 20:18: 'Mary Magdalene came, announcing to the disciples, "I have seen the Lord," and that He had said these things to her.'

Those scholars who are inclined to statistical studies, point out that within the sacred texts of the four Gospels, she is named at least 12 times, which is more than most of the apostles. Carol Ann Morrow, an American Catholic researcher points out that all these references point to her as a courageous woman, brave enough to stand by Jesus in his hours of suffering, during his death and beyond.

Non-canonical gospels such as those Philip, Thomas and the Acts of Peter portray her as a thinking disciple – someone who often asked intelligent questions when the other disciples were confused by Jesus's teachings and his new philosophy. In fact, these versions record that Jesus had a special place for her in his affection, because of her wisdom and understanding.

In later Christian Iconography, she is most often portrayed in acts of devotion to Jesus – washing Jesus's feet, anointing him, or sitting at his feet to listen to him. It was she who wept for Christ, as he was nailed on the cross; she stood by the cross to support him in the final hours of suffering, even when some of his prominent male disciples had fled. She was present at his burial. It was she who discovered the empty tomb of Jesus after his resurrection, and was bidden to inform the other disciples of the same. In fact, John says that after his rise from death, it was before her that Jesus first appeared.

Many Biblical traditions identify her with Mary, the sister of Martha; some say that she was a sinner who was forgiven by Jesus; however, the Eastern Orthodox Church holds her as a distinct figure, a great woman saint of the Catholic Church.

Why was this remarkable woman, who first announced the resurrection of Jesus, labelled as a 'fallen woman' and sinner? The Jewish

[15.] 16:9.

Talmud tells us that the town of Magdala had an unsavoury reputation, and was subsequently destroyed because of the immoral practises carried on in its vicinity. Perhaps it is because of this tradition, that the idea developed that she was a 'sinful woman', and may be the one who was brought to Jesus by the Pharisees as an adulteress. It must be stressed however, that there is not an iota of genuine evidence in the gospels to suggest such a bad reputation.

Mary Magdalene thus, became a woman who has been sorely misrepresented in subsequent times. From the sixth century AD, she was perceived as a 'fallen woman'. But St Augustine referred to her as 'the apostle of apostles'.

THOUGHT FOR REFLECTION

Who was Mary Magdalene? Was she the penitent sinner forgiven by the grace of Jesus? Or was she the intelligent, independent disciple who supported his ministry with her personal wealth, and rose to become one of his beloved disciples? Whoever she may have been, she was there at the 'beginning of a movement that was going to transform the West'; and her fame lives on to inspire the faithful.

The Saint who Baptized
Lord Jesus Christ

John answered, saying to all, 'I indeed baptize you with water; but One mightier than I is coming, whose sandal strap I am not worthy to loose. He will baptize you with the Holy Spirit and fire. His winnowing fan is in His hand, and He will thoroughly clean out His threshing floor, and gather the wheat into His barn; but the chaff He will burn with unquenchable fire.
Amen, amen, I say to you, unless one is born of water and the Spirit, he cannot enter the Kingdom of God. That which is born of the flesh is flesh, and that which is born of the Spirit is spirit.'

– John 3:5

THE Christian ceremony of baptism is one of the Seven Sacraments of the Christian Church; frequently called the 'first sacrament', the 'door of the sacraments', and the 'door of the Church', it is a deeply symbolic and significant event in the life of the true believer. The word baptize is derived from the Greek verb baptidzo which means 'to immerse'. The process of baptism consists of immersion, submersion and emergence. When a person is baptized in water, his or her body is totally immersed in the water and brought out again. The deeper significance of water baptism is that it symbolizes the death, burial and resurrection of Jesus Christ and the believer's assertion and identification with the same. Thus, water baptism is a physical act that should indelibly mark the mind of the person being baptized with the reality of his union with Jesus Christ. It serves as an outward sign and testimony of an inward grace.

One of the most memorable and thrilling accounts in the gospels is the baptism of Jesus, narrated in all the canonical gospels. The man who had the privilege and grace of performing this unique act was Jesus Christ's cousin, the man who boldly proclaimed the arrival of the Messiah to his contemporaries, and who is therefore venerated today as the precursor of Jesus, St John, the Baptist.

Zachary, the father of John the Baptist, was a priest of the order of Abia. Zachary's wife was Elizabeth, who was a cousin of Our Lady, the mother of Christ. Zachary and Elizabeth, we learn from St Luke, 'were both just in the eyes of God, walking in all the commandments and justifications of the Lord without blame; and they had no son, for that Elizabeth was barren.'[16] For long, they had prayed to God to bless them with a child. When they were very advanced in years, and had almost given up hope, an angel appeared before Zachary as he was performing his priestly duty of offering incense before God in his temple. The angel said to him, 'Fear not, Zachary, for thy prayer is heard; and thy wife Elizabeth shall bear thee a son, and thou shalt call his name John: and thou shalt have joy and gladness, and many shall rejoice in his nativity. For he shall be great before the Lord; and shall drink no wine nor strong drink: and he shall be filled with the Holy Ghost, even from his mother's womb. And he shall convert many of the children of Israel to the Lord their God. And he shall go before him in the spirit and power of Elias; that he may turn the hearts of the fathers unto the children, and the incredulous to the wisdom of the just, to prepare unto the Lord a perfect people.' [17]

For a few moments, Zachary was so stunned when he heard the angel's prophesy, that he stood in utter disbelief. For he and his wife were so old, that it seemed impossible that Elizabeth could conceive

16. Luke 1:6-7.
17. Luke 1:8-17.

now. For his incredulity, the angel said that he would be struck dumb as a temporary punishment, until the miracle that was promised to him came to pass, and his son would be born.

Thus was St John the Baptist conceived, with the grace of God. When his mother was six months pregnant, her cousin, the Virgin Mary received the Annunciation of Jesus's birth and came to see Elizabeth. It is told to us in the Gospels that the baby in Elizabeth's womb 'leaped for joy' for he realized that he was in the presence of his Saviour, who was also in the womb of his mother, Mary.

When John was born, speech miraculously returned to Zachary. This and the fact that an aged mother had given birth to a son, made all the people wonder: 'What a one, think ye, shall this child be?'[18]

Of John's early life St Luke tells us only that 'the child grew, and was strengthened in spirit; and was in the deserts, until the day of his manifestation to Israel'.[19] Possibly, St John was sent into the desert to escape the cruel order on the Massacre of the Innocents, promulgated by Herod. Later accounts also tell us that his father, the pious priest Zachary, was put to death by Herod before the altar of God, as he had prophesied the coming of the Messiah.

However, St Luke's Gospel takes up the life story of the Baptist after a gap of thirty years, when he begins his public ministry. Up to this he had led the life of a hermit in the desert; now he came out among the people to deliver his message. 'In the fifteenth year of the reign of Tiberius Caesar... the word of the Lord was made unto John, the son of Zachary, in the desert. And he came into all the country about the Jordan, preaching.'[20] He was not dressed like a townsman, but wore simple, primitive clothes. But the people of Jerusalem and Judea were drawn to him by the magnetism of his ascetic personality, and were convinced of the truth of his words, when he proclaimed the arrival of a Messiah among them. 'Do penance: for the kingdom of heaven is at hand,' was his constant refrain.[21] And the men who flocked to him in large numbers, believed him implicitly.

St John lashed out at the hypocritical Pharisees and Sadducees, warning them to mend their ways, for fear of God. 'For now the axe

[18.] Luke 1:66.
[19.] 1:80.
[20.] Luke 3:1-3.
[21.] Matthew 3:2.

is laid to the root of the trees. Every tree, therefore, that doth not yield good fruit, shall be cut down, and cast into the fire.'[22]

The people beseeched him to tell them what they should do to prepare for the Messiah. His reply was indeed significant. 'He that hath two coats, let him give to him that hath none; and he that hath food, let him do in like manner.'[23] Some people who came to him were public officers; on them he enjoined not to exact more than the rate of taxes fixed by law[24]. To the soldiers (probably Jewish police officers) he recommended not to do violence to any man, nor falsely to denounce anyone, and to be content with their pay[25].

To confirm the good dispositions of his listeners, John began to baptize them in the River Jordan, saying that, 'Baptism was good, not so much to free one from certain sins, as to purify the body, the soul being already cleansed from its defilements by justice.'[26] This feature of his ministry, more than anything else, attracted public attention to such an extent that he was surnamed 'the Baptist' even during his lifetime[27].

Even as he was engaged in baptizing people, St John did not allow them to mistake him for the Messiah. He always insisted that his was only a forerunner's mission: 'I indeed baptize you with water; but there shall come one mightier than I, the strings of whose shoes I am not worthy to lose: he shall baptize you with the Holy Ghost and with fire: whose fan is in his hand and he will purge his floor; and will gather the wheat into his barn, but the chaff he will burn with unquenchable fire.'[28]

The Precursor, as he is called, had been preaching and baptizing for quite some time, when Lord Jesus himself came from Galilee to the Jordan, to be baptized by him. Now, the question might arise: why, should He who is sinless seek John's 'baptism of penance for the remission of sins'?[29] The Church answers very appropriately that

---

[22.] Matthew 3:7-10; Luke 3:7-9.
[23.] Luke 3:11.
[24.] Luke 3:13.
[25.] Luke 3:14.
[26.] Josephus, 'Antiq.', XVIII, vii.
[27.] by Christ, Matthew 11:11; by his own disciples, Luke 7:20.
[28.] Luke 3:16, 17.
[29.] Luke 3:3.

this was the occasion preordained by the Father when Jesus should be manifested to the world as the Son of God; then again, by submitting to it, Jesus sanctioned the baptism of John.

However, St John was at first reluctant to perform so momentous a task. 'But Jesus stayed him, saying: I ought to be baptized by thee, and comest thou to me?'[30]

God was allowing this to happen with good reason. Jesus answering, said to him, 'Suffer it to be so now. For, so it becometh us to fulfill all justice. Then he suffered him. And Jesus being baptized, forthwith came out of the water: and lo, the heavens were opened to him... And, behold, a voice from heaven, saying: This is my beloved Son, in whom I am well pleased'.[31]

After this baptism, Jesus went on to preach his message through the towns of Galilee, while John continued his ministry in the valley of the Jordan. It was at this time that 'the Jews sent from Jerusalem priests and Levites to him, to ask him: Who are thou? And he confessed, and did not deny: and he confessed: I am not the Christ. And they asked him: What then? Art thou Elias? And he said: I am not. Art thou the prophet? And he answered: No. They said, therefore, unto him: Who are thou, that we may give an answer to them that sent us? What sayest thou of thyself? He said: I am the voice of one crying in the wilderness, make straight the way of the Lord, as said the prophet Isaias'[32].

As we saw earlier, this had indeed been anticipated by the angel when, announcing John's birth to Zachary, he foretold that the child would go before the Lord 'in the spirit and power of Elias.'[33]

St John's calling had been fulfilled. But martyrdom awaited this extraordinary messenger of God. Various Biblical accounts help us to put together the story of his later life. Herod, the cruel dictator, contracted an incestuous and adulterous marriage with his niece, called Herodias. When St John denounced his adultery Herod and Herodias were both incensed against him, and had him thrown in prison. The accounts say that when more and more people began to flock to St John for baptism, Herod falsely imagined that if he stopped St John, he could

[30.] Matthew 3:14.
[31.] Matthew 3:15-17.
[32.] John 1:19-23.
[33.] Luke 1:17.

somehow stop the Messiah. Whatever the reason, St John the Baptist was imprisoned. But even in prison, he continued to be a champion of truth and justice, and a firm believer in Jesus Christ. It is said that a group of people once approached him, when he was in prison, and asked him whether Jesus was really the Messiah. John bade them go to Jesus and ask him, 'John the Baptist hath sent us to thee, saying: Art thou He that art to come; or look we for another?'

Before these people who came to him with John's message, Jesus performed several miracles: and he replied thus to their query, 'And answering, he said to them: Go and relate to John what you have heard and seen: the blind see, the lame walk, the lepers are made clean, the deaf hear, the dead rise again, to the poor the gospel is preached: and blessed is he whosoever shall not be scandalized in me.'[34] And Jesus proclaimed John's prophethood thus: 'This is he of whom it is written: Behold, I send my angel before thy face, who shall prepare thy way before thee. For I say to you: Amongst those that are born of women, there is not a greater prophet than John the Baptist.[35]

But Herodias who hated him and wished to avenge herself on him, took the help of her daughter, Salome, from a former marriage, to put an end to the prophet. Salome danced before Herod at a magnificent feast, and in his intoxicated state, the dictator offered to her any gift that she might ask of him; at her mother's insistence, Salome asked that the head of St John the Baptist might be brought to her on a dish.

Herod, who still had the fear of God despite his many sins, was taken aback at the request. In his heart of hearts, he knew that St John was innocent. But the die had been caste; his word was given. St John was summarily executed to satisfy the cruel whim of a dancing girl and her wicked mother.

St Augustine remarks: 'Thus was done to death the greatest "amongst them that are born of women", the prize awarded to a dancing girl, the toll exacted for an oath rashly taken and criminally kept.'

John's disciples, hearing of his death, 'came, and took his body, and laid it in a tomb'[36], 'and came and told Jesus'[37].

---

34. Luke 7:20-23; Matthew 11:3-6.
35. Luke 7:24-28.
36. Mark 6:29.
37. Matthew 14:12.

Thus ended the remarkable life of the Precursor, who had recognized his saviour even when he was in the womb of his mother; who had the singular honour of baptizing the Saviour, and who lived and died for truth and faith.

THOUGHT FOR REFLECTION

Gurudev Sadhu Vaswani has given us a profound message in one of his poems which is like a prayer; 'In all circumstances and under all conditions, in sorrow and suffering remember that God knows the best. Whatever He does is for our benefit. What may seem to us, to be an obstacle, a difficulty, or just misfortune, has been sent to us with a definite purpose. Whatever happens to us, whatever befalls us, has a hidden meaning, which we are often unable to see or comprehend.'

Sorrow, grief, hardship, loneliness and insecurities are given to us to make us strong in spirit, to endow us with moral courage, or what I call muscles of the spirit. Difficulties give us courage and strengthen our will power. They put us through a process of cleansing and purification.

Gurudev Sadhu Vaswani said to us: 'Blessed is the Truth seeker. For his life is tragedy and tears.' Every suffering is a gift from God. It is the gift that will help you in self-growth. To avoid suffering is to shut yourself away from the beautiful life. The supreme vision of beauty comes from the cross!

Paradise Regained: Christ's Suffering and Resurrection

'When we get to Jerusalem,' he told them, 'the Son of Man will be betrayed to the leading priests and the teachers of religious law. They will sentence him to die and hand him over to the Romans. They will mock him, spit on him, beat him with their whips, and kill him, but after three days he will rise again.'

– Mark 10:32-34

⟨symbol⟩

The moving story of Jesus Christ's death on the Cross is recorded in all of the four canonical gospels as well as in the writings of the Apostle, St Paul. The most heart-rending aspect of this sequence of episodes is the fact that the death is unfair, unjust, cruel and gruelingly painful; and it is visited on the Son of God who is sinless and innocent of all the false accusations so ruthlessly laid on him by his own people. Though Jesus suffers unjustly, he knows that it is God's will that he should thus suffer, and faces his ordeal unflinchingly.

Jesus preached love and forgiveness. But that was hardly the reason why his enemies feared him. The Jewish high priests were afraid of his growing popularity among the people. They felt that he was undermining their authority and their established systems of prayer and worship. As for the Romans, they were apprehensive that he could spearhead a mass rebellion, a people's movement which could threaten the Roman rule of Judea. Each one of these groups was thus, operating out of their own vested interests.

Judas Iscariot, one of the apostles, in the meanwhile, conspired with the temple priests and the lawmakers as to how he could help them arrest Jesus.

It was under these gathering clouds of suspicion and betrayal that Jesus and his disciples met to celebrate the Jewish festival of Passover. The ritual Passover meal was held at the house of one of his followers, where the twelve apostles gathered together for what has come to be known as The Last Supper. The Gospels describe the events that followed in minute detail.

As they were about to eat, Jesus said to them:

'I have very much wanted to eat this Passover meal with you before I suffer. I tell you that I will not eat another Passover meal until it is finally eaten in God's kingdom.'

He then broke the bread and handed it round to each of them. 'This is my body, which is given for you. Eat this as a way of remembering me!'

When the meal was over, he took a cup of wine in his hands and said to them, 'This is my blood. It is poured out for you, and with it God makes his new covenant. The one who will betray me is here at the table with me! The Son of Man will die in the way that has been decided for him, but it will be terrible for the one who betrays him!'[38]

One by one they questioned, 'I'm not the one, am I, Lord?' Jesus explained that even though he knew he would die as the scriptures foretold, his betrayer's fate would be terrible: 'Far better for him if he had never been born!' The apostles first argued among themselves about which one of them would betray Jesus and then it turned into which one of them was the greatest of the disciples. Jesus said to them: '… he who is greatest among you, let him be as the younger, and he who governs as he who serves. For who is greater, he who sits at the table, or he who serves? Is it not he who sits at the table? Yet I am among you as the one who serves …'

Simon Peter protested that he would go to prison, indeed go to his death with Jesus. But Jesus said to him, 'I tell you, Peter, the rooster shall not crow this day before you will deny three times that you know me.'

Jesus then went out to pray in the Mount of Olives. He urged the disciples too, to pray that they might be preserved from temptation. He knelt at a stone's throw away from them and prayed, 'Father, if you are

---

38. Luke 22:15-20.

willing, take this cup from me; yet not my will, but yours be done.' An angel of God appeared before him and strengthened his resolve. But he was in intense mental agony. Beads of sweat gathered on his forehead, and when they dropped down to earth, they were like drops of blood.[39]

But the disciples had fallen asleep, exhausted by the sorrow that Jesus had prophesied. He awakened them and said to them: 'Are you still sleeping and resting? The time has come for the Son of Man to be handed over to sinners. Get up! Let's go. The one who will betray me is already here.'

Even as he was speaking, Judas approached him with a big mob carrying swords and sticks; Judas came up to Jesus and kissed him. (This was the sign that had been agreed upon between him and the Pharisees.)

As the mob laid hands upon Jesus and arrested him, all the disciples fled.

Then, those who had seized Jesus led him to Caiaphas the high priest, and the Sanhedrin, where the scribes and the elders had gathered. Peter followed him, but at a distance, as far as the courtyard of the high priest.

Now the chief priests and the whole council were seeking false testimony against Jesus that they might put him to death, and only false witnesses came forward. They accused him of asserting that he would destroy the Temple of God. Jesus remained silent. And the high priest said to him, 'I adjure you by the living God, tell us if you are the Christ, the Son of God.'

Jesus said to him, 'You have said so. But I tell you, from now on you will see the Son of Man seated at the right hand of Power and coming on the clouds of heaven.'

That was enough for his enemies. The High Priest tore Jesus's robes and said, 'He has uttered blasphemy. What further witnesses do we need? You have now heard his blasphemy. What is your judgment?' They answered, 'He deserves death.'

Then they spat in his face and struck him. And some slapped him, saying, 'Prophesy to us, you Christ! Who is it that struck you?'

At this time, a servant girl came up to Peter, who was sitting in the yard and said to him, 'I have seen you with Jesus of Nazareth.' Peter said, 'I don't know what you are talking about.' He went out of the gate, where another girl said to her friends, 'I have seen him; he was with

---

[39.] Matthew 26: 36-75.

Jesus at Galilee.' Hastily, Peter denied it. 'I don't even know the man,' he said.

After a little while, those standing there went up to Peter and said, 'Surely you are one of them; your accent gives you away.' Then he began to call down curses, and he swore to them, 'I don't know the man!' Immediately a rooster crowed. Peter remembered Jesus's words to him; he went away and wept bitterly.[40]

Jesus's enemies wished to make his execution legal and official. In the morning, he was taken before Pontius Pilate. Judas, who had been responsible for his betrayal, returned the thirty pieces of silver that he had got from the Pharisees. Out of remorse, he hanged himself.

Governor Pontius Pilate knew that Jesus was innocent. His wife also begged him not to have anything to do with the trial and condemnation of an innocent man. But Pilate was helpless. Jesus said nothing to defend himself, and the mob, incited by the priests, were crying for his blood. 'Crucify him!' they chanted.[41]

'Are you the king of the Jews?' asked Pilate.

'You have said so,' Jesus replied. The chief priests accused him of many things. So, again Pilate asked him, 'Aren't you going to answer? See how many things they are accusing you of.' But Jesus still made no reply, and Pilate was amazed.[42]

'Why? What crime has he committed?' Pilate asked them. They only cried out louder, 'Crucify him! Crucify him!'

Disgusted by the mob, Pilate washed his hands with water. 'I am innocent of this man's blood,' he said. 'It is your responsibility!'

The crowd cried out, 'His blood is on us and on our children!' Jesus was flogged and handed over to them for crucifixion.

The soldiers stripped Jesus's robes and put a scarlet cloak on him. They twisted some thorns and put a crown of thorns on his head. They put a staff in his right hand. Then they knelt in front of him and mocked him. 'Hail, king of the Jews!' they said. They spat on him, and took the staff and struck him on the head again and again. After they had mocked him thus, they took off the robe and put his clothes on him. Then they led him away to crucify him.[43]

40. Matthew 26: 36-75.
41. Matthew 27: 1- 5.
42. Mark 15: 2-5.
43. Matthew 27: 23-31.

As the soldiers led him away, a large number of people followed him, including women who mourned and wailed for him. Jesus turned and said to them, 'Daughters of Jerusalem, do not weep for me; weep for yourselves and for your children.'

Two other men, both criminals, were also led out with him to be executed. When they came to the place called Golgotha, they crucified him there, along with the criminals; one on his right, the other on his left.[44]

Pilate had a notice prepared and fastened to the cross. It read: 'Jesus of Nazareth, the King of the Jews'. Many of the Jews read this sign, for the place where Jesus was crucified was near the city, and the sign was written in Aramaic, Latin and Greek. The chief priests of the Jews protested to Pilate, 'Do not write "The King of the Jews", but write that this man claimed to be King of the Jews.'

Pilate answered, 'What I have written, I have written.'

When the soldiers crucified Jesus, they took his clothes, dividing them into four shares, one for each of them, with the undergarment remaining.

This garment was seamless, woven in one piece from top to bottom. 'Let's not tear it,' they said to one another. 'Let's decide by lot who will get it.'

Thus it came to pass that the scripture might be fulfilled that said, 'They divided my clothes among them and cast lots for my garment.'[45]

Jesus said, 'Father, forgive them, for they do not know what they are doing.' The people stood watching, and the rulers even sneered at him. They said, 'He saved others; let him save himself if he is God's Messiah, the Chosen One.' The soldiers also came up and mocked him. They said, 'If you are the King of the Jews, save yourself.'[46]

One of the criminals who hung there hurled insults at him: 'Aren't you the Messiah? Save yourself and us!' But the other criminal rebuked him. 'Don't you fear God,' he said, 'since you are under the same sentence? We are punished justly, for we are getting what our deeds deserve. But this man has done nothing wrong.'

Then he said, 'Jesus, remember me when you come into your kingdom.'

[44] Luke 23: 26-32.
[45] John 19: 19-24.
46. Luke 23: 34-38.

Jesus answered him, 'Truly I tell you, today you will be with me in paradise.'[47]

Near the cross of Jesus stood his mother, his mother's sister, Mary the wife of Clopas, and Mary Magdalene. When Jesus saw his mother there, and the disciple whom he loved standing nearby, he said to her, 'Woman, here is your son,' and to the disciple, 'Here is your mother.' From that time on, this disciple (John) took her into his home.

Later, knowing that everything had now been finished, and so that the scripture would be fulfilled, Jesus said, 'I am thirsty.' A jar of wine vinegar was there, so they soaked a sponge in it, put the sponge on a stalk of the hyssop plant, and lifted it to Jesus' lips.[48]

It was now about noon, and darkness came over the whole land until three in the afternoon, for the sun stopped shining. And the curtain of the temple was torn in two. Jesus called out with a loud voice, 'Father, into your hands I commit my spirit.' When he had said this, he breathed his last.

The Roman centurion, seeing what had happened, praised God and said, 'Surely this was a righteous man.' When all the people who had gathered to witness this sight saw what took place, they beat their breasts and went away. But all those who knew him, including the women who had followed him from Galilee, stood at a distance, watching these things.[49]

The next day was the Sabbath and the Jews wanted the bodies taken down. One of the soldiers pierced Jesus's side with a spear and blood and water rushed out. He realized that Jesus was already dead.

Now Joseph of Arimathea, who was a disciple of Jesus, asked Pilate for the body of Jesus. With Pilate's permission, he came and took the body away. Joseph was accompanied by Nicodemus, who brought a mixture of myrrh and aloes, for the burial. Taking Jesus's body, the two of them wrapped it, with spices, in strips of linen. This was in accordance with Jewish burial customs. At the place where Jesus was crucified, there was a garden, and in the garden a new tomb, in which no one had ever been laid. Because it was the Jewish day of Preparation and since the tomb was nearby, they laid Jesus there.[50]

[47.] Luke 23: 39- 43.
[48.] John 19: 25-30.
[49.] Luke 23: 44-49.
[50.] John 19: 38-42.

Now on the first day of the week Mary Magdalene came to the tomb early, while it was still dark, and saw that the stone had been taken away from the tomb. So she ran and went to the disciples Peter and another and said to them, 'They have taken the Lord out of the tomb, and we do not know where they have laid him.'

Peter and John went with her to the tomb and found that this was indeed so. Then they returned home.

Mary stood all alone, weeping outside the tomb, and as she wept she stooped to look into the tomb. And she saw two angels in white, sitting where the body of Jesus had lain, one at the head and one at the feet. They said to her, 'Woman, why are you weeping?' She said to them, 'They have taken away my Lord, and I do not know where they have laid him.' Having said this, she turned around and saw Jesus standing, but she did not recognize him. Jesus said to her, 'Woman, why are you weeping? Whom are you seeking?' Supposing him to be the gardener, she said to him, 'Sir, if you have carried him away, tell me where you have laid him, and I will take him away.'

Jesus said to her, 'Mary.' She turned and said to him in Aramaic, 'Rabboni!' (which means Teacher). Jesus said to her, 'Do not cling to me, for I have not yet ascended to the Father; but go to my brothers and say to them, "I am ascending to my Father and your Father, to my God and your God."' Mary Magdalene went and announced to the disciples, 'I have seen the Lord' – and that he had said these things to her.

That evening, when the disciples were together, with the doors locked for fear of the Jewish leaders, Jesus came and stood among them and said, 'Peace be with you!' He showed them his hands and side. The disciples were overjoyed when they saw the Lord. To them Jesus said, 'Peace be with you! As the Father has sent me, I am sending you.' And with that he breathed on them and said, 'Receive the Holy Spirit. If you forgive anyone's sins, their sins are forgiven; if you do not forgive them, they are not forgiven.'[51]

He said to them, 'This is what I told you while I was still with you: Everything must be fulfilled that is written about me in the Law of Moses, the Prophets and the Psalms.'

Then he opened their minds so they could understand the scriptures. He told them, 'This is what is written: The Messiah will suffer and rise

[51.] John 20: 1-22.

from the dead on the third day, and repentance for the forgiveness of sins will be preached in his name to all nations, beginning at Jerusalem. You are witnesses of these things. I am going to send you what my Father has promised; but stay in the city until you have been clothed with power from on high.'

When he had led them out to the vicinity of Bethany, he lifted up his hands and blessed them. While he was blessing them, he left them and was taken up into heaven. Then they worshiped him and returned to Jerusalem with great joy. And they stayed continually at the temple, praising God.[52]

Thought for Reflection

It was said of Jesus, when He suffered intense pain and agony on the cross: 'He came to save others; how is it that He cannot save Himself?'

That remark was obviously made in ignorance; for suffering is a gift consciously chosen and willingly accepted by saviours and saints, helpers and healers of humanity.

Gurudev Sadhu Vaswani puts it so beautifully: 'Suffering is the benediction which God pours upon His beloved children to whom He would reveal the meaning of His Infinite mercy – reveal Himself, His wisdom and His love!'
Saints and holy men receive the arrows of pain as gifts from the all-giver. Alike in sunshine and in rain, they rejoice, give gratitude to God and sing His Holy Name. Every great one of humanity has had to bear his cross.

When we bleed and are in pain, let us remember that the will of God is working through us: and through suffering and pain, God's will is purifying us, preparing for the vision of light!

[52.] Luke 24: 44-53.

CONFUCIANISM

BRIEF INTRODUCTION

CONFUCIANISM IS KNOWN AS 'THE SCHOOL OF THE SCHOLARS'. IT is an ethical and philosophical system based on the teachings of the Chinese sage Confucius. Although there have been attempts to make Confucianism a religion, and defy Confucius himself as a saviour, it is essentially a way of life taught by Confucius in the sixth to fifth century BC. Regarded by some as a philosophy, and by others as a religion, Confucianism is perhaps best described as an all-encompassing humanism, although it is not very much concerned with spiritual matters. It originated in China but has spread to Korea, Taiwan and Vietnam. Most people who adhere to the teachings of Confucius follow Chinese traditional religion, which is a blending of Confucianism, Buddhism, Taoism, and age-old local practises and beliefs.

K'ung Fu Tzu (551-479 BC) was a contemporary of Gautama Buddha. (Confucius, the name we know him by, is a Latin rendering of the original Chinese). Though he was forced to take up a tedious government job to earn his living and look after his mother, his heart lay in the study of the ancient classics, which offered him both delight and peace.

We do not know who his teachers were, but it is widely believed that Confucius was well-versed in all the arts valued by ancient China – rituals, music, archery, charioteering, calligraphy, and arithmetic – and he was self-taught in the classics which he had always loved. Very soon, he quit his job to become a teacher of the people, and was elevated to the position of a respected and admired man, 'a travelling university' as he was often called. Followed by his devoted students, he moved about in an ox-cart, drawing wisdom from the incidents of everyday life that he and his students witnessed, as they travelled across north-eastern and central China. Like Socrates, he moved among the common people, listening to their problems and worries, and counselling them to live a life based on virtues and ethical principles.

Sadly, his teachings were not accepted by the rulers and their circles of influence; in fact, many records speak of Confucius's frustration at not finding acceptance in the larger political arena; but he had an ever-growing number of personal followers, gaining a great reputation as 'a man of vision and mission'.

Confucius often claimed that he never invented anything but was only transmitting ancient knowledge; however, he did produce a number of new ideas. Many western admirers say that the revolutionary idea of replacing the nobility of blood with one of virtue, was first proposed by Confucius. *Juniz* was a term which had meant 'nobleman' before Confucius; but slowly it assumed a new connotation in the course of his writings, more or less as 'gentleman' did in English.

In the two millennia after his death, Confucius's principles gained wide acceptance in China, perhaps because of their basis in everyday ethics, humanitarian values, emphasis on personal relationships, and respect for morality and common Chinese tradition and belief. He advocated familial loyalty, reverence for ancestors, and respect for all elders among the younger generation. Troubled by the moral laxity and social disharmony of the times, he urged the people to value humanism, justice, truth and morality. Rather than setting out a code of ethics or a formal set of dogmas and rules, he encouraged his disciples to think for themselves, learn their values from the ancient classics, and foster virtue and goodness by personal example rather than doctrinal precepts.

Few followers of Confucius today have a clear belief in any Divine existence, or in after-life. Yet they believe in the world of spirits and souls, and some even practise ancestor worship. As such, there is no concept of God in Confucianism.

Some of the chief concepts of Confucianism are: *ren* (humaneness or benevolence); *li* (ritual norms), *zhong* (loyalty to one's true nature), *shu* (reciprocity), and *xiao* (filial piety). Together these constitute *de* (virtue). The essence of all his teachings may be summed up under this one word '*Jen*'. The nearest equivalent to this difficult word is 'social virtue'. All those virtues which help to maintain social harmony and peace like benevolence, charity, magnanimity, sincerity, respectfulness, altruism, diligence, loving kindness, goodness are included in *Jen*.

His golden rule is: 'What you do not want done to yourself, do not do unto others. The injuries done to you by an enemy should be returned with a combination of love and justice'.

How Confucius Became a Teacher

If you think in terms of a year, plant a seed; if in terms of ten years, plant trees; if in terms of 100 years, teach the people.

– Confucius

⟡⟡

THE CHINESE SCHOLAR, BU MING, POINTS OUT TO US THAT THE three great souls who exercised the greatest influence on Chinese life and culture, namely the Buddha, Confucius and Lao Tse, were all born around the same time, within a few years of each other. They were all born during what is known as 'the spring and autumn era' of China's history, and continue to be venerated and respected by Chinese people till today. According to Bu Ming, Lao Tse was born on 15 February in 571 BC in Qu Ren Li, Ku County, Chu Country (now Luyi County, Henan Province). Five years later on 8 April in 566 BC, Sakya Muni was born in today's Nepal. Another fifteen years later, Confucius was born in Qufu, Shandong Province on 27 August in 551 BC. He adds: 'The three saints came to the world in the same era, was it a historical coincidence or an arrangement by the gods?'

Bu Ming also tells us that Confucius, who was a scholar with a voracious appetite for learning, visited the Zhou Province to learn all about Zhou ceremonial systems and culture in which he was passionately interested. At that time, it is said, Lao Tse was the *ShouCang Shi Shi* (the chief curator of the National Library or the Museum of History) and a *Zhu Xia Shi* (Imperial historian) in the Royal Palace at Luo Yang, the capital of Zhou. In other words, he was the authority on those very systems that Confucius was keen to study. Speculations and legends have been built around the meeting between the two great Masters. But we do know that after completing his tour, Confucius made a statement that has been passed down for many generations, 'In an abundance of theories, I would follow the Zhou State.' Confucius's original attempt was to undertake a comparative study of the systems of Zhou with those of the states of Xia and Shang. The fact that at the end of his study, Confucius decided to promote the system of Zhou is an indication that he had indeed learnt a great deal during this historical trip.

When he returned to Lu Country after visiting Zhou and learning Zhou's ceremonial observance system, Confucius was renowned and reputed as a great scholar, and more and more students flocked to come and study with him. We can safely say that Confucius was the first person in the history of Chinese education who taught privately to students. Before his time, schools were run by the government. Confucius promoted his private school, received students of various kinds, and popularized education to ordinary people. He spread knowledge to society and contributed a great deal to ancient education. But during these early days, Confucius was also engaged with several official assignments and tasks entrusted to him by the state government.

When Confucius was 35 years old, he went to the Qi State. Duke Jing of Qi asked him how a country should be governed. Confucius said to him, 'The emperor should act like an emperor, officials should act like officials, fathers should act like fathers, and sons should act like sons.'

He added at a practical level, 'The most important thing in governing a country is to be thrifty with the budget and eliminate any waste.'

It is said that Duke Jing valued Confucius's advice so much that he wished to grant Confucius some land in Ni Xi. However, his courtiers and ministers were not at all happy about the prominence given to the scholar; who was not an aristocrat by birth, like all of them. The duke's adviser Yan Ying dissuaded him from giving away the land saying, 'This kind of scholar is very good at talking. You cannot control them with laws. They are proud, willful and opinionated. They care a lot about ceremonies like funeral arrangements and are willing to exhaust all their possessions for grand funerals. They lobby everywhere and seek for positions and pay. Therefore, you cannot use them to govern the country. Now, Confucius stresses appearance, dress and personal adornments, defines complicated ceremonial etiquette for going to and leaving the court, and painstakingly promotes the rule of manners. Even after several generations, we won't be able to master and be fluent with these unnecessary and overly elaborate formalities. If you really hope to change Qi's customs, I am afraid his teachings are not going to be of great help to you.'

Rightly or wrongly, Yan Ying's advice did have an impact on the duke's decision. From then on, although Duke Jing still politely met with Confucius, he no longer asked for any advice on governance or ceremony. Some of the minor officials of Qi country were planning to harm Confucius physically. When Duke Jing heard about this, he said to Confucius, 'I am old and I cannot give you the kind of position or protection you deserve.' So Confucius left Qi and returned to the state of Lu.

Back in Lu, Confucius achieved a great deal in political administration, offering his services to the state in several important matters. He also had several important accomplishments to his credit; some people say that his position was enhanced to that of the Prime Minister of Lu. But his path as a government official was not smooth. Once during a ceremony held by the duke to offer sacrifices to Heaven, the Royal Counsellor San Huan intentionally did not give part of the sacrificial offering to Confucius, who was acting in the role of a consultant to the ceremony at that time. Now, as Confucius himself had taught, this was one of the most severe punishments in Zhou's system of etiquette. From then on, Confucius knew that he would not really have much of a future in the government of Lu anymore, so he left his country, wandering around in an ox-cart to give lectures to promote his ideas.

There is an amusing anecdote narrated to us about Confucius and his disciple. One day, a person named Zixia started asking Confucius about each of his close disciples.

'What kind of a person is Yenhui?' he was asked, at first.

Confucius said, 'Yenhui is more compassionate than I!'

'What kind of a person is Zigong?'

Confucius answered, 'Zigong is more eloquent than I.'

Zixia persisted with his questions. 'What about Zilu? What kind of a person is Zilu?'

Confucius answered, 'Zilu is more courageous than I am!'

Zixia inquired further, 'Then what about Zizhang? What kind of a person is Zizhang?' And Confucius replied, 'He is more solemn than I.'

By now, everyone was thoroughly bewildered, and the disciples in question were embarrassed and confused. How could they be more compassionate, more eloquent, more courageous, and more solemn than the Master?

Confucius explained, 'Yenhui knows about compassion, but doesn't know when not to be compassionate. Zigong is articulate, but doesn't know when to be silent. Zilu knows about bravery, but he doesn't know when to be afraid. Zizhang is serious and stately, but doesn't know when to accommodate and compromise with others. If you were to add all of their talents together and exchange them for all of my imperfections, I wouldn't take them!'

In his own way, the Master was teaching them the essence of moderation in everything!

One tale may be taken as an illustration of his consideration of differences. Zi Lu asked him a question, 'When we hear a good proposal, should we put it into practise at once?'

'You should always first ask someone with more experience,' Confucius answered. Ran Yu asked him the same question, sometime later. To him Confucius replied, 'Of course you should put it into practise at once.' A third student who had heard both answers, was puzzled by their apparent contradiction, and asked Confucius to explain the difference.

'Ran Yu always hesitates when making a decision,' the sage said. 'Therefore he should be encouraged to be bolder. Zi Lu tends to make hasty decisions. Therefore he should be reminded to be cautious. It's only natural that different people should get different answers.'

Confucius was not a young man when he undertook this life as a wandering teacher. He was nearly 50 years old. But he continued to work tirelessly, travelling to different countries along with his faithful students to promote his ideas. However, none of the state governments would accept his ideas. When he was 68 years old, Confucius returned to Lu. But Lu did not give him an official position either. In fact, Confucius stopped seeking any state assignments after this time. He continued his teachings to his beloved students. It was at 72 years of age, in 479 BC, that Confucius breathed his last.

An interesting legend has come down to us about the last days of Confucius. During the last days of his earthly journey he was confined to bed. He was surrounded by his many disciples. He wanted to give them the 'last' teaching. Opening his mouth wide, he told them, 'Look inside and tell me, what do you see?'

The disciples looked into the mouth and said, 'Master, we can only see your tongue.' Confucius then asked them, 'What is in *your* mouth?'

The disciples replied, 'In our mouth, there is a tongue and there are also teeth.'

Confucius then said to them, 'The teeth are strong and firm. But the tongue is soft and fleshy. We are born with our tongue, which is formed before the teeth; even a newborn infant has a tongue. Teeth come afterwards, but fall off with growing years. But the tongue remains with man throughout his life. This is because the tongue is fleshy and soft. It lasts a lifetime due to its softness. Therefore, be soft spoken, be sweet spoken.'

Confucius's love of virtue and wisdom is praised by his disciples in *Analects,* where he is described as one 'who in the eager pursuit of knowledge, forgot his food, and in the joy of attaining to it forgot his sorrow'. Whatever traditional records of the past, whether history, lyric poems, or rites and ceremonies which promoted virtue, he sought out and taught to his disciples. He was a man of an affectionate nature, sympathetic, and most considerate towards others. He loved his disciples dearly, and won from them their undying love, loyalty and devotion.

THOUGHT FOR REFLECTION

The education that is being given in our schools and colleges today merely emphasizes book-learning. Students are asked to study a few books, 'cram' certain facts, memorize them and reproduce them. We 'pump' dry facts and figures into their unresponsive heads, for we have forgotten the true meaning of the word 'education'. 'Education' according to its Latin origins, means 'drawing out'. That is what education is – a drawing out process. Alas, we have turned it upside down, into a pumping-in process!

I recall the words of Gurudev Sadhu Vaswani: 'What constitutes a school? Emphasis is often put upon the building or furniture. But the school, as I think of it, is not the place but the atmosphere that the teachers and students move in. Fellowship of teachers and students – that is what makes the school. So it was in ancient India. The centre of the school – the *ashrama* – was the guru, whereby he meant not a pedagogue, but a teacher who carried with him a purifying atmosphere.'

ZI GONG REDEEMS SLAVES

Do not be concerned that no one may recognize your merits. Be concerned that you may not recognize theirs.

– Confucius

ZI GONG WAS A SENIOR DISCIPLE OF CONFUCIUS, WELL-LOVED BY the Master. Zi Gong came from a prosperous merchant background. He was a well-respected citizen and occasionally employed for official work by the State of Lu, where he and other disciples of Confucius lived. He is reported to have performed diplomatic tasks for the state of Lu despite having no office, because of his skills in speech. He is said to have become quite a rich man in later life.

Confucius lived during a war-torn era when many of the Chinese states were at constant strife with one another. In the course of these constant battles, it often happened that citizens of one state, who were captured by enemy states, were made slaves in the conquering kingdom. Many poor citizens of Lu were thus, held in slavery in neighbouring countries. The State of Lu had a policy which officially recognized and rewarded those who paid the ransom to regain the freedom of their enslaved fellow citizens.

Once, Zi Gong, who was on a diplomatic mission to another state, found several of his fellow citizens living there in slavery. Out of his own funds, he paid a heavy ransom to free several Lu people and bring them back home. This act was deeply appreciated by the state authorities who offered to pay Zi Gong a rich reward for his act of generosity. However, Zi Gong was very conscious of two facts: first, that he was a devoted disciple of Confucius; and that he himself came from a wealthy family. Therefore, he politely declined the reward. Having declined it, he considered himself very noble and selfless.

However, when he told Confucius about it, his teacher was not very pleased. He pointed out to Zi Gong that most of the people of Lu were quite poor, and could not afford acts of generosity like his own. When an illustrious citizen like Zi Gong turned down rewards, he would create the impression that accepting state rewards was shameful. This would only hinder the efforts of other people who took the initiative to free their fellow citizens and thus, stall the government's plans to rescue her enslaved people.

Therefore, Confucius pointed out, although Zi Gong's behaviour was good for his own name, it would exert a negative influence on the country; the refusal to accept rewards for a noble task done, would be good for a short while; but in the long term, it would not be good for the state or its citizens. In fact, it would become the bane of the country in the future.

THOUGHT FOR REFLECTION

Cultivate the soul through service! In other words, become aware that you are only an instrument of God. He is the One Worker – you are but His tool, His agent. Therefore, renounce all idea of egoism, of the narrow self and become an instrument of the eternal *shakti* that shapes the lives of individuals and nations.

It is good that those who seek to serve others bear this in mind: that service is meant to purify the mind, heart and intellect, and to move us on the path of God-realization. They are also blessed with the unique, selfless joy that comes from serving those in affliction, and bringing the light of love into dark, unhappy lives. These are the genuine feelings to be nourished by those who save others – and not vanity, ego and self-seeking pride.

Let me appeal to you: do not seek to serve others to prove your superiority. This brings disgrace to you and it degrades those whom you 'serve' in this spirit. It destroys the very spirit and concept of service. True service is free from the contamination of the ego.

MENCIUS'S MOTHER

He who learns but does not think, is lost. He who thinks but does not learn is in great danger.

– Confucius

ＭENCIUS WAS NOT ONLY ONE OF THE MOST WELL-KNOWN philosophers in Chinese history but also among the foremost followers of Confucian philosophy. Many regard him as the true transmitter of the Master's teachings. In fact, his work *Mengzi* became one of the canonical texts of the Confucian tradition. Mencius himself was held in great esteem as the greatest Confucian thinker after Confucius himself, and his teachings have been very influential on the development of Confucian thought, right up to modern times. Here is a beautiful story about his growing years and the stellar role played by his mother in making, moulding and shaping her son's character.

Meng Ke (that was the name Mencius was given at birth) was born in Zou County, Shandong Province. When he was just three years old, his father passed away. It was left to his mother Zhang to assume the responsibility of bringing her son up. To this day, Zhang is held up as an exemplary female figure and mother. One of the most famous Chinese phrases coming from her story is, 'Mencius's mother moved three times.' And that is the essence of our story! Why and how and when did Mencius's mother move?

In the early years after she was widowed, Mencius and his mother lived near a cemetery. As a young child, Mencius frequently saw burials and started to mimic those who cried during the funeral ceremonies.

Zhang was alarmed by this, and decided that such an environment was not good for her son. So she decided to take up her lodging near a busy market.

Here in this crowded market area, there were shops everywhere. The businessmen were always chatting to each other, discussing trade matters and exchanging stories about their travels. Most of them were loud and boastful. Now, Mencius started to imitate the businessmen, talking loudly and boasting about where he had gone and what he had done. His mother was apprehensive, as she did not like the idea of her child becoming loud-mouthed and boastful. After careful consideration, they moved again.

But by now, Mencius's mother had learnt a valuable lesson; this time she chose a dwelling near a school. Here, most of the people who moved about in the locality were teachers, scholars or intellectuals, who were serious in their demeanour and spoke with propriety and decorum. Growing up in such surroundings, Mencius began to acquire the essential etiquette of a scholar and a gentleman. He was a well-behaved young boy, a *juniz* in the Confucian manner, talking and moving about like a perfect gentleman, graceful and courteous towards everyone he met.

Mencius's mother was very pleased: 'This is the right environment for my son to grow up,' she said to herself. By now, she had taken to weaving cloth at home, in order to earn a livelihood.

When Mencius started going to school, he stayed away from class one day, and sneaked out to play with his friends. He heard other children playing outside and decided to sneak out of the class to join the other children. When he returned home, his mother was weaving. As soon as she saw his dirty clothes, she knew what had happened. She asked: 'Did you just get out of class?' 'I skipped class,' he answered honestly.

His mother took him to the loom. She took out the piece of cloth that she had just woven, and cut it in half with a pair of scissors. 'Look at this piece of cloth,' she said to her son. 'It is useless, as it is not whole. If you want to be a true scholar, you must study wholeheartedly. Otherwise, you will end up like this piece of cloth. It took me a long time to weave it, inch by inch. Now I have cut it in half and it is worthless. If you do things by half, you will also end up like this useless piece of cloth.'

Mencius was greatly inspired by his mother and the lessons she taught him. And from then onwards, he began to bloom as a student and a human being. His greatest passion was for studying and learning. With his mother's support and help, Mencius mastered the six classical arts and became one of the most well-known scholars of his day.

THOUGHT FOR REFLECTION

When babies are born, they are wrapped up in a warm bundle, and laid close to the mother – for it is believed that the process of 'bonding' begins even at this early stage.

This 'bonding' is very special – for it involves recognition through the senses, of the mother; awareness of the mother as the closest, most loving, most important being in the consciousness of the child; and familiarity with the person who is going to play a vital role in the child's growth, and the start of a loving relationship which will mean the most to both child and mother.

This is why I urge all mothers, not to leave their children in the care of *ayahs* or paid servants. However busy you may be, however affluent you may be, do not 'delegate' this precious duty to another! How can anyone else replace you, the mother who has cherished and nourished the child in their womb, and given him/her the precious gift of birth and brought him/her out into this wonderful, bright world? How can anyone else be a substitute for you? Therefore, keep your child close to yourself; care for him/her personally, in those crucial formative early years.

Emperor Yu Shun

The Master said, 'Towering! ...that Shun and Yu should have possessed the world yet treated none of it as their own.'

– Analects

Yu Shun was a legendary ruler of ancient China, and has been remembered in Chinese history as one of the three Sovereigns and five Emperors. Shun came from a very humble background; but his great virtues and merits so impressed Emperor Yao, that he was given a prominent administrative position during the emperor's reign. Shun carried out the tasks entrusted to him with such integrity that he gained the respect and confidence of the people and their ruler. Eventually, the emperor actually appointed Yu Shun as his successor when he decided to give up the throne. It is said that Shun politely declined the offer, asking instead that someone more virtuous and noble than himself be entrusted with the task. But eventually, he agreed to take on the onerous duties of the emperor. In later centuries, both Yao and Shun were glorified for their virtue by Confucian philosophers. Shun was particularly renowned for his modesty and filial piety. Here is his story.

Legends tell us that Shun's mother died when he was an infant; his father, who was blind, married a second wife. Shun had a step brother, Xiang, who was arrogant and cruel. Between them, the stubborn and insensitive father, the overbearing and tyrannical stepmother and the vicious and scheming brother made Shu's life a veritable hell. But he continued to love and support them. All the hard work was reserved for

Shun; but he only got the worst food and clothes. He never ever ignored his responsibilities towards the family; he never ever compromised on the love and respect he showed to his parents. For years together, he put up patiently with their hostility and ill will, until one day, he had to run away from home, when the cruel stepmother and her son conspired to kill him. But when things became normal, he actually returned to his family, who were in dire straits without him. And so it was said: 'The family couldn't kill Shun when they wanted to, yet when they needed him he was always around.' Living in such an uncongenial and miserable family environment, Shun's integrity, nobility, patience and virtue were only tempered like burnished gold. He developed a man's greatest asset: strength of purpose and high moral character. Eventually, his stepmother drove him away from home, and Yu Shun was forced to seek his livelihood elsewhere. But wherever he went, he made a mark!

Interestingly enough, Yu Shun made tremendous contributions to the development of Chinese pottery. In those early days away from home, Shun took up work as a potter in Zhufeng Village by the Yellow River. History reports that, 'Shun made quality pots and earthenware, beautifully done with no flaws.' Shun's craft and his workmanship were remarkable. The pots that he made were not only flawless and skilfully crafted, but also beautiful, reasonably priced, and durable. It was Shun's habit to pay particular attention to the quality of clay that he used; he was equally careful about the firing temperature, and took his time to knead and mould the clay and prepare it the right way. This made his pots durable and solid. People thronged to buy his pots and other potters came to learn his special techniques from him. Shun was always happy to share his skills with everyone; but he was kept very busy, catering to the demands of several customers who came from far and near to buy his famous pots. As his business grew and prospered, Shun remained constant in his approach, never ever compromising on his time, efforts or the quality of his wares. Most remarkable of all, the ever increasing demand for his pottery did not tempt him to raise his price or monopolize the market. He was happy with his moderate profits, and remained dedicated to his ideals of quality and integrity.

Gradually, he developed a sophisticated and advanced technology of using a potter's wheel in those ancient times. His fame spread all over the Yellow River area. Many potters set up their business in the area, wishing to emulate his remarkable success. But they were inclined to cut corners, compromise on labour and material, and focus only on profits. They were not ready to prepare the clay properly; they tried to shorten the firing process and save on fuel and time. As a result, their earthenware was not properly fired and broke easily after being used for a short time. The potters continued to make huge profits, but their products were of very poor quality.

Shun opened a new pottery business at a place called Wei; this became a sort of model workshop where he studied and mastered even more advanced techniques which he willingly taught to all the potters in that area. He also focused on making pottery more exquisitely beautiful and decorative.

When the potters became jealous of Shun's growing popularity and prosperity, they remonstrated with him, saying that he was deliberately trying to put them out of business. But Shun heard them out patiently and said to them, 'I did not come here to compete with you or steal your customers away from you! How I make my pots is my business; but I cannot force a single customer to buy my pots! If people choose not to buy my pots, I cannot force them; equally, if everybody wants to buy my pots, I can't refuse them. Dear friends, just think about it: we all make pots, yet why do people buy my pots and not yours? Why is that?'

The potters said, rather grudgingly, 'Your pots are durable and reasonably priced. Our pots are fragile and expensive. So people buy from you, not from us. Aren't you doing this deliberately to take business away from us? You undercut the price and don't allow us to make profits.'

Shun said to them, 'Consider the clothes and fabrics that we buy for our family's needs. If the fabrics tear or their colours start to fade after a single wash, would you buy from the same shop ever again? Would you pay good money for low-quality products? Then how could you expect me to make low quality pots and drive my customers away?'

The potters were not satisfied. They said, 'We were doing quite well before you came here. We had our share of customers and we made decent profits. After you came, everything has changed. It is not that our pots have become fragile all of a sudden. But ever since you opened your pottery no one buys our pots.'

Shun pointed out to them, 'People used to buy from you because there were no options available to them. They did not buy from you because they liked your pots, but because they found nothing better.

When we have years of big crop failures, do we not eat bran and grass? When they had only poor quality pots available to them, you were doing the same as forcing them to eat bran scraps and grass roots. Isn't that so?'

The potters responded, 'We are craftsman who live off our skills. We only know about making money and becoming rich. We don't care about being nice!'

Shun said, 'That is not so. Wealth exists within kindness. Without kindness, where could you find wealth?'

He went on to tell the angry potters, 'The difference between humans and animals is kindness and goodness. If I do not cheat others, then they also will not cheat me. If I cheat them, then they must cheat me. In order to become rich, you have cheated others by selling them fragile pots. However, everybody wants to make money and become rich. If people in all the trades think like you and make shabby products of poor quality, I ask you, could anyone make money? What you make is only earthenware, and you have to buy countless other commodities from others. You only have one product to compete with many other products, so how could you win? Even if you make more profit on the pots, you don't know how much more money you have to spend on other worthless products! Without kindness and goodness there can be no wealth, so isn't it wise to be good and kind?'

The potters were struck by Shun's words of wisdom, and under his guidance, they gradually changed their ways. They began to practise honesty and integrity in their business. They moved away from cost cutting and shoddy quality to make strong and durable pottery.

Later, when Emperor Yao identified Yu Shun as a potential leader and good administrator, Shun was made successively minister of instruction, general regulator and chief of the four peaks region, and wherever he was sent to work, he restored order, discipline and a good work culture within a short period of time. Eventually, as we saw, Emperor Yao rejected his own sons as unworthy of inheriting the throne and made Yu Shun his successor instead.

It is said that when a wise and genuine person takes over the reins of leadership, morals come first and guidance is emphasized. He did not use strict laws and harsh punishments to enforce his power. It is said that people actually became more kind and honest during his reign. There was no need for repeated demands or coercion. All that was needed was to teach and pass on the spiritual obligations, and then everybody improved their characters and was kind. There wasn't much that needed to be done, yet the world was well ruled and everything was in order.

The book *Historical Records: Records of the Five Emperors* evaluates Emperor Shun as follows: 'When Shun was a farmer at Mountain Li, the local people gave him their land; when he was a fisherman at Lake Ze, the local fishermen let him stay in their houses; when he was a potter at the Yellow River, the earthenware in that area was not of poor quality. The first year he was there, more residents gathered; the second year he was there, a city was built; by the third year, a great metropolis was established.' Wherever he worked, there would be a trend towards courtliness and kindness; wherever he went, people followed him. Thus Sima Qian praised Shun, 'Civilization and kindness in the world started with Yu Shun.'

THOUGHT FOR REFLECTION

According to what are called factors of economic development, a country's 'well-being' and 'prosperity' are determined not just by those statistics that we call gross national income (GNI), or even by what that country produces, the gross national product (GDP). We have to consider instead, a whole range of other factors such as 'quality of life', which my sensitive readers will realize, is much more than mere 'standard of living'. The nature of society and conditions of public life; the public services and amenities available to the people; life expectancy; education; family life and family welfare; community life; employment opportunities and job security; political freedom and social security; equality of genders; equitable distribution of wealth; opportunities for advancement; the sustenance and protection of the environment – these and other issues contribute to the overall well-being of the people.

PLANTING THE SEEDS OF GOODNESS

When you see a good person, think of becoming like her/him.
When you see someone not so good, reflect on your own weak
points.

– Confucius

CONFUCIUS REGARDED HIMSELF AS A TEACHER WHO TRANSMITS, rather than innovates. Above all, he chose to transmit through his teachings, the treasure of wisdom from the great classics of the ancients. What follows is a story from the legends of the ancient Qing Dynasty.

Zhang was a merchant broker's employee during the annals of the Qing dynasty. On one occasion, he was sent by his master to transact a business and collect an outstanding payment from a trader who lived in a city across the Yangtze River. It was the season when the New Year holiday was fast approaching. Zhang planned to carry out his errands as quickly as possible and return home in time for the New Year celebrations. Tying up his Master's gold and silver coins in a cloth bag, he left home very early and managed to catch the first ferry, but when he reached his destination, he realized that the city gates had not yet opened. He sat in the empty market square, and waited for the gates to open. But in a short while, he dozed off, with his cloth bag as a pillow.

When he awakened sometime later, the city gates were just opening. In his hurry, Zhang rushed in through the gates, completely forgetting the cloth bag he was sleeping on all this while. It was only half an hour later that he realized that he had left behind him all the money he was carrying. He rushed back to the marketplace, but it was now crowded with people, and the bag was gone.

Zhang was worried; his brows were furrowed with anxiety, and he looked around to see if there was someone who would come up to him and return his bag. An elderly man approached him and asked him, 'What is the matter? You seem to be looking for someone or something.' Zhang explained his predicament to him. The old man listened carefully to him, and then invited Zhang to his home, which was close by.

When they entered his home, the old man said to Zhang, 'I found a bag on the road when I opened the door this morning. But I don't know if it is yours. Can you tell me what was inside your bag?' Zhang replied, 'Inside the bag are two envelopes, each with a certain amount of gold and silver coins. The larger one belongs to my Master and the smaller one is mine.'

The elderly man checked the contents of the bag, which were exactly as Zhang had described. He promptly returned the bag to Zhang.

Zhang was so moved and relieved that his eyes were filled with tears. He wished to express his appreciation and gratitude for the old man and offered him some of the silver coins from his personal funds. But the old man smiled and replied, 'Had I loved money so much, I would not have told you about the bag, would I? I did what I considered to be the right thing to do. I don't think we should do good for the sake of rewards. Doing the right thing, doing what is good must be its own reward.'

Zhang asked the elderly man his name; he thanked him profusely and left to complete his work.

When Zhang was waiting by the river for the ferry to return home, there was a great commotion. A sudden gale had occurred on the river; strong winds had arisen and several boats had capsized, and many passengers were drowning. Zhang saw all the disturbance and the misery all around him, and the thought came to his mind, that the old man had literally saved his life earlier that day, by returning all the bullion to him. Now, it was his turn to save other lives with his money. Using his own silver, he hired people to rescue those who were drowning. Several dozen people were saved by his compassionate impulse.

The survivors crowded around Zhang and thanked him profusely for saving them. One of them happened to be the son of the elderly man who had returned Zhang's lost bag to him. He was on his way home to Nanjing after finishing business in the north area of the Yangtze River. Zhang was amazed to hear this. He then narrated his own story to those present, and everyone was thrilled to hear about the twin miracles. They remarked in unison that it must be the heavenly law in operation: good is always rewarded with good. The young man took Zhang home to meet his family. Later on, the two families were united, when Zhang offered his daughter's hand to the young man in marriage.

Zhang realized the power of a good deed; the elderly man did not keep the fortune he found for himself; nor did he ask for a reward for doing a good deed. He not only saved Zhang in a crisis, but also planted a seed in his heart to do good deeds, thus laying an opportunity for his own son to be saved later. And so we have the ancient Chinese saying, 'Doing good deeds without seeking repayment will inspire others to be compassionate and resolve your own tribulation; helping people in need will inspire them to do good deeds and you will receive help from others.'

Thought for Reflection

'No man is an island,' wrote the poet John Donne. The 'others' as we think of them are not apart from us. We and others are parts of the One Great Whole. We must not cut ourselves off from others. If we wish to live a healthy, happy life – mentally, morally, spiritually – we must be concerned about the welfare of others, specially our less fortunate brothers and sisters. The selfish man, who is interested only in his own welfare and that of his near and dear ones, is never a happy man. It is only when we go out and make others happy, that happiness flows into our own lives.

This is one of my favourite sayings from the famous Methodist preacher, John Wesley:

Do all the good you can, by all the means you can, in all the ways you can, in all the places you can, at all the times you can, to all the people you can and as long as you can.

HINDUISM

BRIEF INTRODUCTION

INDIANS ARE THE PROUD INHERITORS OF A RICH HERITAGE — THE heritage of what people call 'Hinduism'. To tell you the truth, I do not like to use the word Hinduism — for the Hindu faith, I believe, is not an 'ism' — it is not a creed or a dogma. I recall the words of my revered Master, Gurudev Sadhu Vaswani: 'Creeds are broken reeds, and dogmas divide.' The Hindu faith is not a dogma — it is a path, it is a way of life. We should therefore, speak of the Hindu outlook, or the Hindu spirit, or the Hindu faith.

I love to think of Hinduism as a faith without a beginning or an end. It has existed since the very remote past. Therefore, if it is necessary to call it by a name, that name must be Sanatana Dharma — the Eternal Religion.

The term Sanatana Dharma has also been translated as 'righteousness forever' or 'that which has no beginning or end'. By its insistence on these eternal truths, Hinduism implicitly postulates that these truths, first received by the rishis, can be found out by anyone who seeks them through devout and relentless pursuit.

THE PATH OF SHREYA

Beyond the senses is the mind. Beyond it is the brain or intuition.
Beyond that is the great soul (the Atman). Beyond that great soul
is the non-manifested or the invisible (or the Supreme Divine
called as the avyakta).

Above that non-manifested is the Purusha (the all-knowing
and all-pervading Atman). He is all-pervading and is devoid of
any particular mark or characteristic. On knowing Him to be
so, the Jiva is liberated and attains immortality.

The form of the Purusha does not remain before the eyes. No
one ever sees it with the eyes also. It can be seen only through a
fully controlled mind and strong will power and intellect. Those
who have known it to be so attain immortality.

– Katha Upanishad, Ch. VI

THE KATHA UPANISHAD BEGINS WITH THIS MEMORABLE STORY. A
poor brahmin called Vajasravas once decided to perform a yagna. This
was no ordinary yagna; it was the '*Vishwajeeta yagna*', for which it is
stipulated that a man must donate all his wealth, all his possessions, in
return for assurance of heaven.

Now, the poor brahmin was not rich in the wealth of this world, and
the 'treasures' that he offered in the yagna were just a few very old cows,
and a few battered vessels. That was all he had, and that was all he could
offer to those participating in the yagna.

The poor brahmin had a very intelligent son, called Nachiketa. The young lad watched his father's 'treasures' being given away and he was both saddened and puzzled. He thought to himself, 'What kind of heaven will my father attain by giving away cows that cannot even walk, leave alone calve or give milk?' His concern for his father was genuine; he knew that in a yagna, a man had to offer the best that he had. His father had a son – himself, Nachiket, who was sound of mind and body, and pious and intelligent as well. 'What is my father doing, keeping me back, and offering worthless gifts as offerings? If the yagna is to achieve its purpose, he must surely give me away, for a son is a man's richest treasure. It is better that my father gives me away as an offering. I am his dear beloved child. If he gives me away, then this yagna will truly be blessed.'

Without further ado, the boy marched up to his father who was giving away the 'gifts' and demanded of him, 'Father, have you given me away yet?'

That was his ploy to remind his father that his son was ready to be given away, to ensure the success of the yagna. The father, who certainly had not interpreted the injunction to give away his wealth so seriously, just ignored the boy and his cheeky question.

But Nachiketa was not being cheeky. He loved his father, and he venerated the scriptures and the rules of the sacred yagnas. So he repeated his question, 'Father, am I not your treasure, your most valuable possession? Have you given me away to someone?'

When this embarrassing question was repeated a third time, the father lost his patience and shouted, 'Yes, I have! I have given you away to the lord of Death!'

Nachiketa was certainly taken aback: but it was an abstract issue which haunted him. 'Some people rate me among the best of the youth; others think I am no more than average; what could my father gain by offering me to the lord of Death?'

The boy realized that his father had spoken in anger; but the words had been uttered; and their promise had to be fulfilled. Nachiket decided then and there, that he would offer himself to Yama, the god of Death, as his father had said.

It is said that Nachiket comforted his distraught father, and travelled alone to the bounds of the world, to reach the abode of the lord of Death. Not finding Yama at home, the boy waited for three days and three nights to meet him. Three days and three nights the boy sat patiently, without food, without water, without a wink of sleep!

When Yama returned home, he was amazed to see the young boy waiting outside his gates. Here was an *atithi*, a guest, at his door, a youngster who had been left unattended, with no courtesy extended to him, no hospitality shown, not so much as a drink of water offered to him, leave alone food to eat! Our scriptures enjoin us to treat visitors like gods: *atithi devo bhava*! Yama felt it was a grievous offence that had been committed, although it had been inadvertent and unintentional on his part.

He approached the boy with great affection and regard and said to him, 'O, young Brahmin! You have lived in my abode for three days and three nights without food, water and sleep! Allow me to make up for this lapse by offering to you three boons – one for each day you have been kept waiting.'

Let me invite you to guess, what do you think the young boy asked for? I wonder what you would have asked for, if you were in his place!

First and foremost, Nachiketa's thoughts move out to his father. He knows that his father has sent him here in anger. 'May my father be saved from anger,' the boy thinks. Aloud, he tells Yamaraja, 'O, Lord, so bless my father that he may be freed from the disease of anger. When I happen to meet him or when he chances to meet me, may I find him free from anxiety and anger, in calmness of mind, and reconciled to me in every respect.'

Yama is well pleased with the filial piety of the boy, and says to him, 'So be it! Whatever you wish will happen. Seeing you freed from the jaws of death, all traces of anger will disappear from your father's heart. Reunited with his son, he will indeed be restored to peace and joy. His love and affection for you will revive, as before.'

What is the second boon which Nachiketa seeks? First and foremost, he had been concerned about his father. His second thought moves out to this sad, sad world. 'There is so much suffering upon earth,' he thinks. 'But there is so much happiness in the heaven world. They are not troubled by hunger or thirst here. They never fall sick, they never grow old. They are all so happy here. How can people be taught to free themselves from the sorrow and suffering of the world, and find their way to heaven?'

And so Nachiketa tells Yamaraja, 'The second boon I ask of you is this: kindly show us the path which the people can take that will lead them to happiness and then to the heaven.'

Yamaraja is, again, well pleased with the boy's selfless desire to help others. He replies, 'My dear one, this is not a big issue at all. I will tell you about a yagna, which if anyone performs, will definitely reach the heaven world. Suffering will not touch him; he will experience all joy and happiness in the heaven world. You are so young and yet you are filled with the spirit of humane compassion, that I shall name this yagna after you – from now on, it will be called Nachiketa Yagna.' And Yamaraja proceeds to explain the yagna, promising that whosoever performs the yagna with faith and piety, would attain heaven.

What is the third boon he asks for? This young child says to his mentor and kind benefactor, the lord of Death, 'I know for sure, that many people attain to the heaven world, but they all come back. They come back into this cycle of birth and death. O, how they are crushed in this ever revolving wheel! Pray teach me how they may be freed from this terrible, crushing burden!'

Does not Kabir say to us:
Chalti chakki dekh kar, diya Kabira roye,
Dui paatan ke beech mein, saabit bacha na koi.

Yamaraja is amazed at the boy's wisdom and his determined quest to seek the ultimate Truth about life and the goal of life: liberation. Kindly, he tells the boy, 'You have asked a very difficult question. Even the Devtas do not know of this way. Even the gods have quarrelled over the issue. It is abstruse and complex, and you are very young. Ask for something else instead, and I will happily grant it to you. Land, cows, horses, elephants, gold, silver, the kingdoms of the earth, whatever you ask I shall give you – ask for wealth and a long life, sons and grandsons. It will all be granted to you. Beautiful girls will be in your service who will sing songs for you, and fill your life with pleasure. I will give you everything, but do not ask me to give you an answer to this question.'

Nachiketa tells him, 'I could of course ask you for land, cows, elephants, all the pleasures and the wealth of this world – but Lord, you know and I know, these are ephemeral, they are but passing pleasures. They may be mine today, but gone tomorrow. How can I call them mine? I seek from you that treasure, the treasure of truth, which is truly lasting; and who better than you, the lord of Death, to give me the right answer to this question? Show me the path to true and absolute freedom, tell me how one may know his true self, because I know he will not be able to attain God, unless he attains self-realization. His senses, his knowledge are of no avail to him in this quest for truth. Therefore, Lord, I seek nothing else from you, but this sacred truth.'

Yamraja sees that this boy has faith; he has sincerity; he has purity; he has tenacity of purpose, he is free from temptation and above all he has that deep inner longing to know the truth and realize it in his own right. The lord of Death realizes that if anyone is entitled to know the sacred truth, it is this young Brahmin lad.

And thus begins one of the most memorable discourses recorded in the Upanishads – the two paths of *shreya* and *preya*, the preferable and the pleasurable. Yamaraja tells Nachiketa the path to God realization is the path of shreya. Neither the senses nor the mind can help us attain this path, for they only pull us outwards, to the external world. If we want to attain God, we must go within, within the temple of the heart, where the Lord Himself is seated. Only the one who goes within attains God while the one who runs outwards moves further and further away from God.

It is the way of meditation. Sitting in silence, he opens one curtain after another. There are so many curtains. These curtains hide the light that shines inside every one of us. He draws closer and closer to the living light within. Hence, this way is the way of self-control. It is the way of self-knowledge, self-annihilation, service and sacrifice.

Yamraja tells Nachiketa, 'My dear one, above the senses is the mind and above the mind is the *buddhi* – the power of understanding, the power of discrimination. Above the *buddhis* the *atman*, but over and above the atman is the *paramatma*. Even above the parmatama is the unmanifest (*adheestha*). But above it all is the *Para Brahma* – who transcends both the manifest and the unmanifest, because He synthesizes both of them inside.'

Yamaraja tells Nachiketa that when all desires die within the mind and when all doubts are dispelled, then verily does man attain to the Supreme.

In the end Yamraja tells Nachiketa, 'My child, this path, which I have told you today – it is a narrow path, a difficult and slippery one. As you walk on this path, you will have to face so many trials and tribulations, and a time will come when you feel you are walking on the edge of a razor. You will have to face all these difficulties. But if you persist in your efforts unflinchingly, and continue on this path with faith and piety, you will attain to the Supreme.'

THOUGHT FOR REFLECTION

The Upanishads speak to us of the choice that we have before us. Here, it is referred to as shreya and preya. Shreya is the good; preya is the pleasant. It is the pleasant that attracts us; we are seekers of pleasure; we run after pleasure – and finally, we are so caught up in pleasure, that we are entrapped. But it is the choice we have made!

The path of shreya, the path of good is a steep path; it is a rough and a rugged path; it is a stony and thorny path. In contrast, the path of preya is smooth and slippery, you can glide on the path without any resistance – but you slide to your doom! When you move on the path of shreya, you struggle, you suffer, but you are moving towards your higher destiny.

Now, the choice is yours. Whatever the path you choose, you exercise your choice. Now, if I have chosen the path, and I have encountered a bitter experience which I cannot swallow, how can I question God's justice? Is it fair on my part to ask, 'Is God Fair?' Is it fair to blame God for the choices that I have made? Seek to perform your duty; but do not lay claim to its fruits.

Herein lies the secret of the turning point in our lives, from preya to shreya. In itself karma is not evil; it becomes evil when it is mixed up with desire. Verily, desire-tainted action leads continually to the wheel of birth and death. Even those who seek the heaven world, says Sri Krishna, are slaves of desire. Therefore, we must not seek after the fruits of performing our *swadharma.* Freedom from desire is the ultimate freedom. He who does not desire the fruits of his karma is the conqueror of desire!

We must understand that everything that happens to man is of his own doing. In other words, man is the builder of his own destiny. Destiny is not something that has been imposed on him. He is the builder of his own destiny. He is the creator of his own fate; he is the architect of his own future. God has given man complete freedom of choice. Every one of us, every human being has been given this freedom of choice. We can choose between good and evil; we can choose between shreya and preya.

HIS IS THE VICTORY

Om. May Brahmin protect us both (the preceptor and the disciple)!
May Brahmin bestow upon us both the fruit of Knowledge! May
we both obtain the energy to acquire Knowledge! May what we
both study reveal the Truth! May we cherish no ill feeling toward
each other! Om. Peace! Peace! Peace!

– Peace chant from the Upanishads

THIS PROFOUND AND DEEPLY SYMBOLIC TALE IS NARRATED AT THE END
of the *Kena Upanishad.*

The Kena upanishad derives its title from the first word in the text –
meaning 'by whom?'

By whom ordained does the mind go towards its desired object?

By whom ordained does the *prana* (breath) go forth?

By whom is willed the speech that we utter? Who is that God
who directs our ears and eyes?

The answer is given in crystal clear terms: 'He [Brahmin] is the ear
of the ear, mind of the mind, speech of the speech, verily, he is the life
of life and the eye of the eye. On knowing Him the wise ones are freed
and on departing from this world, become immortal.'

The rishis have taught us that he cannot be comprehended by the
senses or the mind alone.

In the last two sections of this upanishad, a story is narrated to
explain this great Truth.

In the days of yore, there was a great battle between the gods (devas)
and the demons (asuras) in which the devas emerged victorious. Of

course, it was a victory obtained by Brahmin for them; but in their elation of triumph and in foolish arrogance, the devas began to exult over their supremacy and their glorious victory.

Brahmin took the form of an effulgent spirit and appeared before them; but in their ignorance, they failed to realize who he was. They summoned Agni, the god of fire, and said to him, 'Do thou approach this spirit and find out who he is.'

Agni approached the Divine Being, who asked him 'Who are you?'

'I am Agni,' he replied. 'I am known as Jataveda – or the all-knowing one.'

'What is the nature of your power, that you are so well-known?' enquired the Divine Spirit.

'I can burn everything that is before me – whatever is on this earth,' replied Agni, who is regarded as one of the primary gods, for it is He who first receives the oblations poured in the sacrificial fires of the yagnas.

The Divine Being placed a straw before him and said, 'Burn that.'

Agni rushed upon the straw in all his burning intensity, but could not even touch the straw.

Disappointed, he returned to the devas and said, 'I could not ascertain who that Divine Being is.'

Puzzled and confused, the devas requested Vayu, the god of wind to approach the Divine Being and ascertain His identity. Vayu approached the Divine Spirit in all speed. 'Who are you?' asked the Divine Being. 'I am Vayu and I am Matarisva (one who travels in space).'

'What power is in you?' enquired the effulgent Being.

'I can blow away and carry away everything on earth.'

The Divine Spirit placed a straw before him and said, 'Blow that away.'

Vayu blew with all his might but could not move the straw at all. Crestfallen, he too returned to his brother gods and confessed that he could not discover the identity of the Spirit who had dazzled them by his appearance.

Now, the devas turned to their leader, Indra, and said to him, 'O mighty one, it is you who must tell us who this Divine Being is.'

'So be it,' said Indra, and approached the Divine Spirit. But the moment he was near, the Spirit disappeared from sight. At that very moment, in the same place appeared a beautiful lady, bedecked in gold. She was Uma Haimavati, daughter of Himavan, the Himalayan god.

'Who is this adorable one?' Indra asked her.

(At this point, Chapter IV of the upanishad ends. Thus the answer to Indra's question is given after a pause, at the beginning of Chapter V.)

Uma replied, 'Verily, he is Brahmin, and His indeed was the Victory which gave you such glory.'

Indra now understood the nature of Brahmin and realized that His was the victory for which the devas had claimed credit.

Having approached him closely, Agni, Vayu and Indra were exalted as the greatest among the devas.

Among them, Agni is associated with the eyes and Vayu with the ears. Not by the eyes or the ears (the sense organs) can Brahmin be known.

Indra symbolizes the intellect (*manas*). The intellect approaches closest to the Brahmin, but finds that Brahmin is not really within its grasp. It is only with the help of superior consciousness or higher awareness (characterized by Uma) that the intellect finally approaches true comprehension of the Divine Spirit. He is known as 'Tadvana' (the adorable One) and whoever knows Him, is loved by all.

The pause or break between Chapter IV and Chapter V (between the question 'Who is He?' and Uma's answer 'He is Brahmin,' signifies that it is only through reflection, contemplation and meditation that one can ultimately come to know Brahmin

THOUGHT FOR REFLECTION

One of the reasons why we do not connect with God is because God has not become real to us. To many of us, God is a distant being. He is a far off, shadowy presence, dwelling on a distant star. I ask so many people, 'Where dwelleth God?' With an uplifted finger, they point to the heavens above, as though God dwelt way beyond our reach. True, God dwells in the heavens above, but there is not a nook, not a corner on the earth, where he does not dwell.

Alas, many of us do not feel His presence. He is not yet real to us.

What we need, above all else today is the rediscovery of the great truth that God is – that He is real; that we need to renew our faith in Him.

Yudhishthira Ascends to Heaven

That learned man who recites this history of sacred days in the midst of a listening auditory becomes cleansed of every sin, conquers Heaven, and attains to the status of Brahma. Of that man who listens with rapt attention to the recitation of the whole of this Veda composed by Krishna-DwaipayanaVyasa (the Island-born), a million sins, numbering such grave ones as Brahmahatya and the rest, are washed off. The Pitris of that man who recites even a small portion of this history at a Sraddha, obtain inexhaustible food and drink. The sins that one commits during the day by one's senses or the mind are all washed off before evening by reciting a portion of the Mahabharata...

The high race of the Bharatas is its topic. Hence it is called Bharata. And because of its grave import, as also of the Bharatas being its topic, it is called Mahabharata. He who is versed in interpretations of this great treatise, becomes cleansed of every sin. Such a man lives in righteousness, wealth, and pleasure, and attains to Emancipation...

– Mahabharata, Kisari Mohan Ganguli

For many of us, the story of the Mahabharata, the world's longest epic, stops with the victory of Kurukshetra. The killing of Duryodhana, which marks the victory of the Pandavas and the fulfilling of Draupadi's vow, actually happens at the end of the ninth Parva of the epic. There are nine more books (Parvas) to follow. Not many of us are familiar with these sections. The last three sections are rarely read; for they are highly philosophical and metaphorical in content.

Thirty-six years after the Kurukshetra war had ended, Sri Krishna was killed in his kingdom of Dwarka, accidentally shot by an arrow from a hunter's bow. The entire Yadava clan had almost perished, fighting each other in an intoxicated condition. The purpose of the Krishna avatar had been fulfilled, and it was time for Sri Krishna to cast aside his human form and merge with Lord Vishnu.

In the meanwhile, Arjuna, who had been helping Yudhishthira to administer righteous rule in Indraprastha, had heard that all was not well in Dwarka, and had rushed out to help his great friend and mentor, Sri Krishna. By the time he reached Dwarka, the city had already been sunk in the rising waters of the sea, and old men, women and children were the only survivors in the once prosperous Yadava stronghold. Depressed and saddened, Arjuna valiantly tried to lead the survivors back to safety, but they were attacked by fierce ruffians and bandits. Arjuna found to his utter shock that his valour and his powerful *astras* (weapons) were of no avail to him, now that Sri Krishna was no more. In this demoralized state, he was met by the great sage Veda Vyasa, to whom he confessed that he had failed to defend and protect the people who had come to him for refuge. He added, moreover, that he had lost all desire to live after the death of his guide and guardian, his divine teacher, Sri Krishna.

The wise sage thereupon explained to Arjuna that the Sri Krishna avatar was at an end; and that the Pandavas too, had served the purpose for which they had been given their human births. 'The time has now come for you and your brothers to renounce worldly life and seek *vanaprastha* – the stage of retirement to the tapobana, to seek ultimate liberation,' he told Arjuna.

To Arjuna, the whole world seemed barren and life had become blank and dark, after the passing away of his divine teacher, and he saw no purpose in prolonging a life that had become bereft of all joy, for the sake of royalty and pomp. The sad tidings he brought back from Dwarka had the same devastating effect on his four brothers and Draupadi, their wife.

Together, the Pandava princes decided that they would appoint a successor to the throne of their kingdom and seek the highest goal of life.

Neither the pleas of the people nor the entreaties of the courtiers and the young prince Parikshit could now deter them. Having crowned Parikshit the King, the Pandava brothers donned the garbs of ascetics. Yudhishthira set out of his palace, followed by Bhima, Arjuna, Nakula and Sahadeva, with Draupadi bringing up the rear. The pleading citizens walked behind them for a distance, crying bitterly. But there was such radiance and joy on the faces of the six elders of the clan that the people realized it would be impossible to persuade them to return. Their minds were made up.

And yet, it was not a party of six that left the kingdom; for in the footsteps of the five brothers there followed a dog, who was so faithful and affectionate that it would not leave them!

Our great scriptures tell us that it is time which puts fetters around us; and it is time which breaks those shackles eventually. Resolutely and firmly, the royal personages who until the previous day had lived the life of wealth, power and luxury, turned their back on their worldly life and walked the way of renunciation, as humble pilgrims seeking liberation. They carried nothing with them, except the garments of bark they wore. However, Arjuna was still carrying his mighty bow Gandiva and two quivers of arrows. As they approached the great Eastern sea, their way was barred by a mighty figure, whom they recognized as the god of fire, Agni.

'Out of this ocean, O Arjuna, I brought this Gandiva, to be your support. Now that you have done with war and worldly victory, cast your weapons back into the ocean where they belong. If it is God's will that you should need them in later births, they will come to you of their own accord.'

His brothers urged him to follow Agni's injunction. Thus, Arjuna standing on the shore of the sea, hurled his dearly held bow, Gandiva into the salty waters before him; the two quivers were also thrown away.

The pilgrims moved on, walking over the sacred Bharathvarsha in a ceremonial circle, as one last act of worship to the land of their birth. Eventually, they came upon the erstwhile site of Dwarka, and saw with great sorrow, that no trace remained of their dearly beloved Lord's kingdom.

'Thus had Sri Krishna foretold events,' they recalled solemnly. 'All things shall pass away and naught shall remain.'

Moving on, the party of pilgrims soon reached the great Himalayan range with its deep forests and mighty snow-clad peaks. This was indeed the home of ascetics and rishis who had chosen a life of meditation. Beyond Rishikesh and Badrinath, the abode of Nar and Narayan, loomed the great Mount Meru, the abode of the gods. As they walked up the steep and thorny path, each one of them confronted the many sins of commission and omission with which their lives had been stained. They were not terrible sins, but each in his or her own way, had been guilty of vanity, pride, arrogance, falsehood and such other vices. They realized that they had not lived perfect lives and repented deeply; and in the knowledge that they must seek forgiveness of the Lord for these wrong doings, one by one they fell on the wayside. Draupadi was the first to go; she was followed by Nakula, Sahadeva, Arjuna and Bhima, until at last, only Yudhishthira was left, with the faithful dog following in his footsteps. He, the Lord of righteousness and justice as his people called him, did not shed tears or sigh in sorrow; for he knew that this was the great law of karma that was now overtaking his loved ones.

As he walked resolutely up the lonely mountain, he heard a deafening peal of thunder and saw a shining golden chariot descend on the path before him. Out of a cloud of light stepped Indra, the king of the devas.

'Aryaputra! The Lord has ordained that you shall ascend to heaven in your human form,' said Indra. 'Therefore, I bring you my own chariot. Get in and it will be my privilege to take you to the heaven world.'

'I can never go to heaven leaving my loved ones behind,' asserted Yudhishthira. 'We have lived and died for each other. Now, how can I enter the heaven world leaving them behind? It is either all of us, or none of us.'

'That is just like you to speak so clearly and fairly,' smiled Indra. 'But you must realize that your beloved brothers and your wife have reached the blessed land before you. All you need to do is enter heaven, and you will be reunited with them for eternity. Therefore, do not delay; come into this chariot.'

Yudhishthira bowed in deep gratitude and stood aside, as he signalled for the dog to get into the chariot. But Indra stopped the dog. 'The heaven world is not for dogs and such lowly creatures,' he said. 'It is the abode reserved for blessed souls like you. Leave this dog behind; it would be no cruelty to the creature, for it knows nothing of the life eternal!'

'I cannot commit such a grave sin, O Devendra, as to abandon a creature that has shown such loyalty and devotion to me. I am at the end of my life now, and this whole life would be wasted if I commit such a dastardly act now.'

'But this is not right! Don't you know how sacred and blessed is the realm you are about to enter? Heaven would be defiled by the presence of a dog. Quit this unbecoming stubbornness and seek your own salvation, O Pandava King,' Indra said to him admonishingly.

But Yudhishthira's mind was made up. 'I cannot, indeed I will not do such a deed, so unworthy of an Aryan,' he said. 'If I so easily cast away one who has shown me such devotion, how can I find it in my heart to enjoy the prosperity you speak of?'

'Realize, O King, you have achieved immortality!' said Indra. 'You are renowned as the fair and the just. I say to you, there is no place in heaven for men with dogs.'

'Let it not be said of me that I abandoned anyone who had sought my protection, shown me loyalty or one who is too weak to protect himself. I refuse, out of my own desire to protect my happiness, to abandon this dog!'

As he spoke these words, the dog vanished, and in its place stood a resplendent being, who was none other than Dharma, the God of righteousness. 'All hail to thee, Yudhishthira,' he said. 'Truly, there is none on earth equal to thee! Thou hast refused to board the very chariot of the celestials for the sake of a humble creature that followed thee with devotion! May you ever dwell in the realm of eternal bliss!'

Forthwith, Yudhishthira the righteous and the just, ascended the divine chariot of Indra, blessed by the Lord of Dharma, and entered heaven in his mortal form. On alighting from the chariot, he was greeted by the celestials who were eager to meet him and welcome him amidst themselves. But he looked in vain for the much loved forms of his brothers and Draupadi. They were nowhere to be found.

'I feel ill at ease without my loved ones,' he said to Indra. 'Where are my brothers and my dear wife, Draupadi? I pray you, lead me to them.'

'This is indeed strange, O King, that you have entered the realm of bliss and you refuse to let go of your earthly bonds,' said Indra with disapproval. 'This is the region of the Gods! Look around you and behold the celestial spirits! Your brothers and wife have all attained to the levels they deserve. Each of them is in their own place. Overcome your human affections and enjoy your hard-earned heaven!'

'There is no heaven for me without my loved ones,' said Yudhishthira firmly. 'I pray you, lead me to wherever they may be!'

As he looked around for his brothers in the heaven world, Yudhishthira's eyes fell on Duryodhana and his Kaurava brothers. Shocked and grieved, he exclaimed, 'I cannot believe what I see! Was it for this that we fought the war of justice and dharma? Was it for this that we killed our kinsmen and friends? I refuse to dwell in the region where spirits like them dwell. I beseech you, lead me at this very minute to where my brothers dwell.'

Indra tried to reason with him thus: 'Yudhishthira, you are well-versed in dharma shastras. Do you not know that all feuds cease in heaven? By dying the death of brave soldiers on the battlefield, your Kaurava cousins have also reached their celestial abode. Dwell here in joy yourself! How can you continue to nourish enmity in heaven?'

'If people like my cousins deserve heaven, then this place is not for me,' said Yudhishthira. 'As for me, I have no wish to dwell in the company of the unrighteous, even in heaven. I pray you, take me to my brothers. I do not wish to dwell in the celestial regions without them.'

The Devas summoned a celestial messenger and bade him to lead Yudhishthira to the nether regions where his brothers dwelt. And now, the Pandava king began a journey even more arduous and grueling than the one he had followed thus far. Gloomy, dark, dreary and polluted was the way they walked, the messenger leading and Yudhishthira following close behind; and not just dreary and dark, but infested with dangers; on either side of the narrow path raged blazing fires; stinging insects flew across the path; terrible and foul odours made them suffocate; the path was strewn with the mortal remains of human bodies; and a spirit of nameless terror seemed to haunt them in the twilight zone.

Yudhishthira was anguished by what he saw around him. Was it to such a region that his loved ones had been sent? If that was indeed so, he would choose to dwell with them, rather than choose celestial bliss.

They came upon a river, which seemed to be flowing with boiling water. Here, the very ground seemed to be made of iron; the very leaves on the trees seemed to be as sharp as swords; clouds of vapour rose all around, from cauldrons of boiling oil, in which mortal beings were subjected to horrendous tortures. Rivulets of blood circled the ground.

How much farther must we travel from here?' Yudhishthira asked his guide. 'I pray you tell me, what is this world we have come to? Where dwell my brothers?'

'Thus far and no farther will I walk with you, O King,' replied the messenger. 'I leave it to you to decide if you wish to move on in search of your brothers. However, should you be weary of the way and fearful of what lies ahead in these nether regions, you have the right to return with me to heaven, at this point.'

For a moment, Yudhishthira's spirits fell. Overwhelmed by the horrible vapours and the dreadful landscape around him, the eldest of the Pandavas was about to turn around, when he heard sobs and wails around him. 'Stay, O stay and do not leave us alone in our misery!' the voices cried out. 'Our pain and anguish is somewhat lessened by your presence with us. Do not take away the radiance and the blessed relief you have brought with you to this dreadful world!'

Yudhishthira stopped short in his tracks. The voices seemed so familiar! 'Where are you?' he called out. 'It is you Arjuna, isn't it? I can hear you, dear Draupadi. Are Bhima and the twins with you here?'

Time seemed to stand still as the truth dawned on him. Duryodhana was in heaven with his brothers; the Pandavas and Draupadi were in this hell; this was the justice of the Universe; and he was expected to go back to the abode of the gods who had perpetrated this. The royalty and the upright nature of the king asserted themselves in him, and he said to the messenger, 'Return to your heaven without me; there can be no celestial comfort, no eternal bliss for me without my kinsmen. I will not leave these wretched souls in their misery and seek my salvation and comfort; here in this hell will I dwell with them, as long as they are condemned to be here!'

'It shall be as you wish,' replied the messenger. In a trice, he disappeared, carrying the king's message of refusal and defiance to Indra. But no sooner had he left, that light gradually began to filter through the surrounding gloom. The pall of vapours and odours seemed to lift, as if by magic. A cool breeze began to blow across the hot region. The horrendous sights, the boiling river, the cauldrons of oil, the rivulets of blood and the scenes of torture disappeared and as Yudhishthira lifted his hands to his eyes to shield them from the sudden light, he found himself surrounded by the devas.

'Hail to thee, King!' they saluted him. 'Blessed indeed are you, and blessed are your loved ones. The illusions are now ended. To you, the righteous and the just, hell was shown as an illusion. Happy are they who suffer for a while, and then enjoy the fruits of their good deeds. You and your brothers and your beloved Draupadi, have seen hell as but a mirage. Now we welcome you to the celestial abode of the gods where all of you rightly belong. Here, take a dip in the sacred river where you will divest yourself of all human grief and enmity; cast off your human body here and arise to the realms of glory!'

The Lord of Dharma said to him: 'Wisest of men, this is the third time I have tested you. You chose to stand up for the faithful dog which followed you; you turned your back on heaven for the sake of your loved ones; and you chose to remain in hell for the sake of your brothers. It is inevitable that kings and rulers must go through hell if only for a while. So it was that, for the thirtieth part of a day, you too were doomed to suffer the pangs of hell. Neither the illustrious Arjuna, nor the valiant Bhima, nor your twin brothers Nakula and Sahadeva are really in hell. The sinless Draupadi too, is safe amongst us. Behold, this is actually *swargaloka*. Therefore, cease grieving.'

Yudhishthira, the Dharmaputra, was transfigured. His mortal frame dropped away and he was now an inhabitant of swargaloka, a god. With the disappearance of the human body, all trace of anger, grief and hatred also dropped away. Then Yudhishthira saw his elder brother Karna and all his brothers and also the sons of Dhritarashtra. Every one of them was free from anger and hatred, all having attained the state of the gods. In this heavenly reunion, Yudhishthira at last found peace and real happiness.

———⟨⊰◈⊱⟩———

THOUGHT FOR REFLECTION

Heaven can wait!

Sadhu Vaswani never longed for the joys of the heaven world. He did not aspire to mukti, salvation, liberation from the cycle of birth and death.

The question was put to him more than once, 'Is there anything higher than mukti?' He answered, 'I do not ask for mukti. I fain would be born, again and again, if only that I might be of some help to those that suffer and are in pain!'

Gurudev Sadhu Vaswani reminds us of a saint who, for the love of God, became a servant of humanity. After completing his mission of help and healing on earth, so the story tells us, he moves on to the heaven world. He is about to enter the portals of paradise, when he hears a cry of agony, 'I am in anguish and pain: is there no one to help?' The cry comes from a corner of the earth. And the saint says, 'Not for me the joys of the heaven world. Back to the earth must I go, to help a brother or a sister in need.'

Such was Gurudev Sadhu Vaswani. Towards the close of his earth-pilgrimage, pointing one day to a street-dog, he said, 'I would not mind being reborn as a dog, if thereby I could give relief to some in suffering and pain!'

On one occasion, he said, 'I would wish to enter hell to give love to those that burn there in the fires of selfishness and greed!'

Heaven can wait!

THE TALE OF JADABHARATA

He is the Soul of the Universe; He is Immortal; His is the Rulership; He is the All-knowing, the All-pervading, the Protector of the Universe, the Eternal Ruler. None else is there efficient to govern the world eternally. He who at the beginning of creation projected Brahma (i.e., the universal consciousness), and who delivered the Vedas unto him – seeking liberation I go for refuge unto that effulgent One, whose light turns the understanding towards the Atman.

— Shvetashvatara-Upanishad, *VI.17-18*

THIS ANCIENT LAND OF OURS IS REFERRED TO IN OUR SCRIPTURES as Bharatavarsha, the land of Bharata. Have you wondered how our country got this name?

Bharata was a great and famous ruler, who was the sovereign of this land, in the days of yore. His story is told to us in the Vishnu Purana as well as in the Srimad Bhagavad. Bharata was married to a virtuous queen called Panchajani, and ruled his kingdom for a long, long time. He had five sons, and ensured that they were well educated, that is, well-versed in the shastras and the laws that govern rulers. When his sons were well settled, his thoughts turned to vanaprastha and sannyasa – retirement to the forest, to seek the ultimate truth and the goal of liberation in the great tradition of India's rishis.

Leaving his kingdom in the safe hands of his sons, King Bharata retired to the *tapobana*, where he lived a life of austerity and meditation.

He built a little kutiya for himself with dried leaves, grass and reeds on the banks of a river. Every day he would rise early in the morning, take a bath in the sacred river and sit under a tree chanting the name Divine. When he needed to, he ate the fruits and berries that grew in the vicinity. He had no thoughts save those of God and liberation.

One day, as he sat in meditation, his *tapasya* was shattered by the plaintive cries of a creature. Startled, he opened his eyes and saw that on the far side of the river, a roaring lion stood, ready to pounce on a pregnant doe. Terrified of the lion, the mother deer jumped into the river. She swam against the strong currents for a while, but the exhaustion of crossing the river was too much for the mother deer; she died midway across the river, after giving birth to the fawn she was carrying. The newborn fawn was carried by the swift currents.

Sage Bharata saw that the fawn was in danger of drowning, and his heart, which was full of compassion for all living beings, melted at the sight of the innocent and defenceless creature. He got up from his yogic posture and swiftly rescued the fawn from the river. He took it into his kutiya, to warm the shivering creature before a fire, and gently bring it back to life. He, who had so effortlessly turned his back on his kingdom, his queen and sons, now lost his heart to a little, motherless deer!

This beautiful act of compassion proved to be a critical stumbling block in his life as a seeker! When he meditated in the daytime, his mind kept wandering with his pet, hoping that the fawn would not have strayed too far into the forest; at night, when he tried to commune with the Divine, he was anxiously waiting for the loved creature to return home quickly. In short, the love for the frail and beautiful animal became the obsession of his life.

Our scriptures tell us that what we think, we become. The Gita echoes this truth when it tells us that our dying thoughts determine our lives in the next birth. When Sage Bharata was on his deathbed, he could think of nothing but his pet deer; who would take care of my beloved creature when I am no more, he thought with anguish; he looked at the beautiful animal one last time, with tear-filled eyes, as his breath departed from his body.

In his next birth, Bharata was born as a deer – the most *saatvic* and delicate of deers. It was only a dumb animal for all people who saw its form; but no karma done by us is ever lost; due to its good karma, it remembered all that had happened to it in its previous birth. It resolved that it would not allow any attachments to distract it from the goal of life. It left its mother and its clan and came to live near the tapasvis in the forest. This creature never went out into the forest with other animals; it haunted the hermitages of the rishis; it gazed piously into their yagna fires; it stood and listened to their holy chants and it fed on remains of their prasad which they kindly gave away to the deer that had become a part of their hermitage. Thus having expiated its karma, it passed away and was reborn as the youngest son of a Brahmin family.

In those days, Brahmins led very simple lives; they ate simple, saatvic food; they read and recited the scriptures; and lived a life of devotion and piety.

Bharata, who still remembered the details of his previous lives, saw that this human life was his best chance of finally attaining liberation that he had craved all these years. In his infancy, the young lad decided that the best way for him to keep his focus on the goal of liberation, was to keep silent and not utter a word to anyone. That way, he thought, he would not be distracted by any worldly concerns, while he would dwell constantly on God in his heart. His father attempted to teach the Vedas to him, but the boy seemed hardly interested. He would wander aimlessly, with a faraway look in his eyes, or seem to search for some precious thing that he had lost. He was strong and healthy; but he would not utter a word.

His family took him to be a dumb idiot and called him Jada (dunce); his brothers and their wives treated him like a servant and dumped all the difficult tasks on him. He did everything that he was told to do without complaint. And when things went wrong and he was beaten up by his brothers, he would sit under a tree and brood on his future silently. There was no resentment, no anger in him. The constant practise of silence and contemplation brought wisdom to him. He was now a ripe *jnani*, whom the world saw only as an idiot.

One day, as he was sitting under the tree and gazing blankly into the blue beyond, he was accosted by the servants of a king who was passing through the area. One of the king's palanquin bearers had hurt his foot on the stony ground, and they desperately needed a strong, able-bodied man to become the fourth palanquin bearer. They saw Jadabharata and assumed that he was a lazy dullard whiling away his day under the tree. 'Hey, you!' they called out. 'Come with us and bear the royal palanquin on your shoulders.'

Jadabharata was used to following all orders implicitly; obediently he ran up to the palanquin and carried it on his shoulders. The king was, in fact, on his way to the ashrama of Rishi Kapila, in quest of spiritual knowledge. He now proceeded on his journey, borne by the jnani Jadabharata; but it was a rough ride. He was jolted and hustled and often pulled to one direction, subjecting him to painful jolts and shocks. He lifted the curtain of the palanquin and found that it was a stupid looking man, bearing the front left of the palanquin, who seemed to be twisting and hopping on one foot, who was the cause of this bumpy ride.

Now, the truth of the matter was that Jadabharata was aware of every little insect and tiny worm that crossed his path, and he was walking slowly and carefully, often sidestepping to avoid crushing them. Thus, his walk and his pace were not in keeping with the steady jogging pace of the rest of the palanquin bearers. Unaware of all this, the king shouted angrily at him. 'Hey you boor,' the king called out in great wrath, 'You are so strong in body. Is it so tough for a big man like you to carry my palanquin for a while? How come you are so tired so soon? Can't you look where you are going?'

Jadabharata turned round and lifted the palanquin off his shoulders, forcing the other servants to put the palanquin down in haste. The king climbed down and shouted angrily, 'Who do you think you are? How dare you behave in this fashion?'

For the first time in that lifetime, Jadabharata spoke a few words; he spoke them with a smile; he spoke them softly. But the impact of the first words he uttered was unbelievable!

'Who do you think you are? Who do you think I am? Who exactly are you and I? Who is the "you" you speak of? Who is the boor you despise? Is there anything, any creature in this wide world that is not actually "you" or a part of you? Who am I and who are you? What you have seen is only my body and your body. But I am not my body and nor are you your body. My atman is neither strong nor tired, nor is it carrying your palanquin upon its shoulders. Our atmans or souls are real and they are the self that matters. Is not all creation a part of that great self? And can that self ever be weary or tired?'

There was such clarity in his expression, such a radiance in his eyes, that the king fell at the 'idiot's' feet and took the dust of the ground under his feet and applied it on his forehead. 'Forgive me sire,' he cried.

'I know now that you are no ordinary man. You must be a *brahmajnani*. I beseech you in all humility; impart to me the true knowledge of the self.'

Thereupon, Jadabharata, until then presumed to be the village idiot, spoke to the king of the individual self and the universal self, the *jivatman* and the *paramatman*; he discoursed eloquently on the goal of life, the quest of truth and the desire for mukti or liberation; he taught the king the great truth that we are not the perishable bodies we wear, but the immortal atman that dwells within each one of us. To understand that the atman is a part of the divine self and to seek union with the Divine is the ultimate quest; to become aware of this oneness is to attain mukti.

'Therefore, O King, detach yourself from all other worldly bonds; sever all relationships that are transient and seek that which is eternal,' he concluded.

The king's life was transformed. He renounced his worldly life and went into the forest to seek the great truth that he had learnt from Jadabharata. As for Jadabharata, he returned to his silent stance and went back to live among his people. In silence he lived the rest of his life, mistaken for an idiot, while he contemplated on the highest truths in his heart. And when he came to the end of his earthly pilgrimage, he attained to the liberation that he had sought so earnestly in his previous births.

—————◦◇◦—————

THOUGHT FOR REFLECTION

You become what you think. Therefore, think thoughts of liberation.

Meditate and be liberated. When you sit in meditation you will be shown the way. You will get direction towards your goal.

It is not without significance that in the Kathopanishad, Yama, imparting true knowledge to the young Nachiket, tells the seeker: 'The fire that leads to heaven is hidden in the secret place of the heart.'

The fire is within us; the divine spark is within us! The question therefore is, how may we kindle this spark?

The answer is simple: *Kar dhyan, pao padnirvan*! (Meditate and discover the light within!)

Meditation is the art of quietening and calming the mind so that our inner consciousness is stilled and becomes more aware. In the state of detachment that ensues, the practitioner attains to a higher level of consciousness.

As we evolve on the path of *abhyasa*, meditation opens up possibilities of vital spiritual experiences. These are not just confined to out-of-body, or floating experiences, but deeply intuitive experiences that make us aware of the higher dimensions of life, leading us on to the highest realm.

THE SUPREME POWER OF GURU BHAKTI

Guruh pita gurur mata
Gurur devo gurur gatih:
Sive ruste gurus trata
Gurau ruste na kascanah

The Guru is father, the Guru is mother, the Guru is God,
the Guru is the refuge. If Shiva becomes angry, the Guru will
intercede on your behalf; if the Guru is angry, you will be
without help.

– Kularnava-rahasya12

※

THE FOLLOWING STORY IS NARRATED IN THE BRAHMA VAIVARTA
Purana and is also part of the Shree Guru Charitra.

In the beginning of the yugas, Lord Brahma created the cosmos,
and along with it, the four Vedas, which were the repositories of all
wisdom, enunciating a code of conduct for the upkeep of dharma or
righteousness. He also created the four yugas and the yugapurushas
as their guardian deities. It was the responsibility of each of the four
yugapurushas to undertake the responsibility for the upkeep of dharma
in his yuga or age. Each age and its yugapurusha had their own unique
characteristics as Brahma enunciated them.

'The purusha of the Satya Yuga [Golden Age]', Brahma said, 'would
be endowed with pure Satwaguna. In this age, there would be but one
religion and all men would be saintly and contemplative by nature,

163

often engaged in tapasya; no religious rituals would be performed by anyone. The age would be without disease; hatred, anger and enmity were to be totally absent. There would be no evil thought in men's minds. Sorrow too would be absent.'

The purusha of Treta Yuga (Silver Age), according to Brahma, would have satwa and *rajas* mixed in him. The people of Treta Yuga would resort to external and ritualistic disciplines and austerities, especially of performance of sacrifices, etc., to attain their worldly desires.

The purusha of Dwapara Yuga (Bronze Age) would be predominantly rajasic, and always carry bows and arrows in his hands. But even so, he would be tranquil-minded and compassionate. In this age, the Vedas would be split into four and people's acquaintance with the Vedas, become lesser and lesser. The power of the mind would decline greatly and truth would no longer be as strong as it used to be. Desire and disease would begin to dominate and many men would fall into sin.

The Kali Purusha, according to Brahma, is possessed of tamasic traits; the people of Kali age will be materialistic, rejecting all higher and nobler values of life; many of them would become atheists and indulge in unwholesome and evil practises. Moral values will sink to the lowest level in the age of the Kali, and Kali will tempt and lead people astray towards evil and sin. People will fall slaves to sense-pleasures, especially the cravings of the tongue and the passions of lust.

Lord Brahma, however, warned Kali Purusha to guard himself against ever bringing harm to those who were devoted to the Guru. He was warned never to interfere with people who practised the ultimate virtue of the Kali Yuga, namely Guru Bhakti. Brahma emphasized that in this age, the Guru would hold the highest spiritual status, higher than those of the gods themselves. And Brahma also guaranteed that whosoever is devoted to his Guru, would ever be protected against all odds and harm. The Guru's grace would be as a talisman, an impregnable armour around his disciples and devotees. Brahma cautioned Kali Purusha that if he meddled in the lives of the true devotees of the Guru, he would himself incur God's wrath and no one would be able to help him, not even the Great Trinity.

And to illustrate the power of Guru Bhakti to Kali Purusha, Brahma narrated the following anecdote to him.

On the banks of the sacred River Godavari, where Maharishi Angiras, the son of Brahma, had set up his ashram in ancient times, there dwelt several rishis, who were ever engaged in their spiritual pursuits. Many young disciples sought the ashram to learn at the feet of these rishis, who were realized souls, well versed in the shastras. Vedadharma, son of the great Paila Maharshi, was one of these rishis. He was highly venerated both on account of his profound wisdom and his spiritual stature. Indeed, he was the worthy son of a worthy rishi. Many students flocked to sit at his feet and learn the great truths of the ancient scriptures. Sandipak was one of them.

One day, the rishi began to speak to his disciples of the great law of karma. 'The law of karma is the law of the seed,' he explained. 'As a man sows, so he shall reap. No one can escape the bonds of karma. Every thought, every word, every deed that we sow in the field of life will have its consequence on our lives, now or in future births, for the moral law is inexorable and inescapable.'

The rishi added, thoughtfully, 'I too, carry the burden of karma from my previous births. Though I have managed to expiate most of them through penance, I am only too well aware that some amount of prarabdha karma still persists, which I will have to expiate in this lifetime. I know I will have to go through a period of intense suffering, which is inescapable for me. The time has come for me to leave you, my dear disciples, and live the rest of my life in solitude. It is going to be a period of intense suffering and hardship which I cannot escape and will have to suffer.'

'Very soon now, I shall be overtaken by a dreadful disease, which will keep me in its grip for a long, long time. I am going to need the services of just one of you, that is, only if any of you are willing to submit yourself to this great ordeal. Remember, you will have to constantly attend upon me, nurse me and relieve me of my sufferings to whatever extent you possibly can. Let me also warn you, the disease that is going to overtake me is most loathsome and you will not be able to bear my presence, leave alone take care of me. I think the one who chooses to serve me will be subject to the utmost strain and suffering. Under the circumstances, I can well understand it, if none of you volunteers for this painful duty.' And the rishi broke off, studying his disciples in silence.

When Rishi Vedadharma put hundreds of his disciples to this test, all of them were found unworthy. Only one could pass the tough test – Sandipak.

No sooner had the Guru finished speaking this, than Sandipak touched the Guru's feet, prostrated himself there and prayed that he may be given the chance and privilege to serve him. He said, 'Sire, what greater blessing can there be than serving the Guru, under all circumstances, through trying times and rewarding times, through joy and sorrow, in pain and good health? I pray you, confer this great blessing upon me!'

Vedhadharma accepted the young man's offer. He announced that they would set out on a pilgrimage to the holy city of Kashi, for the dreaded disease that was about to overtake him could prove fatal, and like all pious Hindus, he would like to breathe his last on the banks of the holy Ganga at the feet of Lord Vishwanath.

Having entrusted his other disciples to the care of his brother rishis in the ashram, Rishi Vedadharma set out with Sandipak for the holy city of Kashi. Here, they settled down at a small kutiya on the northern bank of the Manikarnika Ghat, sacred to Lord Shiva.

Things came to pass exactly as the rishi had predicted for himself. He became afflicted with leprosy, and the disease spread rapidly, ravaging his ascetic frame. His leprous sores were smeared with oozing blood, attracting dreadful flies and worms that would not let him rest even for a short while, let alone sleep. He was in acute agony and became peevish and irritable over the least cause. The disease dealt a cruel blow on him, when it caused his total blindness.

All the anger, the pain and the agony, the Guru took out on his hapless disciple, Sandipak. The young man was the constant target of the Guru's impatience and rage. When Sandipak was cleaning the leprous sores on his body, the Guru would howl in pain and accuse the disciple of handling him carelessly. When the disciple brought freshly made broth for him, the Guru would scold him for the insipid food he cooked.

But none of these things upset Sandipak in the least. He continued to serve the Guru with the greatest love and reverence, day after day. He was indeed a devoted disciple, a devoted servant to his ailing Guru. As we may well understand, it is no easy task to care for an ailing, old man, stricken with blindness and afflicted with the dreaded disease of leprosy. Why, these days, we come across the heart-rending cases of old, blind fathers and mothers, left in institutional care, because their own children cannot be bothered to care for them! But Sandipak was exceptional; he devoted his life to caring for his Guru. The physical strain and effort, the Guru's oft-flaring temper, the sleepless nights and constant calls of the Guru – all these, he accepted, as a boon from his Guru. It was enough that the Guru had permitted him to be of service!

His only regret was that he could not alleviate the suffering and the pain of the Guru, no matter how faithfully he served him. If only he could have taken the Guru's pain and suffering on himself, he would have been most happy to do so. But that is not given to us to take on the karma of the Guru! And he knew that Vedadharma was on a sacred penance to expiate all his prarabdha karma, voluntarily. In this case, Sandipak could not take on the Guru's suffering. He hardly slept at night, ever vigilant to press the Guru's feet, fan him gently or otherwise minister to him. He hardly ate anything except the broth left over after the Guru's meal. But his devotion and care were exceptional; never once did he complain; never once did he so much as heave a sigh of weariness.

Such piety and devotion could not go unnoticed by the gods. One day, Lord Shiva appeared before Sandipak and told him that He was mightily pleased with his devotion and dedication to the Guru. 'Ask me whatever you wish,' Lord Vishveshvara said to him, 'and it shall be granted to you as a special boon from me.'

Sandipak craved only for one boon – the well-being and complete cure of his Guru. It was readily granted to him. However, Rishi Vedadharma rejected this offer – for he did not want to be cured, but to expiate his karma. And so Lord Shiva went away – and Sandipak continued to serve his Guru, as before. The stress and strain and constant toil, continued as before. Not once did Sandipak even wonder why his Guru had not accepted the Lord's boon, which would have put himself and his disciple out of misery.

Soon thereafter, Lord Vishnu appeared before Sandipak. 'I am immensely pleased with your Guru bhakti and Guru seva,' he said to the young man. 'Ask of me what boon you will, and it shall be granted unto you.'

'My Guru's command is my wish,' said Sandipak. 'Tarry a while, Lord, while I ask the Guru what he would like to have from you.'

Humbly, he asked the Guru if he should beg healing and well-being of the Guru as a boon from the Lord. The Guru flew into a rage and said that he did not want favours from anyone, and all that he desired was to be left alone to expiate his karma.

Sandipak returned to Lord Vishnu, who had waited for him and said to him humbly, that he had no boon to ask of him.

Now, the holy trinity of Brahma, Vishnu and Shiva appeared before Sandipak and said to him, 'Is it wise for a young man like you to refuse the benevolent kindness of the Gods because of the stubbornness of the Guru? When We, the Supreme Gods, who are higher than any being, are graciously offering you boons, is it not foolish of you to listen to the perverse behests of your Guru and spurn the blessed opportunity that has come to you?'

Sandipak bowed politely before the effulgent deities and replied humbly, 'I know of no higher religion than Guru seva; I know of no other God higher than my Guru. For our sacred shastras teach us that there is none equal to the Guru, and that the Guru is higher than even the highest Gods. What I want above all else is only my Guru's grace and the opportunity to serve him; and not the favour of anyone else. If you are still keen on granting me some boon, please bless me that my devotion to my Guru may grow from more to more and that it may never slacken and waver.' The Gods blessed him accordingly and disappeared.

Actually, Vedadharma had only wanted to test his disciple's devotion and loyalty. He now revealed to his dear disciple that his leprosy was only a condition he had created himself, to identify his true disciple.

Blessed is the disciple who is gifted with such faith and devotion – for he evolves from being a disciple to becoming a Guru!

THOUGHT FOR REFLECTION

Gurudev Sadhu Vaswani tells us: he, who loses himself in his teacher, is the true disciple. He who follows his own will and his own desires is not a true disciple; he who doubts in his heart and is dominated by personal ambition may be intellectually strong; he who argues endlessly and emphasizes the rightness of his own point of view may be an able debater – but a disciple he cannot be: for he is a worshipper of himself.

What are the marks of a true disciple, we asked Gurudev Sadhu Vaswani. The Master outlined the following traits:

1. Humility: When a true disciple was asked whether he was a disciple, he answered, 'I am trying to be a disciple, so help me God!' Humility helps us to avoid several obstacles and evils on the path of discipleship, such as ostentation and pretension.

2. Obedience to the teacher: The disciple must always remember that in obeying his Guru, he obeys God. The teacher may put the pupil to severe tests. The worst may be this – he asks the disciple to be far away from him. For a teacher knows that a raw fruit requires both sunshine and shadow, in order to ripen in maturity. So, the disciple must have the double experience of fellowship and separation: for in separation too, there is union. Spiritual obedience to the teacher, not physical nearness to him, is the mark of a true disciple.

3. Seva or service: The disciple must serve the teacher wholeheartedly. Growing in humility, obedience and service, the disciple will develop intuition and rise to meet his Guru on the Buddhic plan.

ISLAM

Brief Introduction

*I*SLAM IS ONE OF THE TWO MAJOR RELIGIONS OF THE WORLD. THE Muslim population of the world today is estimated at more than one billion, covering four continents and many different areas of the world. It is the dominant religion of North Africa, the Middle East, and certain areas of Asia and Europe.

Etymology tells us that Islam is derived from *sin-lam-mim*, which carries the basic meaning of 'safety and peace'. Other root meanings of the word also connote 'submission' or 'surrender'. Modern scholars translate the term to mean 'losing oneself for the sake of God and surrendering one's own pleasure for the pleasure of God'. The message of Islam was revealed to the Holy Prophet Muhammad, 1,400 years ago. It was revealed through the Angel Gabriel and was preserved in the Holy Quran. A Muslim is a follower of Islam. 'Muslim' is an Arabic word that refers to a person who submits himself to the will of God.

Muslims believe that true Islam dates back to the creation of the world, and look upon Adam as one of their earliest prophets, followed by Abraham, Moses, Jesus (Isa) and Prophet Muhammad, the last in the line. But for the purpose of history, many regard Prophet Muhammad as the founder of Islam. It was to him that God chose to reveal the Holy Quran, and it was he who was responsible for establishing the faith as we know it today.

The fundamental precept of Islam is that God is One and Allah is the proper name for the Almighty God. Allah has other names, that are used to describe his characteristics: the Creator, the Sustainer, the Merciful, the Compassionate, etc. The concept of purity is central to Islamic belief. There are different aspects of purity to be maintained by the faithful. One is through the avoidance of using drugs and alcohol or engaging in gambling. Another is through not eating certain foods, like pork. And finally, there is the matter of maintaining a measure of ritual cleanliness.

Muslim beliefs are often summed up in the following seven principles:

1. *Tawheed* – the unity of God
2. *Risallah* – acceptance of the Prophethood of Muhammad, a messenger of God
3. *Mala'ikah* – belief in angels
4. *Kutubullah* – belief in God's books (like the Quran and the Psalms of David)
5. *Yawmuddin* – belief in a Day of Judgement
6. *Al-Qadr* – acceptance of pre-destination
7. *Akhriah* – faith in a resurrection after death

As a Muslim, each member must carry out five essential duties, called the Five Pillars of Faith. They are:

1. A Muslim must acknowledge that there is no God but Allah and Muhammad is his Prophet.
2. A Muslim must pray five times daily, facing Mecca: at dawn, at noon, in the mid-afternoon, at dusk and after dark.
3. Each Muslim must pay a *zakat*, a voluntary contribution for poor Muslims.
4. A Muslim must fast for the month of Ramadan. During the fasting month, one must refrain from eating, drinking, smoking and sexual intercourse from dawn until sunset.
5. A Muslim must make a pilgrimage to Mecca. Every adult Muslim who is physically and financially able to do so must make this pilgrimage at least once in his or her lifetime.

These practises may be described as the cornerstones of Islam. These are obligations which are required of every Muslim. They are known as: *shahadah* (statement of faith), *salat* (prayers), *zakat* (alms), *sawm* (fasting) and *hajj* (pilgrimage).

MUHAMMAD BECOMES A PROPHET

We have sent thee not except as a giver of glad-tidings and a warner to all the peoples.

— The Holy Quran, Sheba (34):28

⋘⋙

THE AGE IN WHICH PROPHET MUHAMMAD WAS BORN WAS AN AGE OF darkness and ignorance in Arabia. It was as if God had sent His prophet to redeem the people from the slough of depravity and ignorance into which they had fallen.

Islamic historians describe the era as an age of ignorance (*ayyamul-jahiliyyah*) in which, generally speaking, moral rectitude and the spiritual code had long been forgotten. Superstitious rites and dogmas had replaced the tenets of the Divine religion.

It was only a few elders of the Quraish tribe (i.e., the ancestors of the Holy Prophet) and a handful of others who continued to follow the religion of Ibrahim; but countless others were completely given over to blind superstitions and pagan rituals. By and large, the people of Arabia had become idol worshippers, though they knew in their heart of hearts that there was but one God, whom they called Allah. Even the other Abrahamic faiths, Christianity and Judaism, had lost their initial appeal in the region.

Round about 605 AD, when the Holy Prophet was 35 years old, a flood had swept Mecca and the building of the Ka'bah was badly damaged. The Quraish decided to rebuild it. Though most of the people of Mecca were idol worshippers, many of them held the Ka'bah in great veneration, believing that it was the only remaining connection to the Prophets of the past. The rebuilding process began; and when the walls reached a certain height, a dispute arose between various clans as to who should have the honour of placing the Black Stone (Hajar Aswad) in its allotted place. This dispute threatened to become ugly, until it was agreed upon that the first person to enter the precincts of the Ka'bah the next day would settle the issue.

As it happened, it was God's will that the first person to enter the sacred precincts was none other than Muhammad, who was already respected and recognized as 'the Truthful' and 'the Trust-worthy' amongst his people. The Quraish thus had every reason to be pleased. Thus, it was Muhammad who supervised the placing of the sacred stone. God had decided that he would be the one who would lead the Arab people to the dawn of a new faith.

During these years, it was Muhammad's custom to spend a great deal of his time in solitude and meditation. His favourite haunt was the cave in the upper reaches of Mount Hira, to which he would often retire, to contemplate in solitude. This was his habitual practise during the sacred month of Ramadan. No one ever went up to disturb his retreat, except for his wife, Khadijah and his beloved nephew, Ali.

When he was 40 years of age, the Divine revelation came to him. It was not as if his character was miraculously transformed overnight; for he had always been a wonderful human being, a man of integrity whose heart overflowed with love and compassion for his fellowmen. But now the time had come for God to reveal Himself to His chosen messenger.

One day, as he meditated in the solitude of the cave of Hira, the Angel Jibreel (Archangel Gabriel) appeared before him in a dazzling white light and said to him, 'Recite!' The voice echoed and re-echoed through the cave: 'Recite!' the angel commanded, over and over again.

'Recite! In the name of your Lord, who has created all that exists, has created a man from a clot. Read... and your Lord is the most generous, who has taught the writing by the pen, and has taught man that which he knew not.'

Muhammad was shaking with awe and wonder. Slowly, he repeated the words of the Angel. Jibreel disappeared and the cave went dark.

Dazed and overcome, Muhammad stepped out of the cave, unable to understand what had come to pass. He was about to take the path that led to his home, when the Angel called out to him, 'Know Muhammad, you are the messenger of Allah, and I am the Angel Jibreel.'

These were the first *ayats* (verses of the Quran) to be revealed to the Prophet, and the date was the 27th of Rajab, 40th year of the Elephant (610 CE).

The flow of the Divine messages which would continue for the next 23 years had begun, and the Prophet had been proclaimed to lead his nation, to destroy the practises of superstition, ignorance, and disbelief, to set up a noble ideal of religious belief and to show humanity the path to the light of faith and celestial bliss.

As for the Prophet, he was perplexed by this new experience, and made his way home, where he was met with great support and understanding by his loyal and loving wife, Khadijah. It is said that when he entered his home, he was still shivering with the impact of the experience he had undergone. Khadijah wrapped him up in blankets and calmed him. Ever the angel of compassion and love, she comforted him and counselled him, before she took him to her venerable and learned cousin, the Ebionite Waraqah ibn Nawfal, a pious Christian of those times. Waraqah was widely read in both Jewish and Christian scriptures. Islamic historians tell us that on hearing Muhammad's account, he immediately stated that Muhammad had indeed been proclaimed the Prophet, and that his revelation had come from God Himself. 'This is Namus [meaning Gabriel] that Allah sent to Moses,' he told his nephew-in-law. 'I wish I were younger, so that I could live up to the time when you will most need my support, when your own people would turn you out.'

Shocked, Muhammad asked him, 'Will they really drive me out?' Waraqah answered in the affirmative and said, 'This has indeed been the fate of the prophets before you. Anyone who came with a message similar to yours has always been treated with enmity and hostility by their own people. You too, will be denied and persecuted. You too, will meet with abuse and hatred. If I should be alive until that day, then I would support you strongly. I would stand by you and God.' Waraqah then kissed Muhammad on the forehead and went away. A few days later, he died.

Khadijah was the first to accept Islam – that is, the faith in the Prophethood of Moses and the belief that the only God was Allah. For long, she had known that her beloved husband was the very soul of truth, integrity, compassion, honesty, charity and trust. She knew he had sought the truth with single-minded devotion all these years. Near and dear ones like Ali followed suit. After Ali, Muhammad's adopted son Zaid became a convert to the new faith. He was followed by Abu Bakr, a leading member of the Quraish tribe and an honest, wealthy merchant, and Muhammad's childhood companion.

The Prophethood had begun!

Waraqah's prophetic words also came true. For the first few years, the Prophet preached the faith only among a select few; but later, he was commanded by the Angel to preach the truth openly, in public. And that was when ugly enmity began to raise its head in Mecca, the land of his birth. The influential men of the Quraish tribe took a strong offence to his teachings. They felt he was undermining their authority in the state. They spread the malicious rumour that he was an atheist and trying to destroy the faith of their ancestors.

Insults and threats were heaped on him. His enemies incited people to stone him and attack him wherever he went.

The Prophet's uncle Abu Talib, an old man, was alarmed by the antagonism and hatred that his nephew had to face. In his anxiety and fear, he said to the Prophet, 'My dear nephew, the Quraishites are strong and powerful – and they hate you! Heed my words: fear their power; do not provoke their wrath. Give up your preaching and return to your trade, I entreat you!'

Prophet Muhammad was unafraid. To the old uncle whom he loved and respected, Muhammad said gently but firmly, 'Be not afraid for me! God will help me to stand by the truth – or give me death!'

May I say to you, whenever my beloved Gurudev Sadhu Vaswani narrated this story to us, he would exclaim, 'Truth, though she lead me to the gallows! Truth, though she take me through the fire!' Such was the Prophet's allegiance to the Truth he believed in, that he did not care for his own life!

He learnt from his friends that his life was in danger, and that fierce men had been sent out to kill him under cover of the night. Prophet Muhammad was constrained to leave his home at that dark hour. With him was his friend and faithful follower, Abu Bakr.

In hot pursuit of these two devoted servants of God, were the men who were out to kill the Prophet. They were wary, they rode strong steeds, and in their hands they carried drawn swords and sharp spears.

Abu Bakr saw them from a distance and was terribly frightened. In abject terror, he said to the Prophet, 'They are coming! They will be upon us soon. They will slay us with their sharp swords. Our bodies will lie on the desert sands to be devoured by wild animals!'

The Prophet was silent. In his heart he felt sure that God was with them and that they were safe.

Nearby was a cave. Prophet Muhammad and Abu Bakr hid themselves in the depths of the cave. The party of persecutors rode up after some time. They halted at the mouth of the cave. Their horses were neighing and their leader's order to halt was heard inside the cave.

Abu Bakr began to tremble like a leaf in the wind. 'What shall we do now?' he whispered. 'There are so many of them – and we are only two!'

Quietly answered the Prophet, 'Not quite, friend! We are not two, but three! The third is Allah! And when He is near, we need not fear!'

It is then that a miracle came to pass. Just after the two fugitives entered the cave, and a short while before the persecutors arrived, a huge spider had crawled to the entrance of the cave and woven its web across the entrance. Seeing the web, unbroken and whole, the persecutors said to themselves, 'Nobody could have gone inside that cave. Don't you see the spider's web covering the entrance? See, it is undisturbed. Had anyone gone inside, the web would have been torn apart. Let's not waste precious time, let's move on!'

Thus were the Prophet and his companion saved, by the grace of Allah!

THOUGHT FOR REFLECTION

Unlike the founders of the other great faiths of the world, Prophet Muhammad was born relatively recently, in the late sixth century AD, about the year 570. Many details are available to us about the life of the Prophet, who is held in such great reverence by the followers of Islam, that he is never ever mentioned without the prayer 'Peace Be Upon Him'.

The Prophet's actions and words were remembered and later recorded (known as Hadith), so that Muslims in future generations to the end of time could try to act, speak and live as he did. He has served as an example for all Muslims in all periods to modern times. Being the virtual ruler and military leader of the whole of Arabia by the end of his life, he still remained a humble, modest, simple man, always gentle, always soft-spoken, always kind to the least of his people. He will remain a model example for all of humanity.

While other religions are named after their founders, such as Christianity and Buddhism; after a tribe or ethnic group, such as Judaism; Islam (peace, submission, surrender to the will of God) is unique because its name represents its outlook on life and reflects its universal nature.

In other religions, even monotheistic faiths, people are exhorted to approach God through an intermediary, such as a saint or an angel or a Prophet or a teacher. However, it is only in Islam that a person is required to pray to God directly.

The teachings of Islam, even though they do cover religious rituals and morality, also extend to all other aspects of life. The Prophet Muhammad's mission encompassed not only spiritual and religious teachings, but also included guidance for such things as social reform, economics, politics, warfare and family life.

By maintaining a balance between man's spiritual and physical needs, the teachings of Islam suit the needs of society as a whole.

WEALTH AND POVERTY

Three things destroy, and three things save. As for the three things that destroy, they are: greediness that is obeyed, and desires that are followed, and a person becoming self-conceited (and proud) with himself. As for the three things that save, they are: the fear of Allah in secret and public, moderation in poverty and richness; and fairness in anger and pleasure.

— Reported by al-Bazzar (#80)

⚜

THE HOLY PROPHET OFTEN HELD MEETINGS WITH HIS COMPANIONS and followers, who were happy to gather around him and listen to his words of wisdom and guidance. One day, during such a meeting, a very poor man appeared at the entrance to the assembly. He was dressed in very shabby rags. He saluted the assembly: 'Peace be upon you.' Looking around for a place to sit, he spotted a vacant place and sat down to listen to the Prophet.

The Prophet had always taught his companions that all Muslims were brothers and equals in the sight of Allah; and in an assembly of the faithful, one should not insist on one's wealth or status; everyone should sit wherever he finds a place, regardless of his status. Now, the poor man had followed this teaching; and it so happened he had taken his seat next to one of the wealthiest men in the assembly.

The rich man was not comfortable with this; he was disturbed and upset, and tried to collect the edges of his robe around himself, so that the poor man's rags did not touch his robes.

The Prophet observed this and said to the rich man, 'Perhaps you are afraid that this man's poverty would affect you in some way?' The rich man was quick to deny this. 'Oh no, Messenger of Allah,' he said. 'Perhaps you were worried that some of your wealth would rub off on him, perhaps even fly away to him?'

The rich man was acutely embarrassed, for he had indeed felt reluctant to sit next to a poor man. But he protested, 'Indeed, not, O Messenger of Allah.'

'Perhaps you were afraid that your clothes might become unclean if his clothes touched them?' enquired the Prophet. 'No, O Messenger of Allah.'

'Then why was it that you drew yourself away and gathered your robes around you?' Now the rich man was constrained to admit the error of his ways. He said, 'I confess and repent for what I have done. It was indeed the most undesirable thing to do. I beg your forgiveness for this act. And to make amends for it, I offer to give away one half of my wealth to this Muslim brother so that I may be forgiven.'

But even as he said this, the poor man rose and said, 'O, Prophet of Allah, I beg to inform you that I do not accept this offer.' Everyone present in the assembly was taken aback by this statement. They whispered to each other that the poor man was indeed a fool to decline such an offer of wealth.

However, the poor man explained: 'O, Prophet of Allah, I humbly decline this offer because I am afraid that if I am wealthy, I too, might become vain and arrogant like this brother, and look down upon my Muslim brothers and ill-treat them, as he did to me.'

The assembly thus learnt a valuable lesson that day that even the smallest gestures reveal what one feels in the heart; and that arrogance and discrimination are not acceptable in the sight of God and His prophet.

THOUGHT FOR REFLECTION

Peace and prosperity on this earth are possible only through the spirit of selfless sharing. If I had a million tongues, I would appeal to you with each one of them, especially to my young friends who are going to be tomorrow's leaders and opinion makers – seek not power! Seek service! The selfless attitude of caring and sharing must come naturally to all of us!

Therefore, I urge my friends: Let us do as much good as we can, to as many as we can, in as many ways as we can, on as many occasions as we can and as long as we can.

How can the world be peaceful and prosperous if one fraction of its people lives in luxury and opulence, while the majority live in poverty and deprivation? Therefore, we must all learn to share what we have with others! Let us set apart a portion – say one-tenth – of our earnings to be utilized in the service of those less fortunate than ourselves.

To some of us, who are unable to make two ends meet, or live within their income, this may at first appear a very difficult thing to do! But we will find eventually, that in the measure in which we share what little we have with others, we will be truly blessed – and this world will be a better place for our humble endeavours!

THE THREE FRIENDS

At the moment when the coffin of a person is being lifted and carried, the concerning soul follows its corpse and regretfully calls: 'O you my children and my relatives! Beware that the world does not cheat you as it did me. I gathered wealth regardless of it being lawful or unlawful and left all of it for others. Now I am left with its burden upon me while they enjoy the fruit of it; therefore, avoid that which is similar to what happened to me.'

– Hadith of Prophet Muhammad

ONCE THE PROPHET MUHAMMAD, THE MESSENGER OF ALLAH WAS sitting amidst his companions (Sahabah) in the mosque, when all of a sudden he said to them, 'Today I shall narrate a story to you, and reveal a threefold riddle which you must try to solve.'

Upon hearing the word 'riddle', the assembly became eager to listen most carefully to the words of the Prophet. The entire congregation was hushed. Prophet Muhammad began his story.

Once, there lived a man who somehow realized that his life was drawing to a close. Very soon, he realized, he would be face-to-face with death. Now, what feared him most about this realization was that he felt he would be very lonely in the grave. He thought to himself that what he needed above all else now, was the support of true and loyal friends who would help him, may be even accompany him beyond death.

Determined to seek the help of his most trusted friends, he went to the house of his very best friend. He knocked on the door, and was warmly welcomed by the friend.

'I have come to you in dire need,' the man said to his friend. 'Can you help me?'

'Of course I will help you!' assured the friend heartily. 'After all, what are friends for? Tell me what you want and I will provide all of it in an instant.'

Gently the man explained that it was not material help that he needed. 'I do not have long to live,' he explained. 'It is after my life ends that I require your help.'

Frowning, the friend said, 'I assure you I will buy the best place in the graveyard for your burial. And I will provide the finest shroud to cover your dead body. Beyond this, who can do anything for you?'

The man was disappointed and moved on to his next friend. Having arrived at his door, the man explained his predicament and told his friend that he needed support and companionship beyond death. Could his friend help him out?

The second friend said, 'You know I have always been there for you throughout our lives. I can extend all the help you need here in this life. But what can I do for you when you are dead? I can carry your corpse to the burial ground and assist in your burial.'

Now, the man was close to agony and despair. Yet he headed towards the house of a third friend, hoping against hope. 'How can I expect him to give a different answer,' he thought to himself.

And he headed for the house of the third friend, very sure that he would receive the same answer. But when he confronted the third friend with his problem and pleaded for his help and support, he was pleasantly surprised by the answer he received. 'Tell me, and I shall help you in any way I can,' volunteered the third friend, most eagerly.

'I don't think you understand,' said the man reluctantly. 'I do not need your help here in this life. I am about to die, and it is after death that I need all the help I can get.'

The friend replied, 'Do not worry my dear friend! In death, as in life, I shall be with you. Let me assure you, I shall accompany you to the grave, I shall be there with you in the grave, and even when the angels of death arrive to question you and take your account, I shall support you, and then assist you on the *Pul-e-Sirat* [bridge] and lead you safely to heaven.'

The man was happy and relieved to hear this answer. A short while later he passed away in peace; undisturbed by fear and insecurity.

Having narrated the above story, Prophet Muhammad turned and asked his companions if any of them could identify the three friends in the story.

Everyone was silent, trying to figure out the significance of the story that they had heard. When no answer was forthcoming, the Prophet solved the riddle himself.

'The man in the story is every man, and his story is the story of every human being. All of us must die one day, and confront our death bravely.'

'The first friend in the story is money, worldly wealth; it can help us in life, but it is useless to us after death.'

'The second friend stands for our loved ones, namely our family, our kindred, our sons and daughters. We live and strive for their comfort all our life, but all they can offer to us after death is a shoulder to carry us to the grave.'

'The third and most important friend is *Aamal* [deeds]', concluded the Prophet.

'Everything we have in this life, loses its value in the hereafter. It is only our good deeds, our noble actions which will accompany us all the way through, till we reach our eternal life.'

THOUGHT FOR REFLECTION

Man's life is so crowded with mundane activities, that he rarely has time for self-study and introspection. He seldom finds himself in that expansive, tranquil mood of silence and reflection, where he can listen to God, and chant the name Divine in the heart within.

It is said that the worldly desires are like the salty waters of the sea. Such waters can never quench man's thirst. On the contrary, his thirst increases and his craving for fresh water grows even more acute! To drown yourself wholly in this worldly life is akin to quenching your thirst with salt water.

Work is a great boon. But we must remember, work is a means, it is not an end. Livelihood must never be confused with life. Do not make your work the objective of your life on this earth. The purpose of your life is to cultivate the soul. Hence, even while you are attending to your work, stay connected to the source of all life; stay in constant touch with God. If you give eight or nine hours a day to your work, it should not be difficult to spare one or two hours to your spiritual growth. This will help you achieve the kind of inner peace and bliss that work can never bring to you.

We have much to do to reach our goal. We have to face storms. We have to cross treacherous oceans; we have to climb rocky mountains; we have to be tested by fire. It is tough to get past these tests. One thing can get us across safely: The Lord's grace. By His grace alone shall we reach our destination.

Therefore, let us pray to God, 'Be kind, be compassionate, and make me worthy of thy grace!'

If we want to be worthy of His kindness, we must be kind to everyone around us. Kindness is a great spiritual quality. Be kind to everyone. Be kind to friends and foes alike. Be kind to birds and animals. Be kind to all people. Do not sit in judgement; do not find fault, do not criticize! Do not gossip. Be kind in thoughts, words and deeds. Kindness brings joy to both – to the one who gives and the one who receives! Seek blessings for all.

ALLAH LOVES THOSE WHO LOVE THEIR BROTHERS

None of you truly believes (in Allah and in His religion) until he loves for his brother what he loves for himself.

– Hadith of Prophet Muhammad

THE FOLLOWING STORY IS SAID TO HAVE BEEN NARRATED BY PROPHET Muhammad.

Once three men were walking along a road. One of them was afflicted by vitiligo, a deforming skin disease; the second was bald and the third was blind.

Allah sent His angel to them, to work a miracle in their lives. The angel approached the first man and asked him, 'What would you like above all else?'

The man who was afflicted with skin disease, said with longing, 'Above all else, I would like fair and clear skin, for people look with repulsion on me.'

The angel touched him and lo! His illness was cured completely. His skin glowed in soft, supple radiance.

'Allah be praised,' said the man, tears flowing down his cheeks. 'I can walk and live as a free man among free men.'

'And what would you like to have by way of wealth?' enquired the angel.

'A camel,' the man replied.

Immediately, the angel presented him with a pregnant she-camel and blessed him in the name of Allah and said that his wealth would multiply manifold.

Next, the angel approached the bald man and asked him, 'What would you like most?'

'I would like to have a head full of hair,' the man said immediately. 'People laugh at my baldpate.'

The angel of God touched him and his head was full of hair.

'What would you like to have by way of wealth?' the angel asked him.

'I would like to have a cow,' the man replied.

The angel at once gifted him with a pregnant cow and blessed him in the name of Allah and said that his wealth would multiply manifold.

Finally, he went to the blind man and asked him, 'What would you like most?'

'I beg that Allah may restore my vision so that I can actually see the people and the world around me.'

The angel of God touched him and his vision was completely restored.

'What can I give you by way of wealth?' the angel asked him.

The man said, 'I would like to have a sheep.'

Forthwith, the angel gave the man a pregnant sheep and blessed him in the name of Allah and said that his wealth would multiply manifold.

The three men went their ways and fed and cared for the animals that the angel had bestowed on them. The animals flourished, grew and multiplied so bountifully, that the man with vitiligo soon owned an entire valley of camels; the bald man had a whole valley of cows, while the erstwhile blind man now owned a whole valley of sheep. They lived lives of abundance and prosperity.

After a few years, Allah wished to test them and sent His angel to them once more. But this time, the angel went to each of them in disguise.

To the first man, he went disguised as a leper. 'I plead with you, in the name of Allah, to help me,' he cried. 'Look upon me with compassion; I am so badly disfigured by my disease that I cannot find a living. Allah has given you such a beautiful, bright complexion and so many camels by way of wealth. I pray you, give me just one camel that I may eke out a living with the animal.'

'Look here fellow,' said the man, 'I may appear to be wealthy in your eyes, but I have several obligations. I have no camel to spare for you. So leave this place and go somewhere remote so that people would not be repulsed by your sight.'

The angel revealed himself to the man and asked him, 'Do you remember the time when you too were a repulsive looking leper, and Allah took pity on you and cured you and blessed you with the gift of a camel? Have you not grown to wealth and prosperity with Allah's gift to you?'

The man replied rudely, 'I am not the one you speak of. All my wealth came to me from my grandfather and his grandfather. It is all inherited wealth.'

'If you are speaking an untruth, may you revert to your former condition,' said the angel and went away to find the second man.

Disguised as a bald man, he approached the second traveller and said to him, 'Brother, I am not blessed with wealth or good looks. I pray you in the name of Allah, to give me a cow. I shall work hard and support my family with the animal you give me.'

'Go away,' said the rich man. 'I cannot part with any of my cows.'

'I remember you,' said the angel to this man. 'You were bald and poor and unhappy. Allah blessed you with decent looks and a cow. Don't you remember Allah's munificence to you?'

'I am not the one you speak of,' denied the man hotly. 'My wealth has come to me from generations of wealthy ancestors who lived before me.'

'If you are speaking an untruth, may you revert to your former condition,' said the angel and went away to find the third man.

Disguised as a blind man, the angel now approached the wealthy sheep farmer and said to him, 'In the name of Allah, have compassion on me! I am sightless and I struggle to live. I beg you to give me just one sheep so that I may eke out an existence with the animal.'

The sheep farmer warmly held the blind man by the hand and said to him, 'Brother, I was blind and poor once, as you are now. Allah was munificent. He restored my vision and blessed me with all the wealth that I now enjoy. This wealth is yours, as it is mine. Come and take whatever you please from my dwelling, and Allah be praised!'

The angel revealed himself to the man and said to him, 'Blessed are you in the sight of Allah, for you remembered your former state and

His kindness to you. May you grow in wealth and piety. Allah is verily pleased with you and angry with your two companions.'

Appreciating and giving thanks for the blessings that we receive is a huge part of Islam. We should recognize that everything we have is given to us from the bounty of Allah; we are not deserving of it, rather it is a blessing that has been given to us, and to keep in mind that this is from Allah is something highly recommended as it will increase thankfulness and remove pride and arrogance.

(From Sahih Bukhari: Volume 4, Book 56, *Virtues and Merits of the Prophet [PBUH] and his Companions*, Number 670)

THOUGHT FOR REFLECTION

Would you like to make God your partner? Would you like to walk with Him today and trust Him for the morrow? Would you like to be given the tremendous privilege of issuing cheques on a bank that never fails – the Bank of Providence?

Here are some innovative ways to offer your partner His share of your wealth:

- Spend your birthday, especially your children's birthday, at a home for the aged. You will find that sharing your food with the old people will bring you far more satisfaction than throwing a lavish party.
- Each Diwali, each Christmas, set aside some of your festival spending to buy gifts for those who cannot dream of such luxuries. Don't be content with donations by cheque. Actually go out to deprived areas, hospitals and institutions.
- Sponsor a poor child's education; offer the cost of a surgical process; sponsor a day's meals at an institution – in sacred memory of your departed ones.

Do all of the above in the spirit of offering to God. Do not give with ego and pride; give with humility and love in your heart. It is a privilege to give – for giving blesses the giver as much as the receiver. God is the greatest giver – the All-Giver. He gives and gives and ever gives! And if man is to grow in the likeness of God, he must also become a giver. What a beautiful place this world would be if we share with the poor and the needy all that we cannot, do not use! Truly blessed are they who give to the poor – for they are the ones who will be richly rewarded!

The Simplicity of the first Caliphas

*He it is who hath placed you as viceroys of the earth and hath
exalted some of you in rank above others, that He may try you by
(the test of) that which He hath given you...*

– Holy Quran 6:165

PROPHET MUHAMMAD, IT IS SAID, WAS AN EMBODIMENT OF
simplicity and austerity, which he not only preached, but actually
practised in deeds of daily life. We are told that when he sat among his
faithful followers, strangers could not identify him by his attitude or
demeanour or the clothes he wore. He once forbade the construction of
a stage for his address to the faithful, turning the whole idea down as a
waste of public funds. He insisted on complete honesty and probity in
public life among all his followers. His wife Ayesha once remarked that
on occasions, the kitchen fire was not kindled in their house for a whole
month together, during which they lived just on dates and milk.

A Hadith by Hassan tells us that once the Prophet remarked: 'My
Lord offered to turn the valley of Mecca into gold for me but I said:
"No, my Lord, but let me have enough to eat a day and be hungry
on the other." He said this thrice or so: "When I am hungry I shall
make supplication to Thee and make mention of Thee and when I have
enough shall thank Thee and praise Thee."'

The great leaders who took charge of the faithful after the passing
away of the Prophet, proved themselves worthy followers of this beautiful

tradition of probity, honesty, simplicity and lack of extravagance in public life.

Abu Bakr was a wealthy merchant by family inheritance. In the days of his prosperity in Mecca, he spent all his fortune on helping the poor and promoting the cause of Islam. So much so, the Prophet once remarked, 'I am not aware of a person who can surpass Abu Bakr in beneficence.'

When he became the first Caliph, he lived a life of utter simplicity. It is said that Abu Bakr surpassed all the Muslims of his day in his austerity, his frugality, and the simplicity of his life and outward appearance. He made his public appearances in a simple linen garment and a cloak. It is said that he had but one set of clothes for public wear. It was in this simple dress that he gave audience to the richest and most powerful chiefs of the noblest Arab tribes and to the kings of Yemen who called upon him. Such guests presented themselves before the Caliph dressed in the grandest and richest robes, embroidered in gold thread and wearing rich jewels and splendid crowns. But at the sight of the Caliph, these men grew ashamed of themselves, and were awed by his pious humility and earnest gravity, and often decided to follow his example and renounce their extravagant attire.

On becoming the commander of the faithful, as he was called in those days, Abu Bakr said to his people, 'The weak among you shall be strong with me till, God willing, his rights have been vindicated; and the strong among you shall be weak with me till, if the Lord wills, I have taken what is due from him.' Abu Bakr strictly followed this policy and administered even-handed justice. As a result of this policy, we are told, Madina became a society which was practically litigation free.

The famous historian Edward Gibbon tells us that he attended to his jobs himself. He lived in an ordinary house. He himself ate very frugal meals and slept on the ground. There were no guards to attend to him. 'The pride of his simplicity,' Gibbon says, 'insulted the vain magnificence of the kings of the earth.'

One account narrates that there were two inkpots on the Caliph's desk; one provided by the public treasury and the other bought from his personal funds. When he wrote official letters, he used the first inkpot; when he attended to his private work, he used the second.

It is said that he would give his wife two dinars as housekeeping money. Once, he and his wife were invited to a feast and offered tasty sweets to eat. His wife was so enamoured of the taste of such good food that she remarked to her husband that she wished they could afford to throw such a feast for their friends. Abu Bakr said to her that he had no money for such a luxury; however, he added, if she could save enough money from her housekeeping allowance to afford such a feast, he would not object to it.

From that day onward, she began to skimp and save on the housekeeping money most diligently. At the end of a month, she was actually able to make the sweet dish that she had enjoyed so much at the feast. Happily, she offered it to her husband and her friends. The Caliph praised her for the effort, and enquired how much it had cost her to make the sweet. She made her calculations and said that she had been able to save a certain amount of money over the period of a month, which had gone into the making of the sweet dish. The next day, the Caliph visited his treasury and informed the officials that his monthly allowance should be cut by the same amount. And from then on, he cut the household allowance by half a dirham so that his wife would avoid such extravagance in the future!

If this was the probity and integrity of the first Caliph, his successor, Umar, was indeed a worthy inheritor of the tradition. Mahatma Gandhi narrated the following story about Umar, while extolling the simplicity and honesty of these two great leaders, who governed a vast empire.

Once when Umar was going on his usual rounds in the suburbs of Medina, with his attendant Aslam, he saw a distant fire in the desert. He said, 'There seems to be a camp. Perhaps it is a caravan that could not enter the town due to night fall. Let's go and look after them.'

When he reached there, he found a woman and some children. The children were crying. The woman had a pan of water over the fire. Umar greeted her. (The woman didn't recognize that it was Umar.) Umar asked, 'Why are these children crying?'

The woman replied, 'Because they are hungry.'

Umar asked her, 'What is cooking in the pan?'

The woman replied, 'Only some water to comfort the children, so that they may go to sleep in the belief that food is being cooked for them. Ah! Allah will judge between Umar and me, on the Day of Judgement, for neglecting me in my distress.'

'How can Umar know of your distress?'

The woman answered, 'When he is our Khalifah, it is his business to keep himself informed about us.'

Umar returned to the town and headed to the Baitul Mal (House of Charity) to fill a sack with flour, dates, fat, and clothes, and also drew some money. When the sack was ready, he ordered Aslam to put the sack on his back.

Aslam was shocked; he pleaded that he would carry the sack. Umar refused to listen to him and remarked, 'What! Will you carry my load on the Day of Judgement? I must carry this bag, for it is I who would be questioned about this woman.'

When he reached the woman's tent, the Caliph put a little flour and some dates and fat in the pan and began to stir the pot himself. When the porridge was ready, he served it to the family with his own hands. The meal was over and children were very happy and began to play about merrily. The woman felt grateful and remarked, 'May Allah reward you for your kindness! In fact you deserve to take the place of Khalifah instead of Umar.'

Umar bowed to her and said, 'When you come to see the Khalifah, you will find me there.'

Having narrated the story, Gandhiji said to the Congress members who were with him that all elected members and leaders should adopt simplicity and austerity in their lifestyle.

What a wonderful polity we would have if everyone followed this ideal!

THOUGHT FOR REFLECTION

Somewhere I read about an American, who shifted his home from an old house to a new one. He loaded three trucks with his furniture and gadgets. His new neighbour, seeing three truckloads of modern gadgets, said with surprise, 'My dear neighbour, you have brought three truckloads of machines and goods. Suppose for some reason, any of these gadgets don't work or you feel that you still have to modernize your house, then come to me, I shall teach you how to live without gadgets. I have none of these and I am still very happy.'

Dependency of any kind ultimately becomes the cause of misery. We need to bring austerity and simplicity into our lives. It is said of Leo Tolstoy that he was very fond of luxuries. He was related to the royalty of Russia. He was very fussy about the choice of his clothes. He used to spend a fortune on his attire. But, when he came under the influence of the holy ones, he began to change. He began to question himself, 'What right do I have to wear such expensive clothes?' Once this realization came to him he started wearing ordinary, peasants' clothes. He mixed with his peasants socially. He spent his money buying toys and other gifts for their children.

Many of us accumulate far too many material possessions on the journey of life. We cannot resist the urge to buy and possess things, which, we feel we 'simply cannot do without'. So we buy more and more. We end up dragging our possessions with us wherever we go – and we allow ourselves to be dragged down by them.

'Remember that very little is needed to make a happy life,' Roman Emperor Marcus Aurelius tells us. Alas, we pay no heed to such advice. We want bigger houses, faster cars, more money, more pleasures, more of everything!

We live in an age of sensation. We crave, we attain, we are satiated – and we crave for more. And so it is said that modern man is diet conscious, but spiritually undernourished.

JAINISM

BRIEF INTRODUCTION

$\mathcal{L}$IKE HINDUISM, JAINISM IS ALSO ONE OF THE ANCIENT RELIGIONS OF India, dating back to the prehistoric age. As a formal, institutionalized faith, it is thought to have been established in India, in the seventh century BC. This was a time of great religious upheaval in India, directed against the excessive ritualism of the Hindu faith as it was practised at the time.

A Jain literally means the follower of the Jinas or 'conquerors', highly evolved and spiritually elevated beings, who had mastered the self through discipline, austerity and complete control of the senses. These evolved souls attained enlightenment through their own personal efforts, and became tirthankaras or the great 'ford makers' who not only attained their own liberation, but also showed their followers the way to liberation across the ocean of existence. In all, there were 24 tirthankaras, who at various times rejuvenated and revitalized the faith, the last and most famous among them being Lord Vardhamana Mahavira, the founder of the religion which we call Jainism today.

Scholars agree that Jainism is closely related to the Shramana tradition, a movement that ran parallel to the Vedic tradition in ancient India. The Sanskrit term *shramana*, (derived from the root *shram* or effort, and meaning 'one who exerts effort') refers to men who took to ascetic or renunciate practises, which emphasized individual effort, thought, discipline and hard work as against rituals and mastery of texts, as practised by the Brahmins. In fact, shramanism along with Mimamsa (investigation) and Bhakti (theism) can be said to represent three different strands of ancient Hindu philosophy. Part of the Shramana tradition was absorbed into Hinduism, which provides for the life of renunciation as one of its four ashramas or stages of life; part of the tradition broke away from mainstream Hinduism altogether, rejecting the authority of the Vedas.

Jains identify Lord Rishabha Deva or Adinath (First Lord) as the first tirthankara who lived prior to the Indus Valley Civilization. Lord Rishabhadeva, according to Jain tradition, was a king of the Ikshvaku clan, who contributed greatly to the progress of society, at a time when civilization was progressing from the primitive to the complex i.e., from the Stone Age to the agricultural age. He is credited with having taught his people various occupations and professions like agriculture, animal husbandry, architecture etc., so that they might earn their living, and also with establishing the basic Jain dharma of compassion. At a certain stage in his life, he chose the way of renunciation and asceticism to seek enlightenment. He lived up to the age of hundred; he is said to be the founder of the shramanic tradition (the tradition of continence and austerity), and was responsible for the propagation of the basic principles of Jainism.

Not much is known in historical terms of the 21 tirthankaras who followed Adinath; however, it is said that the 22nd tirthankara, Arishtanemi or Neminatha, is referred to in the Rig Veda and the Yajur Veda, and is described as being a cousin of Lord Krishna. The 23rd tirthankara was Parsvanath, who was the predecessor of Mahavira.

It is thought that Parsvanath gave a new identity to Jainism, and actually set-up an order of ascetics who influenced Lord Mahavira to embrace the faith. But history credits Mahavira with being the official founder of the religion as it is known today.

LORD NEMINATHA

*All breathing, existing, living, sentient creatures should not be
slain, nor treated with violence, nor abused, nor tormented, nor
driven away.*

– Mahavira, Jaina Sutra

$\bowtie$

$\mathcal{I}$N ANCIENT INDIA, THE RAGHU AND THE YADU DYNASTIES WERE
well-known for their culture and civilization. Many Sanskrit poets
have sung the glories of their kings. Ayodhya was the capital of the
Raghu Clan and Dwaraka, the capital of the Yadhavas. Sri Rama and
Sri Krishna have been the greatest names from the two dynasties. In
addition, the Yadu Dynasty also attained the distinction of producing
the 22nd tirthankara, Lord Arishtanemi, also known as Neminatha.

Arishtanemi was the son of King Samudra Vijaya and Queen Shiva
Devi of Souripur in the Harivansh clan. His birth date is recorded as the
fifth day of Shravana Shukla in the Indian calendar. (Roughly around
3100 BC.) When he was conceived, Queen Shiva Devi had seen all the
14 dreams that are seen by a tirthankara's mother.

When he was born, his parents named him Arishtanemi, meaning
'the one whose path is unobstructed'. Vasudeva was the younger brother
of King Samudra Vijaya. He was a charming prince. His senior queen
was Rohini whose son was Balram and his younger queen was Devaki
whose son was Vasudeva or Sri Krishna. Thus Arishtanemi was the first
cousin of Sri Krishna.

Like other tirthankaras, Neminatha also had an inkling of his previous births. In his earlier incarnation, he was Shankh, the eldest son of King Shrishen of Hastinapur. One day, his father, the king, deputed the prince to go and deal with the bandits who were terrorizing the villages around the capital. Prince Shankh, an accomplished strategist, conducted this mission in such a way that he apprehended the leader of bandits without any bloodshed.

On his way back to the palace, he heard the desperate plea for help of a young and beautiful maiden who was being abducted by an inferior deva. Prince Shankh defeated the god and rescued the maiden, who was princess Yashomati. The two young people fell in love and were married soon thereafter. In due course Prince Shankh ascended the throne. In later years, King Shankh often dreamt of taking to a life of tapasya, but one strong force always held him back: and that was his great love for his beloved Queen Yashomati.

Once, an old and renowned astrologer visited the royal palace and King Shankh asked him, 'How is it that I am so deeply in love with Yashomati that all my desires to renounce come to naught?' The astrologer replied, 'O, King, the bonds between the two of you are as deep as several lifetimes. For the last six lives you both have been married to each other, and this is the seventh birth. That is the reason why you have such an intense and deep feeling of love for each other.'

The king asked, 'When will these ties be broken?'

The astrologer replied, 'Two lifetimes from now, in your ninth incarnation, you will be born as Neminath and she as Rajimati. In that birth both of you will be able to break free from this karmic tie of love; you will become a *margadarshak* and she will follow you into a life of renunciation; both of you will attain liberation.'

Now, born in the Yadhava clan as Arishtanemi, the prince grew up in the company of Sri Krishna and Balram. When he was of marriageable age, Sri Krishna took an interest in arranging a suitable match for him; thus the beautiful and virtuous sister of his consort, Satyabhama, a princess called Rajimati was selected to marry Prince Arishtanemi.

The marriage procession set out from Dwaraka towards the bride's palace. Prince Arishtanemi was riding a magnificently decorated elephant at the head of the procession; hundreds of kings, princes and aristocrats, kinsmen and friends of the Yadu clan, followed with their royal regalia and retinues. It was indeed a grand sight!

As the procession neared the bride's residence, a disturbing sight met the prince's eyes. On either side of the road, which had been gaily decorated with arches, flags and buntings to greet the bridegroom's arrival, there were fenced-in enclosures in which thousands of animals, big and small, had been tethered. Over and above the music of the trumpets, instruments and drums and cymbals that were accompanying the procession, the piteous wails of the caged animals rose in a sad crescendo.

Shocked by what he saw and heard, Prince Arishtanemi asked the mahut, who was leading his elephant, about the animals. The mahut explained to the prince that these animals had been supplied by the local butchers in preparation for the grand wedding feast on the morrow. 'After all, this is no ordinary wedding, Your Highness,' he explained. 'Your father-in-law is keen to show the Yadhavas that he is second to none in generosity and hospitality. Tens of thousands of guests will eat at the royal feast to mark your wedding. No efforts will be spared to please their palates. Every guest will be well provided for.'

'All these animals will be killed and served as dishes at my wedding?' asked Prince Arishtanemi, who was utterly overcome with a grievous sense of shame and guilt.

'Just as soon as our procession has passed, they will be slaughtered, sire,' explained the mahut, pointing to the burly men with knives and axes who stood ready near the fencing.

'If my marriage is going to be the cause of the slaughter of so many dumb and defenceless creatures, it is better that I do not marry at all,' vowed the prince. 'Mahut, I say to you, order the fences to be pulled down and all the animals to be released, at once.'

When the mahut conveyed these instructions to the guards, they obeyed instantly. Who were they to question the orders of the bridegroom? All the captured animals fled from the enclosures, for they knew instinctively that they had escaped the butcher's knife by a hair's breadth.

Prince Arishtanemi ordered the mahut to turn back to Dwaraka. A deep sense of disquiet and anguish filled his soul and he made up his mind then and there that he would renounce worldly life, which was so materialistic and insensitive, causing harm to so many creatures.

Alarmed, his parents, uncles and cousins pleaded with him in vain to turn back. They begged him to consider the condition of Rajimati, who would be heartbroken if he refused to marry her. Their pleas fell on deaf ears. 'Elders and cousins of the Yadu clan,' he addressed them, 'it is not just these animals that are trapped and helpless; we too, are trapped by the bonds of our karma. If I permit the slaughter of these animals, I will carry the negative karma of violence and bloodshed for aeons to come! My heart quails at the prospect. For them as for me, true happiness can only be in freedom from bondage. I am determined to break free of my bonds and tread the path of liberation. I earnestly beg you not to stop me.'

As the hapless mahut turned back towards Dwaraka, Prince Arishtanemi removed his rich jewels, ornaments and garments and gave them away. When he reached Dwaraka, he shaved his head, rejected his royal life and went into the forests on the Vijaynath Hills near Dwaraka. It is said that people were so moved by this spectacular event that as many as a thousand men decided to follow him into renunciation. In the Girnar forests, after prolonged fasting, meditation and severe ascetic practises, he attained liberation on the 15th day of the dark half of the month of Ashvin.

As for Princess Rajimati, she had at first been afflicted with profound melancholy. But when she reflected on all that had happened, she too decided to follow the noble example of the prince whom she was not destined to marry. She along with her friends became disciples of Lord Neminatha and took diksha from him for the vows of asceticism. She too was blessed and attained liberation under his guidance.

Thus the astrologer's prediction came true, and the 23rd tirthankara brought salvation to many aspiring souls before he himself attained nirvana.

THOUGHT FOR REFLECTION

We have all been given the freedom of choice. God has bestowed on each and every individual, the right of freedom – the same degree of freedom that God has kept for himself. Man is free to choose – between vice and virtue, good and evil, selfishness and service. Man can choose to be selfish or unselfish. He can choose to be a sinner or a saint. He can choose to move on the path of evil, even become a criminal. He can choose to become a thief or a murderer. Equally, he can choose to move on the way of virtue, he can become a God on earth. The choice is entirely his.

But remember, if the right to freedom of choice is vested within him, it follows that the responsibility for his actions also rests with him; for we cannot have right without responsibilities. At every step on the road of life, we have the freedom to choose the direction in which we move.

Now, if I choose to move on the path of good, I go forward; I progress; I evolve spiritually. If I choose to move on the path of evil, I regress; I am pushed backwards. If I choose wrong over right, evil over good, how can I blame God for what results from my action?

This is the difference between men and animals – that animals do not have a mind or will of their own, to act as per their choice. They act without ulterior motive. They are only impelled by blind instincts. Suppose a man is crossing a jungle; he is confronted by a hungry maneater who leaps on him, attacks him, tears his flesh to pieces and feeds on him! How can any blame accrue to the animal in this terrible incident? The animal was hungry; it killed and ate its victim. It was only acting according to its instincts – for it can act in no other way.

We have no right to take away the life of a creature, just to satisfy our appetites. Life, after all, is God's gift, and when I cannot bestow life on any creature, what right do I have to take it away? When we make the choice between good and evil, right and wrong, we determine the consequences of our own action. If we choose right, we attain happiness; if we choose wrong, we have to confront distress and misery.

The Ordeals of Bhagwan Mahavira

The worthy men of the past, present and the future all say thus, speak thus, declare thus, explain thus: all breathing, existing, living and sentient creatures should not be slain, nor treated with violence, nor abused, nor tormented. This is the pure, eternal and unchangeable law or the tenet of religion.

– Acaranga Sutra

*P*RINCE VARDHAMANA, AS HE WAS KNOWN IN HIS *PURVASHRAMA* (earlier life) renounced his princely life at the age of 30, on the 10th day of the dark half of the month of Kartik in the year 513 before the Vikram Era (569 BC). Taking the vow of extreme asceticism, he wandered the land in deep silence and meditation, living on alms as and when he got them and fasting most of the time. He was set on by dogs, stoned and abused; but he accepted all that came his way with the utmost equanimity.

Many people who saw him were deeply impressed by his penance and austerity; they wished him well in his quest for enlightenment. But there were others who regarded him as an atheist and a rebel who was out to destroy their way of life. Neither praise nor blame affected him. Be it attacks by wild beasts, reptiles and poisonous insects, vagaries of weather or other such calamities, he was neither moved by attachment nor aversion. With perfect equanimity he continued towards his goal.

***

Once a celestial being by the name of Sangam Deva grew envious of Mahavira's growing tapasya shakti. He was determined to distract him and disturb his equipoise. Using his siddhic powers, he inflicted 20 dreadful atrocities on Mahavira – all in one night. To mention just a few, an army of deadly ants ate through his body; swarms of blood-sucking flies and mosquitoes attacked him; venomous scorpions stung him and ferocious wild animals attacked him. Lord Mahavira remained unmoved, the very epitome of equipoise and steady concentration. He did not utter a word in pain or protest. He did not even so much as bat an eyelid or twitch an eyebrow.

And yet the scheming Sangam Deva was not ready to accept defeat just yet. He decided to lure Mahavira with temptations of the flesh. He set celestial damsels to dance and sing before him and entice him into sin. But Mahavira was not in the least moved by these visions. For six long months did this evil god try to tempt him and distract him from his quest, but it was all in vain. In the end, exhausted and defeated, Sangam Deva fell at Mahavira's feet and begged forgiveness. Mahavira offered him forgiveness, for he was compassion incarnate.

***

Once, as Lord Mahavira was leaving a village to traverse a thick jungle, a few villagers begged him not to travel through the woods. They warned him that a deadly cobra known as Chandakaushika lived there, and many men had fallen fatal victims to his deadly venom. They humbly requested him to take another route out of the village.

Through his divine vision, Lord Mahavira was able to see the true nature of the cobra and the secret behind his birth as a deadly snake. Immediately he understood the circumstances under which this soul had the misfortune of being born a serpent.

Several births earlier, he had been an ascetic who stood all day in meditation. But one day, when a frog had climbed over his feet, he had kicked it away without thinking. His disciple reminded him that he had caused harm to the frog and that he ought to confess his act of commission and seek repentance for the same. This angered him so much that he had turned upon the young man blind with murderous hatred and anger; so wildly did he hurl himself that he crashed headlong against a pillar that stood nearby and met his death.

The remnants of his good karma as an ascetic caused him to take rebirth as a god for a brief life; but when this good karma got spent, he was reborn as a bad-tempered man, who became the abbot of a community of ascetics. One day, as he was chopping wood, he tried to attack a fellow monk who kept on arguing with him; while angrily trying to kill this man, he fell on his own axe, splitting his own head. He was then born as the angry serpent, which bit several passers-by and killed them with his deadly venom.

Lord Mahavira saw all this, and realized that the time had come for the poor soul to be liberated once and for all from the vicious cycle of rebirth. Casting a compassionate glance on the frightened villagers, he headed into the forest where Chandakaushika lived. In a short while, he reached the mouth of the deep hole in the earth, where the cobra lived. He sat silently at the mouth of the hole and began to meditate.

The cobra sensed a person in the vicinity and rushed out of the hole; he stung Mahavira's foot with his deadly venom. Blood rushed out from the wound; and lo and behold, it was not red blood, but milky white in colour, as it was infused with Mahavira's infinite compassion. At the sight of this white milk-like blood, Chandakaushika came to his senses; in the meanwhile, Lord Mahavira too, had opened his eyes and cast his glance of sympathy on the cobra. Chandakaushika attained realization: He saw through his previous births and his misdeeds therein; he bitterly repented of his sins and realized that anger had been the root cause of his misfortunes. He circumambulated Mahavira thrice, and curling himself around the lord's feet, he gave up his life, in meditation and fasting. He was reborn as a god.

***

On another occasion, Lord Mahavira was standing in profound meditation on the outskirts of a village. A cowherd who happened to be passing, took him to be a wandering beggar, and left his bullocks near him, asking him to take care of the animals till he returned. Mahavira was totally lost to the world, and unaware of what had been spoken to him. He continued his meditation, and the bullocks wandered away.

The cowherd returned and saw his oxen missing. 'Where are my animals?' he asked Mahavira angrily. Receiving no reply, he picked up sharp pegs of dry grass and thrust them into Mahavira's ears, causing deadly pain but he did not even flinch. In his rage, the cowherd cut off the outer ends of the grass so that the pegs could not easily be removed from the lord's ears. Lord Mahavira wandered with this painful condition for several days, before a kind physician noticed his ears and had the grass removed.

These austerities and trials continued for 12 long years before Lord Mahavira attained enlightenment. This blessed event came to pass on the 10th day of the bright half of the month of Vaishakha in the year 511 before the Vikram Era (557 BC). Lord Mahavira was 42 years of age at that time. He spent the next 30 years of his earthly life preaching his message of Ahimsa (non-violence), *Parasparopagraho Jivanam* (interdependence), *Anekantavada* (the doctrine of manifold aspects), *Samyaktva* (equanimity) and *Jiv daya* (compassion, empathy and charity to all living beings).

THOUGHT FOR REFLECTION

'Awake! Arise!' was Vivekananda's call to the youth of this nation. Indeed, all of us need to be aware, to be awakened. We cannot afford to procrastinate, for we may miss the golden opportunity that this human life offers to us – of getting closer to God, of experiencing his beautiful presence!

How may we become aware, awakened and arise out of the stupor of bondage to the senses? The answer is simple: through the practise of self-discipline.

What is self-discipline? Self-discipline is exercising control over our senses so that they do not impede us from reaching the goal of this human life. It is not an easy task to discipline oneself. But when one takes the first steps on the path of self-control, one will be amazed by all that can be achieved.

As we say, practise makes man perfect. Man has the power to achieve the impossible through constant perseverance and practise.

Indeed, it is possible for each one of us to conquer the mind and bring it fully under control. For this, two things are necessary: *abhyasa* and *vairagya*. It is only with a Guru's grace that we can attain these two qualities. As we cultivate reverence for the Guru, the impulse arises within us to follow the path of abhyasa or self-discipline. Many people make this effort, but only those blessed with the Guru's grace succeed in their efforts. Such blessed souls follow the path of abhyasa successfully, and gradually attain to the state of vairagya. It then becomes possible for them to control the mind, and inner peace soon follows. He who is blessed with inner peace is happy in every state, every condition of life.

Gautama Attains Enlightenment

Your destiny is in your hands. No imaginary external power can help you. Every living being wants to live and be happy. Do not hurt or kill other living beings. Devote yourself to liberate your trapped soul.

– Lord Mahavira

THE STORY OF GAUTAMA SWAMI, ONE OF THE CHIEF DISCIPLES OF Mahavira during his lifetime, has been told in many versions by Jain scholars. Some of them are mythical and focus on details; others are more abstract and philosophical versions.

Indrabhuti Gautama was a learned Brahmin, well-versed in the knowledge of the scriptures. It is said that he was master of 14 vidhyas like, veda, vedang, puran, commentary and logic, etc. When, for the first time, he went to Lord Mahavira, he was extremely proud of his own knowledge. But Lord Mahavira won him over by addressing the deepest doubts and queries that he had regarding the nature of the soul and the mysteries of life. Gautama immediately surrendered to him with his own group of 500 disciples and became himself a disciple of Lord Mahavira.

From early Jain accounts, we get the following picture of Gautama Swami, as he was affectionately known:

'He was a perfect, a complete disciple devoted to Lord Mahavira, in service to him, in devotion to him, in hospitality to him with respect, honour, courtesy. His eyes were without any wanton curiosity, his speech was without any tension, his walking was without any undue haste, he was not affectionate to his food, and when not on fast, used to take only one meal a day. He was indeed serious in nature, but not heavy with thoughts, he was quiet, but not withdrawn, he was always pleasant, happy, simple, frank, bright, knowledgeable, in his meditations noble, possessing highest qualities of virtues ... Guru Gautama Swami was indeed the most devoted, most unassuming, totally submitted disciple to Lord Mahavira.'

Although Gautama was absolutely devoted to Mahavira, it is said that he was the last among the disciples of the last tirthankara to attain *kevalagyana* or enlightenment. His very great love for his teacher was the cause for this delay, so the scholars tell us. His absolute devotion to Mahavira became a sort of attachment from which he could not free himself; Mahavira knew this, and was determined to help his disciple overcome this 'weakness' and attain nirvana, while he, the teacher, was still alive.

Gautama himself was puzzled by the fact that he alone, among all the *ganadharas* (leaders of the community) appointed by Mahavira, had not attained enlightenment. Once he actually posed this question to the Master: 'Bhagwan, I have been your faithful disciple ever since I joined the sanga. I was your very first disciple and have followed, obeyed and loved you faithfully. Yet why is it that so many people who joined your path much later have achieved moksha [liberation], but not me?'

Earlier, when Gautama had posed the same question, Lord Mahavira had told him that Gautama's excessive attachment to the Master was his one weakness. If he could eliminate this, Bhagwan said to him, nothing would stand between him and nirvana.

'Just as greed, lust, and ego, are passions, so are infatuation and attachment, Gautama,' the Master had told him. 'Attachment to objects or persons cause bonding and impedes liberation of your soul. Cut all your bonds and free your conscience of all passions and you too, will reach your goal.'

'Bhagwan,' Gautama had protested, 'have I not given up everything in your service? I own nothing, and I have no desires for anything.'

'It is true, dear Gautama, that you have given up many objects and have cut your ties with many loved ones,' Lord Mahavira explained to him patiently. 'However, you must also free yourself from your love for me, your devotion for me, and your emotional dependence on me. This too is bonding, Gautama! Fetters, golden or otherwise, will not allow a bird to fly free in the sky. Gautama, think about this imprisonment of your soul and set it free. Only then will you be able to reach the safe shores of freedom.'

But this had seemed so preposterous to Gautama, that he rejected it outright at that time. He thought that living in the blissful presence of the Master was surely preferable to an unknown, abstract form of moksha. Passionately, he had said to the Master, 'Forgive me, my Bhagwan, for I cannot obey this. I am nothing without you. I do not wish to attain freedom at such a price! I can live without moksha! I am all right, Bhagwan, where I am – away from my goal, away from the shore, but closer to you! I cannot leave you!'

Now, several years later, he was posing the same question again. In his wisdom, Mahavira decided to give him an indirect answer. He said, 'Dear Gautama, absolutely selfless love, without any attachment is the key to moksha. However, do not lose heart. You and I have been together not for just last 30 years, but during several previous births. With such past association, our souls are now destined to be equal, and this association shall continue.'

Gautama was puzzled by this reply. He thought to himself, 'Have I not redeemed myself? Have I not learnt the art of boundless love and compassion? Do I not love and even revere every living being large and small? Does my love still fall short?' And he was even more perplexed about the Master's assertion that their souls were destined to be equal. 'I don't want to be the Master's equal,' he thought. 'I only want to remain his most devoted disciple, his faithful shadow, forever.'

When the great tirthankara realized that his end was near, he hit upon a way to help Gautama attain the desired goal. The Master determined that Gautama should be sent away from him at this point, as the grief over his death might overwhelm him and make it difficult to reach the goal. It was the Master's will that this, the most devoted among his followers, should not lose the chance of becoming a kevalagyani.

Mahavira therefore sent for Gautama and told him of a great yagna that was to be performed by a group of sages. There was to be a mass animal sacrifice during this yagna. Sadly, in those days, the importance of sacrifices as a symbol of inner renunciation and self-sacrifice were misconstrued and yagnas had become excuses for animal sacrifices. People believed that these sacrifices would please the gods and in return their wishes would be fulfilled.

Gautama, ever obedient to the Master, made his way to the yagna, as instructed by him. When the Brahmins who were officiating at the sacrifice, saw him approaching, they pelted sticks and stones at him, and ordered him to go away. His unkempt appearance and his alms bowl made him appear contemptible and worthless in their eyes. They heaped insults and abuse on him. None of this deterred Gautama. He silently endured their abuse, insults and the injuries they inflicted.

The wife of the leading Brahmin then entered the yagnashala, carrying the offering of milk and rice (kheer) that she had prepared for the gods. On seeing the devout monk standing there, injured and bleeding, she fell at his feet, and offered the kheer to him as alms. To the astounded onlookers, she explained that the ascetic was none other than Indrabhuti Gautama, one of the foremost of learned Brahmins of his time. 'O, Realized One! Forgive us all for the injuries that we have caused you,' she begged of Gautama.

'Collecting alms one may be insulted and despised, but the wise with undisturbed mind sustain their insults and blows, like an elephant in battle with arrows, and is not shaken any more than a rock is by the wind,' Gautama said to her. 'The sage lives detached from pleasure and pain, not hurting and not killing; bearing all, one's lustre increases like a burning flame as one conquers desires and meditates on the supremacy of virtue, though suffering pain.'

The assembly of Brahmins fell at the feet of Gautama and he taught them Mahavira's views on ahimsa.

'There is no quality of soul more subtle than non-violence and no virtue of spirit greater than reverence for life,' he said, quoting the words of Lord Mahavira. 'Therefore, do not injure, abuse, oppress, enslave, insult, torment, torture or kill any creature or living being. All the *arhats* [Venerable Ones] of the past, present and future discourse, counsel, proclaim, propound and prescribe thus in unison: Do not injure, abuse, oppress, enslave, insult, torment, torture, or kill any creature or living being. If you kill any being, it is yourself you kill. If you overpower some being, it is yourself you overpower. If you torment some being, it is yourself you torment. If you harm someone, it is yourself you harm.'

Thanks to the eloquence of Gautama, the animals were saved from slaughter. The Brahmins agreed that from then on, they would abjure all forms of ritual sacrifice. Gautama had obeyed his Master's instructions in letter and spirit.

But, unknown to him, Lord Mahavira had passed away in his absence. When Gautama heard the news, he was overwhelmed by grief, but only momentarily: he realized the greatness of the Master, who had put Universal welfare above his personal interests. What mattered most to him was saving the lives of the innocent animals. Gautama would never again get the chance to sit at the feet of his beloved Master. As he returned, he saw people everywhere, lighting lamps to pay homage to the great tirthankara, who had crossed over to the other shore. Sorrow turned to vairagya, and Gautama realized the Lord's words coming true: he and the Master were indeed one! And enlightenment came to Gautama, at long last.

THOUGHT FOR REFLECTION

What is vairagya?

Vairagya is the knowledge and the wisdom of knowing that whatever we crave in this life, whatever attracts our senses is nothing but maya, an illusion. It is a mirage. This awareness will make you realize the futility of running after material wealth and sensual pleasures. It will make you aware of the Truth of the Absolute Reality.

Vairagya is the spirit of dispassion, detachment. The man of vairagya is without desire, without moha or kama. Desire leads to greed for gold and wealth; sometimes it takes the form of hankering after fame and power and other worldly gains. Many of us are trapped by our excessive attachment to our near and dear ones.

It is when you renounce your worldly pursuits and stop chasing its shadows, that you will be able to create a space within. And when you feel the vacancy, the emptiness in the heart within, there will arise the yearning, the intense longing for the Lord! This thirst, this hunger will grow till streams of tears flow from your eyes, and you will come to realize that the goal of this life is to attain God.

CHANDANA

As gold does not cease to be gold even if it is heated in the fire,
so too, an enlightened man does not cease to be enlightened on
being tortured by the effects of karma.

— Mahavira, Samayasara

WHEN THE GREAT *AVATARA PURUSHAS* WALKED UPON THIS EARTH MANY
were the lives that were touched, even transformed utterly, through
just a momentary contact with them. Such is the power of a realized
soul, that it can offer deliverance and liberation to so many others at a
glance, or through a chance meeting! Even such a transforming power
is illumined for us in the story of Vasumati, which I am about to narrate
to you.

Born a princess, sold into slavery, ill-treated by her mistresses,
disfigured and deformed because they envied her beauty, Vasumati at
long last had the good fortune to have a glimpse of Lord Mahavira.
In that instant, Lord Mahavira recognized her innate goodness, and
Vasumati became Chandan Bala, a saint venerated by all Jains today.

Vasumati was the daughter of King Dadhivahana, who was the ruler
of the historic kingdom of Anga, which had, in the long forgotten past,
been ruled by Karna of Mahabharata. He and his queen, Dharini, lived
with their beautiful and charming daughter, Vasumati, in the capital
city of Champa. The neighbouring kingdom of Vatsa was ruled by
King Shatanik, from his capital Kaushambi, along with his chief queen,
Mrigavati.

Both the queens, Mrigavati and Dharini, were daughters of Maharaj Chetak of Vaishali. The two royal families continued to maintain cordial relations, and lived in peace and prosperity. However, trouble was lurking, for Shatanik was jealous and greedy for greater power. He nourished secret ambitions of annexing his neighbouring kingdom by aggression and invasion – notwithstanding the fact that it was his own brother-in-law, a wise and virtuous man, who ruled the kingdom.

An opportunity for his evil plans was presented to him very soon. Once, when Dadhivahana had gone with his army to assist a neighbouring king, Shatanik attacked Champa. The kingdom and its capital were defenceless in the absence of the ruler and his army. The cruel soldiers of Kaushambi plundered Champa. In those days, looting was considered to be the reward for all soldiers, and even higher ranking officers would join the plunder and take away whatever they could lay their hands on.

The general and chief charioteer of King Shatanik's army led the plunder of the royal palace of Champa. His name was Kakmukh. He was more interested in acquiring concubines from the vanquished kingdom, rather than mere riches. When he entered the royal apartments, his eyes fell on Queen Dharini. He kidnapped Queen Dharini and Vasumati and swore that he would take the queen as his mistress and approached her menacingly. When he attempted to violate her chastity, Queen Dharini committed suicide. Princess Vasumati, who was just a little girl, was utterly distraught. The sight of the little girl and the heart-rending death of the queen, brought about a change of heart for Kakmukh. He consoled the weeping princess and reassured her that she would come to no harm from him, and that he would do everything he could to protect her.

When he returned to Kaushambi, he offered the girl to his wife as a gift from the war. His hope was that she would accept the young girl as a daughter, for they were childless. But his wife was hard-hearted, and did not appreciate his gesture. She would have preferred that he had brought gold and silver as the spoils of his victory, like other soldiers. Moreover, she was struck by the girl's great beauty and grace, and grew jealous of her.

'I do not need a servant like her,' she said to her husband coldly. 'She doesn't look as if she is capable of much work. Moreover, I distrust her looks. I do not want her in my home. Take her away and sell her to someone as a slave. May be she will at least fetch us a decent sum of money.'

Kakmukh was saddened that he could not keep his promise to Vasumati. He had been responsible for kidnapping her from the royal palace. He had also been responsible for her mother's death. He would have loved to make reparation for this heinous act by being a father to the orphaned child; but it was not to be. Vasumati consoled him: 'Do not grieve for me, dear sir,' she said to him. 'All that is happening to me is a result of my past karma. You are not responsible for my fate. Take me and sell me, as your wife says, and I will not hold it against you.' He too, could not stand up against his wife's wishes. So he decided to auction Vasumati in the open market.

In those days, trading of slaves was a common practise. People could buy and sell slaves like commodities. The one who bought a slave would become the lord and master of the slave. The master would 'possess' his slave, body and soul. He could get any work done from the slaves, treat them any way he wished and nobody could interfere. Kakmukh took Princess Vasumati to the market and began to auction her in public. He shouted, 'Is there anyone who will buy this beautiful and charming girl? I am ready to sell her for 20,000 gold mohurs.'

The highest bidder for the girl was a courtesan, who kept a house of ill-repute in Kaushambi. She took one look at Vasumati and realized that the girl would be an asset to her. 'I will give you 30,000 mohurs for her,' she said to Kakmukh. 'I shall train her in singing and dancing and in all feminine charms and she will soon become the most sought after courtesan in Kaushambi!'

Vasumati trembled on hearing these words. She fell at Kakmukh's feet and said to him with tears, 'Sir, you promised me refuge and protection when I lost my mother! I beg you, do not push me into a fate worse than death! I would rather die at your hands than be sold as a courtesan.'

Kakmukh was moved by her pleas, and rejected the courtesan's offer. Luckily for him, a rich merchant called Dhanvaan happened to come along at that time. He was also struck by Vasumati's beauty, and offered to buy her. 'Give her to me without fear,' he said to Kakmukh. 'I shall bring her up as my own daughter!'

Vasumati was sold to the merchant. But his honourable intentions could not come true. Yet again, the merchant's wife took an instant dislike to Vasumati. 'Treat her like our daughter? You must be out of your mind,' she said to her hapless husband. 'No one buys daughters from the slave market. You have paid an extravagant price for her, and I shall get my money's worth out of her. She will be my servant and slave.'

Helplessly he watched, as the girl was reduced to hard work and misery. She, who had once been a princess and could have got whatever she wished for, with dozens of servants to wait on her, was now reduced to being a servant herself. Vasumati had to sweep the floor, wash the utensils and clothes, bring wood from the forest, and look after the cattle. In return, she was provided stale food to eat and torn clothes to wear. But the gracious and charming princess never uttered a word of complaint. Dhanvaan was heartbroken to see the plight of the girl whom he had brought home as a daughter. But once again, Vasumati consoled him. 'Be not grieved, dear father,' she said to him. 'All that is happening to me is the result of my past karma. I accept it all as the will of God.'

Years passed, and Vasumati grew up to be a beautiful and attractive young maiden. The merchant's wife grew even harsher in her attitude. She could never understand her husband's kindness and affection for Vasumati. She was only afraid that he would fall in love with the slave girl, and make her his mistress. She waited for an opportunity to harm Vasumati, and wreak her anger and vengeance upon the beautiful slave.

Once, when her husband had to leave the city on business, she had Vasumati in her power. She shaved off the young girl's hair, beat her up, shackled her hands and feet in iron chains and locked her up in the underground dungeon beneath the house. Then she locked the house and left to visit her parents. She hoped that Vasumati would starve to death by the time she returned.

Dhanvaan returned home earlier than he had anticipated. Seeing his house locked, he enquired after his wife from the neighbours. They informed him that his wife had left home a few days earlier.

'But what about Vasumati?' he asked. 'Did she leave with my wife?'

One of the neighbours said to him that he had not seen Vasumati leaving the house. 'But I had heard a very faint wail coming from the house last night,' she added.

Anxious and desperate, Dhanvaan went around the house, listening carefully at various windows and back doors to see if he could find out anything about Vasumati's whereabouts. At one of the windows, he was startled to hear a feeble cry of pain. Acting quickly, he had the doors of the house broken open and entered within. But Vasumati was nowhere to be found. Where could she have gone? Nobody had seen her leave the place. And what of those wails and cries they had heard?

All of a sudden, the pitiful cry was heard yet again. Dhanvaan was perplexed. Where was it coming from?

'Vasumati! My child, where are you?' he cried out.

He heard a very frail voice answer, 'Father! I am here.'

The cellars and underground dungeons had been abandoned and disused for long. Therefore, it did not occur to him to go downstairs and explore the nether areas of the house. Strangely disturbed by the tortured wails, he looked around helplessly. At last, he realized that they were emanating from below the house. He rushed down the disused steps to the cellar, and was appalled at the sight that met his eyes.

The girl whom he loved in his heart of hearts as his own child, was locked up in an unventilated dungeon. She was virtually gasping for breath, for the foul underground air was suffocating her. And she was unrecognizable! Her long and lovely hair had been chopped off, and her head had been shaved bald. She had been beaten up and her face and limbs were bleeding. Her clothes were torn and tattered. Her limbs were fettered with strong iron chains!

Horrified and distraught, Dhanvaan cried out, 'Dear child! What has happened to you? How were you brought to such a condition?' Vasumati was in no condition to reply. Only a groan of pain emanated from her lips.

Dhanvaan realized the dire condition she was in. The doors to the dungeon were locked. His cruel wife had taken the keys away, for her intention was to leave Vasumati to perish.

'Do not fear, my child,' he reassured her, gathering his wits. 'I shall go out and get help. I shall bring the neighbours and a blacksmith who will free you from this dungeon and those cruel fetters. Keep up your spirits, for I shall return to you very soon! You must know that I love you like a father!'

He rushed upstairs to see if there was anything he could offer to the tortured girl. There was nothing in the house – not a drop of water, not a grain of food! He found a few green grams (channa) in the kitchen, and he took it down to her in a basket. 'Dear child, eat a few of these,' he begged her. 'Keep up your spirits! I shall free you soon from your misery!' And he rushed out of the house to get help.

But God had other plans for Vasumati! In order to tell you about these plans, I am now constrained to leave Vasumati fettered and shackled and confined in the dungeon, and go back in time ...

Lord Mahavira had arrived in Kaushambi sometime earlier. He had been welcomed by the people of the city, and was offered hospitality for his followers and bhiksha for himself by all the leading citizens. But he had graciously declined all the invitations and announced that he would go on a fast. He was in the 12th year of his spiritual life at that time, and the vow he took was unprecedented: 'I will break my fast only when I accept alms from a starving, shaven-headed princess-turned-slave in fetters, dressed in tattered clothes, who offers me green grams with both smiles and tears,' he announced, to the consternation of his devotees and all the assembled people. Would his fast ever be broken under such impossible conditions?

Five months and 26 days after he began fasting, Lord Mahavira opened his eyes and heard Vasumati's cry in his heart. He got up from his meditation and proceeded straight to the house of Dhanvaan, without anyone to show him the way. He encountered Vasumati at her prison. At that moment, a miracle came to pass. The doors to the dungeon opened of their own accord and her fetters broke away.

Weak and emaciated as she was, the moment she met his eyes, such joy flooded Vasumati that she forgot all her sorrows and tried to stand, smiling at him in welcome. But Lord Mahavira seemed to turn away! The poor girl began to cry. At this, he turned back, for all his conditions were now met. Here was a princess-turned-slave in fetters, with a shaven head and in tattered clothes, smiling and crying all at once! In her hands, she held a basket of green grams, which was all she could offer to him at that moment in time! Her fetters fell off and the Mahashraman broke his fast at last!

In the meanwhile, Dhanvaan returned with the neighbours. He was indeed wonderstruck by Vasumati's wisdom and forbearance. She had shown mercy even towards those who had behaved badly with her. Dhanvaan embraced Vasumati and said to her, 'My dear Vasumati! You are like a piece of sandalwood. One may cut or crush or rub sandalwood; but it only spreads fragrance all around in return. Hence, I shall call you Chandana from today.'

When Sri Mahavira obtained enlightenment, many people came to him and became his disciples. But Vasumati was one of his foremost disciples, who devoted herself at the lotus feet of the master and became the first sadhvi of the order he established.

THOUGHT FOR REFLECTION

Whenever suffering comes to us, God always gives us the strength and wisdom to bear the suffering. For these are just two sides of the same coin – sorrow and wisdom; suffering and endurance. Look at the coin – one side is suffering; on the other side is the wisdom and the strength to bear that suffering. Never, ever does God send suffering to us, unaccompanied by the strength and wisdom to cope with it. That is why we continue to live, that is how mankind has survived personal and public calamities, and still continues to survive and flourish. The very fact that we are all alive and breathing, is a testimony to this great truth – that we invariably conquer suffering with God-given strength and wisdom.

We are easily annoyed and upset by every little inconvenience that we have to face. We become angry and frustrated by the ordinary problems of life and start complaining bitterly. We get disturbed and we upset others as well. We must also learn to say, like Chandana, 'Whatever is happening to me is a result of all my karmas. Why should I blame anybody else?' If only we could understand this well, that whatever occurs in our lives, is a result of our previous karma, then it will be easier to live our lives in peace, and bring peace and happiness to those around us.

AIMUTTA MUNI

I desire to free myself from all my sins. I may have pained living beings while walking on the road. While coming or going, I may have crushed living beings, seeds, plants, dew, anthills, spider webs, live water, or live earth. Whatever living beings or souls, on which, with one sense, two senses, three senses, four senses or five senses, I may have inflicted pain, crushed, attacked, covered with dust, rubbed, collided with one another, tormented by turning on one side or completely upside down, moved from one place to another, frightened, bothered or alarmed or separated from life: may all such sins be dissolved.

— *Tassa Michhami Dukkadam,* Iriyavahi Sutra

$\sim$

PRINCE AIMUTTA WAS THE DARLING SON OF KING VIJAYA AND QUEEN Shrimati of Polaspur. The 6-year-old prince was playing on the street near the palace garden with his friends, when he saw a monk – bald, wearing a single white cloth, barefooted and begging for alms. The little prince felt a magnetic attraction to the monk and ran to him. Panting, he said, 'Swamiji, will you please come to my house with me? My mother would be very happy to offer you bhiksha.'

The monk smiled, for he knew the prince, even though the prince did not know him. He allowed the prince to take him home to the palace, where Queen Shrimati welcomed him with reverence and obeisance. In full devotion she uttered '*Maithen Vandami,*' (I bow down my head before you.) For she was well aware of the identity of her revered visitor.

221

To her young son, the prince, she explained that the monk he had brought home was none other than Gautama Swami, chief disciple of Lord Mahavira. She said to the prince that he could offer the monk whatever food he wished to. For the mother was a deeply devout lady and keen to inculcate the virtues into the young prince.

Now, Prince Aimutta loved ladoos. He rushed in and brought a whole plateful of ladoos and started putting them into the alms bowl of the monk. The monk tried to tell him that he really did not need so many ladoos, but the young prince would not listen. He was so thrilled to see the monk and so happy to be able to offer him food.

When the monk was leaving, the prince said to him, 'Swamiji, your bag is heavy; please permit me to carry it for you.'

Gautama Swami said to the prince, 'Aimutta, I cannot give it to you; only those who have received diksha can carry it.'

'What is diksha, Swamiji? And can I receive it?'

Gautama Swami explained to the prince that when one renounced one's home, one's family and all worldly possessions, as well as all social and economic ties and took up the life of a monk, only then could they receive diksha.

'Why is the life of a monk different from ours?'

'That is because a monk avoids all himsa. In worldly life, one commits some form of himsa or the other in every step one takes. Sometimes, one cheats others or is forced to utter lies; at times one speaks hurtful words; one causes injury to beings which are in earth, water and air; thus one's sins accumulate over a period of time. When one becomes a monk, he avoids all such sins, to the extent possible. A monk has no possessions, no home to call his own, and he lives a life committed to ahimsa.'

Aimutta was wide-eyed with wonder. 'Does that mean, Swamiji, that you do not have a place of your own to live? What do you eat? How do you avoid causing harm to other living things?'

Gautama Swami was very pleased with the little boy's interest in such matters. 'We do take food, but we do not accept food which is specially made for us. We do stay in a place, but we do not own the place and we do not stay anywhere for more than a few days. We do not keep any money with us, nor do we buy or sell or transact business with others. This way, we avoid most activities which cause harm and add to our sins.'

In all his sweet innocence, Aimutta said to the monk, 'Swami, can I too, take diksha? My mother also tells me that I must avoid causing harm to others, and adding to my sins.'

'In good time, dear prince, in good time,' said Gautam Swami. But Aimutta walked back with him and heard Lord Mahavira's teachings that day and on several following days. His interest in the teachings grew manifold, until one fine day, he placed before Mahavira, his intense yearning to take diksha.

'That can only be done with the consent of your parents,' Lord Mahavira told him.

'That is easy!' exclaimed the prince. 'My mother never refuses anything that is good for me. I will go to her right away and be back in a trice with her permission.'

He ran all the way home and said to his mother and father, breathless with excitement, 'Dear father and mother, I want to free my life of all sins. Lord Mahavira and Gautama Swami are showing the way for all of us. Please give me your permission to take diksha.'

Now, the parents were devout and pious souls. They appreciated their son's aspirations. But they wanted him to understand what diksha was, in the real sense. So the queen said to him, 'Dear son, diksha is not child's play. It calls for a tough and disciplined life. Can you take on all those hardships?'

'But mother, this worldly life we lead is also full of suffering and sorrow. At least in the life of renunciation, my hardships will destroy my bad karma and give me hope of salvation, isn't that so?'

The mother's heart was both heavy and glad. She put her son to one more test. 'Aimutta, where is the need to hurry? You are very young. And then you have us, your parents. Who will take care of us in our old age? And what about the kingdom! It will be yours to rule one day ...'

'Mother, Lord Mahavira says no one is too big or too small, too old or too young. And he also tells us that we do not know what is going to happen tomorrow. You talk of your old age; who can say whether I will live long enough to take care of you? Who knows when we will die? Who can say which of us will die first? So why should we wait for an appropriate time and miss a golden opportunity that may not come our way again?'

The mother's heart overflowed with love and gratitude, at the wise words uttered by one so young. He not only knew the meaning of diksha, he had also set a high goal for himself.

'What you say is true, my son,' she said. 'I can see that you will make a very good monk. Your father and I give you our blessings. Do not ever forget that your goal is to attain salvation, and be sure to observe ahimsa in all that you do or say or think, all your life. We give you our permission to take diksha.'

And so it came to pass that on an auspicious day, Prince Aimutta took diksha from Lord Mahavira and came to be known as Balamuni Aimutta.

***

Once, as Balamuni was returning from bhiksha, he saw a group of boys playing with bits of wood in a puddle of water. The sight of the water puddle excited the young monk so much that he ran to the boys and started playing with them, splashing his hands about in the water. Together, they were laughing, having fun, and for a brief while, Aimutta was just another child!

A few monks saw Aimutta playing about in the water and remonstrated with him, gently. 'Balamuni, you must not play with water in this fashion. Don't you know that there may be hundreds of living organisms in this water? You must remember that we have taken a vow not to hurt any living things. You have broken your vow and must make due amends for it.'

Aimutta Muni was distraught with grief and shame. 'O, what have I done, what have I done,' he cried. 'I have broken my sacred vows. I do not know how many creatures I have disturbed, playing with the water. I had promised my mother that I would obey all the vows without fail. I have fallen into sin. If my brother monks had not come along, I would surely have been beyond redemption. I must repent now.' And in his sorrow and deep repentance, Balamuni Aimutta rushed to sit at the feet of Lord Mahavira.

'Bhagwan, I have sinned, grant me forgiveness,' he sobbed. And in his deep sorrow, he started reciting the Iriyavahi Sutra. '*Panakkamne, Beeyakkamne, Panag-daga-matti* ... [if I have hurt any living beings of water, green grass, clay ... then I am asking for forgiveness ...],' he prayed repeatedly. And he continued to seek forgiveness through the constant repetition of this sutra; his whole being was imbued with repentance; and the intensity of his piety and concentration were such that the young Balamuni obtained kevalagyana.

When the monks gathered together the next day at Lord Mahavira's assembly, Balamuni Aimutta spontaneously headed towards the section reserved for kevalis. Some of the senior monks noticed this and said to him, 'Aimuttaji! That section is reserved for kevalis. Come and sit with us over here.'

In all innocence, Aimutta Muni responded, 'But I am a kevali too!' This sent shock waves across the entire assembly.

'Aimutta, you are very young, how can you make such a claim?' whispered a senior monk.

But Lord Mahavira said to the assembly, 'Monks, age is no bar to self-realization. Aimutta speaks the truth; he has indeed attained kevalagyana.'

THOUGHT FOR REFLECTION

There are set prayers that some of us offer every day. Millions of Christians all over the world offer the Lord's Prayer, given to them by Jesus: 'Our Father who art in Heaven, Hallowed be thy name ...' Hindus repeat these lines again and again, '*Twameva mata cha pita twameva* ... [thou art our mother, thou art our father ...]' So many of us repeat the prayer of the Sikh Guru: '*Tu mata pita ham balak tere* ... [You are our mother and father, we are your children].'

We say the words, no doubt. But how many of us approach God as we would approach our father? How many of us turn to God, as we turn to our mother? Through prayer, of course! It is not the words of the prayer that matter, but the feeling, the intensity, the devotion with which it is uttered.

Prayer is not at all a complicated matter. Prayer is something very simple. Prayer is like speaking to a friend. Suppose your friend were to come to you, it would be so natural for you to discuss with him your dreams and desires, your anxieties, your worries and your aspirations and achievements, your problems and perplexities and ask him to help you. Do likewise with God. He is the friend of all friends. When all other friends fade away, he is the one friend who will remain. All you have to do is to close your eyes, shut out the world, open your heart and call him with deep love and longing – and there he is with you!

Art, music, spiritual lore, rituals, ceremonies are not needed. What is needed is a heart contrite and lowly, pure and holy – a loving heart eager to wait upon God.

JUDAISM

Brief Introduction

*T*HE HISTORY OF THE JEWISH FAITH, LIKE CHRISTIANITY AND ISLAM, may be said to begin with the myth of creation as outlined in the Book of Genesis. However, this ancient history becomes specifically Jewish, with the Life of Abraham, who is regarded as the Founder of the Jewish religion, indeed, the Father of the Jewish people. Son of Terah, and the father of Ishmael and Issac, Abraham was put to the test by God, who demanded that he should sacrifice his son Issac to establish his faith and prove that he was, 'worthy of becoming the father of a mighty nation, which would be as numerous as the stars in the sky or the grains of sand on the seashore.'

Abraham obeyed the command, and was about to kill his son as a sacrificial offering, when an angel intervened to save the boy. Well pleased with Abraham's faith, God promised the prophet that his descendants would 'inherit the land' (i.e., Canaan, which is the ancient name for the territory that includes modern-day Israel, Palestine, as well as parts of Lebanon, Syria and Jordan, referred to as 'the Promised Land' in the Old Testament). This is called The Covenant of Abraham. Most scholars are of the opinion that this event took place around 1800 BCE. All the ancient Jews trace their physical lineage of birth to Abraham, and in the Bible, Jews refer to themselves as 'the seed of Abraham'. All subsequent prophets refer to God as the God of Abraham, and he is thought to be the first of the prophets of Judaism, Christianity and Islam.

Jews consider Judaism to be the expression of the covenantal relationship between the Children of Israel (later, called the Jewish nation) and God. According to the biblical tradition, God revealed himself to Abraham and also propounded to him the doctrine of a monotheistic God, at a time when most religions of central Asia and Europe were actually polytheistic. God also promised special protection to the Jews, who were hence foreword known as 'the Chosen people'.

Judaism is not just one of the ancient religions of the world; it is also the religious culture of the Jewish people, incorporating a system of Jewish law, custom and practise for the individual and the whole community. The word Judaism is derived from the Hebrew word *Yehudah*, and its distinct feature is a set of beliefs and practises derived from the Jewish Bible, also known as the Tanakh. A religion which claims a historical continuity of over 3,000 years according to the Old Testament, it is the oldest surviving monotheistic faith in the world. Its texts, traditions as well as some of its practices and beliefs are common to all the Abrahamaic religions such as Christianity, Islam as well as the Bahá'í faith.

Interestingly, the sacred texts of the faith describe the Jews as a 'nation' rather than a religion; thus Jews of all denominations are regarded as belonging to one ethno-religious group, wherever in the world they may happen to live. Originating in the Middle East, Judaism spread to many parts of the world including India, Europe, Russia and the United States, both due to voluntary immigration and forced exile and persecutions. Today, many Jews will subscribe to the idea that what we call 'Jewish identity' arises primarily from belonging to an ancient people and upholding its traditions.

THE TOWER OF BABEL

Therefore, is the name of it called Babel; because the LORD did there confound the language of all the earth: and from thence did the LORD scatter them abroad upon the face of all the earth.

– Genesis 11-9

〰

THIS DEEPLY SYMBOLIC STORY IS TOLD TO US IN THE BOOK OF GENESIS. When a deluge was all set to flood the earth, God commanded Noah to build an ark (a boat) along with his family, and seven pairs of every kind of bird and animal, each with its mate. He warned Noah that it would rain continuously for 40 days and 40 nights and all the rest of His creation outside Noah's Ark would be completely destroyed.

Noah did exactly as God asked him to do. Noah and his wife along with their sons, Shem, Ham and Japheth, together with their wives entered the ark. They had with them every wild animal belonging to different species, all kinds of livestock, every kind of creature that moves along the ground as well as all species of birds, everything with wings. Pairs of all creatures that breathe the breath of life came to Noah and entered the ark. The animals going in were male and female of every living thing, as God had commanded Noah. Then the Lord shut him in.

For 40 days the rains poured down on earth and as the flood rose, the ark was lifted high above the earth, rising above the highest mountains. Every living thing that moved on land perished – birds, livestock, wild animals, all the creatures that swarm over the earth and all mankind. Only Noah and his family and the animals he had taken into the ark with him, survived.

Then God said to Noah, 'You may now come out of the ark, with your wife and family. Bring out every kind of living creature that is with you – the birds, the animals and all the creatures that move along the ground so they can multiply on the earth and be fruitful and increase in number on it.'

God then made a new covenant with Noah: never again will the waters become a flood to destroy all creation. Whenever the rainbow appears in the clouds, it would remind men of the everlasting covenant between God and all living creatures of every kind on the earth.

Noah and his family saw the rainbow appear in the sky and they were really happy. The sons of Noah and their offspring spread out all over the earth after the flood. At this point in time, the entire population of the world spoke but one language; everybody understood everybody else's speech. As the people moved eastward, they found a plain in Shinar and settled there. Shinar was the land that later came to be known as Babylon.

The people, who were one community, one nation, then decided to build a city, so that they would not be scattered or fragmented any more. They learnt to bake bricks; they learnt to build with tar (instead of mortar.) And then they decided that they would build a high tower – a tower so high that it would form 'a stairway to heaven'.

Rabbinic literature claims that the builders of the tower were actually defiant secessionists – rebels from the faith. It was their intention, to defy God. 'God has no right to choose the upper world for Himself, and to leave the lower world to us; therefore we will build us a tower, with an idol on the top holding a sword, so that it may appear as if it intended to war with God.'

God saw their city and their tower being built, and He was not pleased with their inordinate ambition. Being united and speaking one language, they felt that there would be no limit to what they could achieve.

God in His wisdom decided that he would 'confound' them. Now, they began to speak different kinds of languages, and could not understand each other. They scattered and gave up on the idea of the tower. The place where their speech became confounded came to be known as Babel. This name is derived from the Hebrew word *balal*, meaning to jumble.

Symbolically the story explains the origin of the variation in human languages. While some scholars see the story as a record of punishment for excessive arrogance and pride in human beings, a more positive interpretation is to see it as a move from cultural homogeneity to cultural diversity. Thus Babel is thought to be the cradle of all human civilizations to come.

The Book of Genesis makes no mention of the destruction of the tower. The people, we are told, just stopped building further. However, the Midrash tells us that the top of the tower was burnt, the bottom was swallowed, and the middle was left standing to erode over time.

THOUGHT FOR REFLECTION

The Fellowship Song

The whole earth is our country,
And the sky is its dome;
The nations are as mansions
In th' Heavenly Father's Home!
We of Chin' and Japan,
Of 'Merica and Ind,
We all are brothers, sisters –
Of Soviet and Sind!

Hindus, Muslims, Christians, all
Buddhists and Bahá'ís –
We share each other's friendship,
And the love that never dies!

One is the faith we live by
One is the song we sing!
With little deeds of service,
We worship Him, our King!

We trust in God, His mercy,
And in ourselves believe!
All that today we hope for
We shall one day achieve!

Hand in hand, we march on still,
A better world to build,
A world of love and laughter,
With peace and plenty filled!

THE LIFE OF MOSES

Moses said to the LORD, 'You have been telling me, "Lead these people," but you have not let me know whom you will send with me. You have said, "I know you by name and you have found favor with me." If you are pleased with me, teach me your ways so I may know you and continue to find favor with you. Remember that this nation is your people.'

The LORD replied, 'My Presence will go with you, and I will give you rest.'

Then Moses said to him, 'If your Presence does not go with us, do not send us up from here.

How will anyone know that you are pleased with me and with your people unless you go with us? What else will distinguish me and your people from all the other people on the face of the earth?'

And the LORD said to Moses, 'I will do the very thing you have asked, because I am pleased with you and I know you by name.'

— Exodus 33: 12-18

$$\approx\!\!\succ\!\!\prec\!\!\approx$$

$\mathcal{M}$OSES WAS A HEBREW, BORN INTO THE TRIBE OF LEVI. THE LEVITES were one of the 12 tribes of Israel. They were regarded as God's spiritual leaders. He was born in Egypt, as the son of Amram and Yochebed of the tribe of Levi. According to the Bible, the name Moses (Mosheh in Hebrew) is derived from the phrase 'From the water I drew him [*meshitihu*]' (Exodus. 2:10).

How did it come to pass that this great Hebrew prophet was born in faraway Egypt? Why were his people slaves in that country?

The Bible tells us that the patriarch of the ancient Israelites, called Jacob, migrated with his family from Asia to Egypt, due to a severe famine in Canaan. The Bible tells us that they were settled in 'the land of Rameses' and that they eventually became property owners there. (Genesis 47:11, 27.) We are also told that Jacob's son, Joseph, became a high-ranking official in Egypt after he correctly interpreted the pharaoh's dreams (Genesis 41:39-45). In fact, so well did he manage the affairs of the state, that when the whole region was struck by a famine, the grain stores of the pharaoh, under Joseph's management, had surplus grain, which could be sold to other nations. Pharaoh was so pleased with his abilities that he made Joseph viceroy (second in command) over Egypt.

With Joseph's help, the 12 sons of Jacob were all settled in the Egyptian province of Goshen. It is said that when their father Jacob, the patriarch of Israel, died, Joseph had Jacob meticulously embalmed and, with the pharaoh's permission, led a huge state funeral back to Canaan, with the 12 sons carrying their father's coffin and many Egyptian officials accompanying them.

But after Joseph's death, Israelites in Egypt lost the respect and status they had enjoyed earlier. Their rising numbers was viewed as a threat to the local Egyptian population. Thus, they were enslaved and used as labourers to build the city of Rameses (Exodus 1:11). In slavery they dwelt in this foreign land, for over 400 years, until Moses liberated them from this condition, and led them out of the land of Rameses and into the Promised Land. The unforgettable story of their journey is told in the Book of Exodus, which literally means, mass departure or migration.

Let us now return to the life story of the man who led the Exodus, in fact, the man who made it possible. When Moses was born to Amram and Yochebed, conditions were really bad for the Jews of Goshen. Bent on harassing them and persecuting them, the pharaoh had passed a law ordering all the newborn male children of the Jews to be killed by drowning in the River Nile. Amram and Yochebed already had two other children, Aaron and Miriam; when Moses was born, they took their newborn son and placed him in a basket of reeds and hid him in the tall grasses of the Nile.

His sister, Miriam, watched over the baby anxiously, from her hiding place, as the basket floated downstream. She saw a group of women and their servants taking their bath in the river. Among them was a princess, the pharaoh's daughter, who was without issue. Hearing the baby cry, the princess rushed to rescue him. She named him 'Moses', meaning 'drawn from the water'. Her desire for a son was now fulfilled, and she took the baby away to the palace with her. Miriam, who had watched her baby brother being rescued, ran back to tell her parents that the baby was safe.

Thus, it came to pass that this child of Hebrew slaves, condemned to death by drowning by the pharaoh, was brought up in the splendour of the Egyptian court as the pharaoh's daughter's adopted son! The princess made certain that he had the best of everything, including education. With hindsight, we may see that it was indeed God's will that the Jews' future liberator was raised as an Egyptian prince. For, if Moses had grown up in abject slavery with his fellow Hebrews, he probably would not have developed the pride, vision, and courage to defy the pharaoh and lead a revolt against him.

The Bible tells us of three major incidents in the life of Moses, before the Exodus. As a young man, he once came across an Egyptian overseer flogging a Jewish slave brutally. He was so incensed that he killed the Egyptian then and there. Fearing the wrath of the pharaoh, he fled to the Midian desert, where he found employment as a shepherd for the priest Jethro. Such was his behaviour and conduct that he was married to Zipporah, his master's daughter. They had two sons, Gershom (meaning a stranger or alien); and Eliezer (meaning the help of God.)

One day, while he was tending his flock on a lonely hillside, Moses was amazed to see a burning bush, which was not being consumed by the fire. When he approached the bush, he heard the voice of God speak to him: 'I have seen the affliction of my people, and I am determined to save them. I want you to go to the pharaoh, and arrange to get the Hebrews out of Egypt.'

Moses was taken aback. 'Lord!' he exclaimed, 'Who am I that I should go to the pharaoh, and should bring forth the children of Israel out of Egypt?'

God said to Moses: 'I know that the king of Egypt will not let you go, but by a mighty hand. For I will stretch forth my hand, and will strike Egypt with all my wonders which I will do in the midst of them: after these he will let you go.'

And still, Moses hesitated. 'I beseech thee, Lord,' he said, 'I am not eloquent; and I have impediment of speech and slowness of tongue.'

Thereupon, God advised him to take his brother Aaron with him; Aaron was a fluent speaker, and bold in spirit, and would play the role of spokesman for Moses. God also gave Moses the power to perform miracles, so that the Hebrews would recognize him as God's messenger and servant.

And thus was the destiny of Moses determined. He took leave of Jethro and returned with his wife and children to the land of his birth, Egypt. Accompanied by his brother, Aaron, Moses went to the pharaoh and informed him that the God of the Hebrews demanded that he should free the Hebrew people. The pharaoh refused to listen to him. Therefore, Moses, in accordance with God's instructions, used the miraculous staff that God had given to him, and brought about the nine terrible plagues (diseases that spread rapidly and can cause death) of Egypt. It was God's will that the Egyptians had to pay the price for their ruler's obstinacy and cruelty.

Thus the Egyptians suffered various disasters such as the following: the water of the Nile turned into blood; the people were attacked by successive infestations of frogs, gnats and flies; their cattle were destroyed by disease; they were afflicted by boils; they were attacked by hail, locusts, and darkness. Each plague was so severe that it brought death and misery to the Egyptians; but the Hebrews were safe and unaffected in Goshen.

The tenth plague was the fiercest of all. Angered by the pharaoh's refusal to listen to Moses' plea, God sent the Angel of Death to kill all the firstborn sons of the Egyptians as a proof of His strength and power. Once again, the Israelites were protected; the Angel of Death would pass over their homes. This last plague was the proverbial last straw that broke the pharaoh's resistance. He was forced to grant the Hebrews permission to leave immediately. This event is still celebrated by Jews as the Feast of Passover.

Now, Moses found himself the leader of an undisciplined collection of slaves, eager to escape from their life of slavery in Egypt, towards their Promised Land and freedom. It was by no means an easy task! Having let them go, the pharaoh went back on his word, and sent his army to pursue them. The Jews found themselves facing the Red Sea before them, and the might of the pharaoh's army behind them. Yet again, God worked his miracle. The waters of the Red Sea parted to allow Moses and his people to pass to the other side. But when the Egyptian army tried to follow them, the waters flooded over them and drowned them.

After many ordeals and troubles, the Hebrews came to Mt Sinai. Here, God commanded Moses to go up to the mountaintop. Up on these heights, he appeared in the form of a cloud of fire, and gave to Moses, the Ten Commandments: a list of moral imperatives that are sacred to the Jews and Christians, but also universally applicable to all devout and pious souls. God spoke them aloud to Moses, and also handed over to him, two stone tablets on which they were inscribed.

The people heard the voices and saw the flames on the mountain; they heard the sound of the trumpets, and saw the mount smoking; and being terrified and struck with fear, they stood afar, and implored Moses to speak to them.

Moses said to the people: 'Fear not; for God is come to prove you, and that the dread of Him might be in you, and you should not sin.' The people answered with one voice: 'We will do all the words of the Lord, which He hath spoken.'

Taking the tablet of the covenant, he read it in the hearing of the people: and they said: 'All things that the Lord hath spoken, we will do, we will be obedient.'

The laws that Moses transmitted to the Jews on that momentous occasion embrace far more than the Ten Commandments. In addition to many ritual regulations, the Jews were also instructed to love God as well as be in awe of him, to love their neighbours as themselves, and to love the stranger – that is, the non-Jew living among them – as themselves as well.

But the sad part of the Exodus was this: only at the very moment God or Moses were actually doing something for them were the Jews loyal believers. The instant God's or Moses' presence was not manifest they reverted to amoral, immoral, and sometimes idolatrous behavior. Like a true parent, Moses raged at the Jews when they sinned, but he never turned against them – even when God did! Once when God declared, wrathfully, that he would blot out the Jews and make of Moses a new nation, he answered, 'Then blot me out too.' (Exodus 32:32.)

The journey to the Promised Land was not easy. For as many as 40 years Moses wandered in the wilderness of Sinai, with his unruly people:

the Jews were not, at that time, the loyal, disciplined, committed and faithful people that they are today. They constantly complained about the food, the climate, and the slowness of their progress towards the Promised Land. Moses was often driven to rage and desperation over their behaviour. Once, he even heard them complain that slavery in Egypt had been better than this wilderness that they were forced to cross now.

Battling against all odds, overcoming many obstacles, Moses led the horde of former slaves, shaping them into a nation, which would become synonymous with determination, courage and patience in the future. Many miracles happened along the way. When food supplies ran out, God sent down what was called 'manna' (spiritual food) everyday for the nourishment of the Israelites. When the people were in need of water, God told Moses to speak to a rock and water would spring from it. Moses' patience was worn down by now; instead of following God's directions implicitly, he struck the rock with his staff. This was to have a devastating effect on his final days.

The saddest event in Moses' life came to pass when God prohibited him from entering the Promised Land of Israel. As they approached the Promised Land, from the heights of Nebo he surveyed the land promised to his forefathers, which would be given to their children. And then Moses, 120 years old, died in the land of Moab and was buried opposite Bet Peor.

———⟨✦⟩———

THOUGHT FOR REFLECTION

The figure of Moses dominates the first five books of the Biblical Old Testament, which constitute the most sacred scriptures of the Jews, and is venerated as the Torah. Moses is not only the most important prophet in Judaism but also considered as the prophet of Islam, Christianity, the Bahá'í faith, the Rastafari and many other faiths. He was a great leader, lawgiver, and prophet of the ancient Israelites, or Hebrews. He was chosen by God to lead Israelites out of their miserable condition of slavery in Egypt, to Canaan, their own Promised Land of Israel. We may well say that it was he who created the true identity of the Hebrews, paved the way for Israel's nationhood and also delivered to them the Ten Commandments. And yet, he did not live to see the Promised Land.

Despite this personal tragedy, Moses impressed his monotheistic vision upon the Jews with such force that in the succeeding three millennia, Jews have never confused the messenger with the author of the message. To quote an admiring biographer, 'He selected and set them apart for a divine purpose and consecrated them to the highest ethical and moral laws. Only a man with tremendous will, patience, compassion, humility, and great faith could have forged the bickering and scheming factions who constantly challenged his wisdom and authority into an entity. Under his inspiring leadership, the Jews evolved into a nation and a people who have earned the admiration and respect of the world for their fortitude, patience and perseverance.'

At a personal level too, Moses set an example to his nation by his extraordinary patience and forbearance. His own brother and sister, Aaron and Miriam turned against him, speaking against Moses and even questioning God's exclusive communications with him. They said, 'Was it only to Moses that God spoke? Did He not speak to us as well?' (Numbers 12:10-14.) But God was displeased with their questioning and especially with Miriam's envy, that he punished her with leprosy. But it is to Moses that the credit goes for healing her and absolving her of the terrible sin of questioning God's wisdom: Moses cries out to the Lord, saying, 'Please heal her, O God, I pray!' And the Lord heeds his prayer. Miriam is cured after being shut out of the camp for seven days. Such was the forgiving, healing nature of this great prophet, who was not only one of Israel's greatest leaders, but also a wonderful human being, chosen by God to lead and teach his people and show them the way ahead.

THE MINORITY VIEW

He who meditates over the words of Torah, finds ever new meanings in them.

— Rashi, commentary to Cant 5.15

THIS IS AN AMAZING STORY NARRATED BY RABBI TUVIA BOLTON.

Baby Yonatan who lived in Warsaw, was acclaimed as a child prodigy when he was barely three years old. People were charmed and thrilled with the radiant child and his brilliant mind. Yonatan became so famous that the King of Poland soon came to know about him. The king was an eccentric and temperamental man who craved for excitement and unusual experiences to stop him from being bored, which he often tended to be. So he took it into his head to send a message to the child prodigy's father: on an appointed day, early in the morning, the father was to put the child on the street outside his home and tell him to go to the royal palace, where the king would be waiting to meet him and take a test of his highly spoken of intelligence. 'Since your boy is reputed to be such a prodigy, the wisest being in Poland, he should have no problem finding his way to the palace,' the king added, sarcastically. 'I would like to see how he navigates his way through the confusing, congested lanes of our city, unassisted by you or his family members.'

The father was dismayed. He lived in a suburb several miles away from the palace. How could his little son walk all the way, indeed, find the way to the royal palace? But in those days, humble Jews did not go around questioning the commands of their king. On the appointed day, Baby Yonatan was dressed in his best Sabbath clothes and put on the road outside his home, with instructions to find his way to the palace, where the king would be waiting to give him an audience. His father blessed him and begged God to protect the child from all harm.

Yonatan set off cheerfully. The citizens were delighted and amazed to see the precocious child, wearing his bright clothes, striding blithely on the streets, so sure of himself and where he was going. 'Godspeed to you,' they called out, waving to the child with love and affection.

After quite a few hours of walking, Yonatan stood outside the gates of the royal palace. The guards at the gate could not believe their eyes when they saw the toddler before them, asking to be let in. 'I am supposed to have an audience with His Majesty,' Yonatan told them politely. 'Will you kindly tell him Yonatan is here as he commanded?'

The king was mightily pleased to receive the young visitor. 'At least today I shall be saved from listening to my boring ministers and courtiers,' he thought to himself. The entire court was charmed by the sight of the tiny tot, so good looking, so self-possessed, who surveyed the court and seemed to be sizing all of them up. The buzz of the court became so loud that the king had to order everyone to be silent.

'So, my little friend, welcome to my court,' he said to the child very grandly. 'How did you manage to find your way here on your own?'

'Well, Your Majesty,' Yonatan answered in his squeaky, high-pitched, childish voice, 'whenever I had a doubt, I stopped and asked the people for directions to make sure I did not lose my way. And of course, God helped me.'

'Aha,' said the king. 'But didn't it ever occur to you that people might say the opposite things and mislead you? For example, one man might have told you to turn right and another might have told you to go straight. What would you have done under these circumstances?'

'It's quite simple, isn't it Your Majesty? The Torah tells us that when we are faced with differing opinions, one should follow the majority. That is exactly what I did. When two people gave me contrary advice, I asked a third man and followed the majority view.'

The king smiled graciously and the entire court broke into thundering applause. But the king now became grave and said to Yonatan, 'My dear child, you must listen to what you yourself have just said: listen to the majority view. Here in Poland, the majority of us are Christians. Should you not follow the majority view, as the Torah tells you to, and give up your Judaism?'

The audience clapped and cheered this piece of royal cleverness. When the laughter and applause had died down, Yonatan cleared his throat and said, 'I do beg your pardon, Your Majesty. I think we have a little misunderstanding here. When I said I followed the majority view, I meant in the matter of finding my way, when I was far from the palace. But now that I am here and I see you before me, even if all your courtiers tell me that I am in the wrong place, I will not believe them. The God of Israel is everywhere and I believe in His presence. No place is empty of Him. So even if the whole kingdom denies His presence, I shall never believe them!'

Baby Yonatan later became one of the most admired spiritual leaders of his community – the chief rabbi of the 'Three Communities' in Germany (Altona, Hamburg, and Wandsbek) and known in rabbinicl history as the great Rabbi Yonatan Eibeschutz.

***

In a strange case of history repeating itself, Rabbi Eibeschutz was asked a similar question by a bishop with whom he was taking a walk. 'If your Torah tells you to follow the majority view, why are you still sticking to a minority religion?'

Rabbi Eibeschutz gazed up at the sky and remarked, 'Just see that amazing eclipse! What a celestial sight!'

The bishop too gazed up at the sky. 'Indeed,' he murmured, 'quite amazing.'

Very soon, a crowd gathered around them and everyone gazed up at the sky and said aloud, 'What a breathtaking eclipse.'

Abruptly, the rabbi turned to the bishop and said softly, 'There is no eclipse today, actually. And I did not see anything particular in the sky.'

The bishop whispered to him, 'Actually, I couldn't see a thing! But since you were so taken up with the sky, I was too embarrassed to say anything to contradict you.'

'You see, bishop,' said the rabbi, 'you know and I know that there is no eclipse today. But all these people are sure that there is one. That is not the majority view the Torah tells us to follow.'

THOUGHT FOR REFLECTION

If you wish to have the vision of the lord, the first step is to develop a bond with God. God cannot be realized through the intellect, through book knowledge and words. God cannot be understood through words, though it is true, we talk about God only through the medium of language. Whenever a tragedy occurs or we go through a trauma, we cry out in anguish: where is God? The question is asked because we have not built up any relationship with God. We must create a relationship with God. We must know God: And knowing God is an experience very similar to that of knowing your own brother, your sister, your friend, your spouse.

Did anyone have to formally introduce you to your mother, father, brother or sister? Did you have to attend lectures or workshops on the importance of family relationships? Did you have to have lessons on building bonds with your spouse and children? These beautiful bonds came naturally to you, didn't they? So it must be with God. Make God real in your daily life. Otherwise you will not be able to experience him or find him by your side. But to forge a relationship with him we must surrender ourselves to him. The act of surrender is very important. All that you have and all that you are, must be surrendered to God; we should think and we should be convinced that we belong to God. This will build an unbreakable bond with him and then God will become as real as the sun in our lives.

Why Do Good People Suffer?

Should a man see suffering come upon him, let him scrutinize his actions; as it is said, 'Let us search and try our ways, and return unto the Lord.'

– Talmud Lament. 3:40

*T*HE TALMUDIC TEXTS TELL US THAT DURING ONE OF HIS DIRECT encounters with God, Prophet Moses asked the Creator about the problem of pain, suffering and evil in the world. His query was particularly related to the way in which suffering is visited on some people – even good people – in a random manner.

The poet Hopkins also expresses this most powerfully in one of his poems: 'Why do sinner's ways prosper? And why must disappointment all I endeavour end?'

Rabbi Louis Jacobs quotes a Talmudic passage (Berakhot 7a), in which Moses asked God why one righteous man enjoys prosperity while another righteous man is afflicted with adversity; why one wicked man enjoys prosperity and another wicked man is afflicted with adversity. If all righteous men suffered and all wicked men were prosperous, some kind of pattern might have emerged, perhaps on the lines that the righteous suffer for their sins here on earth while the wicked are rewarded here on earth so as to be punished by being deprived of bliss in the hereafter. But, as we know, poetic justice of this kind is rarely witnessed here on earth. This leads to the notion among many lay people that suffering and happiness, pain and pleasure are accorded very arbitrarily to the

243

deserving and undeserving alike, leading us to question the very justice of the Universe.

The Book of Job in the Tanakh is specifically concerned with this issue. Interestingly, the story opens with a conversation between God and Satan. Satan tells God that the devout Job is a good and pious man only because he is secure in the abundance of his wealth. Take his wealth and prosperity away, and he will turn to ingratitude and start cursing his Maker. God agrees to allow Satan to put Job through a series of adversities. Job not only loses his wealth and his children, but is also afflicted with a dreadful skin disease. He does not rail upon God as Satan wanted him to do; but he wonders why he is being punished so severely.

The Mekhilta (a Midrash on the Book of Exodus) has the following commentary: 'Do not behave towards Me as heathens behave to their gods. When happiness comes to them, they sing praises to their gods, but when retribution comes upon them they curse their gods. If I bring happiness upon you give thanks, and when I bring sufferings give thanks also.'

A rabbi was delivering a lecture on the teachings of the Torah to a class of Jewish students. They came upon a line which read, 'The truly evolved person is even he, who in the midst of the greatest of adversities, continues to smile.' So the students asked the teacher, 'If we are surrounded by the greatest of adversities, how is it possible to smile under those conditions?'

The rabbi said to them, 'I myself cannot answer this question because I too cannot smile when I am in the midst of any difficulty. I seem to forget how to smile! How can I give you the answer? But there is one man living here in this town, who has faced all kinds of adversities. When he was born, he became an orphan within a week's time. Then he broke his leg and so his difficulties continued. He has gone through all sorts of trials, and has recently suffered a stroke; yet he continues to smile. You must go and ask him how he manages to do it.'

The students went in a row and knocked at the door of this man. The door was opened by a man in a wheelchair, who asked them of the purpose of their visit. The students explained it to him. He said to them, 'You have come to the wrong address because I am one who has had to face no adversity whatsoever! I am 73 years old but in all these years I have not had to face a single difficulty. How can I tell you how to smile in the midst of adversity?'

***

'Why do bad things happen to good people?' asked a man, writing to Rabbi Aaron Moss. 'Why is this world so unfair? Please don't tell me, "We can't understand God's ways." I am sick of hearing that. I want an explanation.'

The rabbi replied: 'Are you sure you want an explanation? Do you really want to know why the innocent suffer? I think not. You are far better off with the question than with an answer. You are bothered by the fact that people suffer undeservedly: as indeed you should be. Any person with an ounce of moral sensitivity is outraged by the injustices of our world. Abraham, the first Jew, asked God, "Should the Judge of the whole world not act fairly?" Moses too asked God, "Why have You treated these people badly?" And today we still ask, "Why God, why"?'

But what if we found the answer? What if someone came along and gave us a satisfying explanation? What if the mystery were finally solved? What if we asked why, and actually got an answer?

'If this ultimate question were answered, then we would be able to make peace with the suffering of innocents. And that is unthinkable. Worse than innocent people suffering is others watching their suffering unmoved. And that's exactly what would happen if we were to understand why innocents suffer. We would no longer be bothered by their cry, we would no longer feel their pain, because we would understand why it is happening.'

So, the rabbi tells us, let us keep asking the question, why do bad things happen to good people? But let us stop looking for rational answers. Instead, let us start formulating a response. Let us take our righteous anger and indignation and burning resentment and turn it all into a force for doing good. Let us redirect our frustration with injustice and unfairness and channel it into a drive to fight the same injustice and unfairness. Let our outrage propel us into action. When we see innocent people suffering, there is only one right response: help them. Let us combat all the needless suffering and pain in the world with goodness. Let us seek to alleviate suffering whenever and wherever we can.

THOUGHT FOR REFLECTION

What is the best way to tackle personal suffering, pain and grief? Here are a few practical suggestions:

1. We must take our mind away from the fact of suffering. If our attention is focused on suffering, it tends to get multiplied manifold.

2. In times of pain and suffering, we must learn to count our blessings. For those of us who are pessimistic enough to imagine that there are no blessings to count, there is a simple exercise. We can take a piece of paper and list all the things in our life which we cannot do without.

3. We must learn to dissociate ourselves from the body, the mind and the ego. This is not easy, but it is the first step towards self-realization. It is the mind that creates all our suffering; once we transcend the mind, there is no suffering at all – only peace and joy.

4. In all conditions and circumstances of life, we must continue to thank the Lord. We must make it a habit, to praise the Lord at every step, in every round of life. Even in the midst of fear and frustration, worry and anxiety, depression and disappointment, let the words, 'Thank you, God! Thank you, God! Thank you, God!' be upon our lips constantly. We will find that we are filled with an amazing sense of peace.

5. Do not try to run away from trouble and pain. They are essential to our growth. God means us to face them and acquire strength and wisdom.

6. Accept the Will of the Lord and fix your minds and hearts on God. Realize that God is always by our side, watching us, guiding us, guarding us and protecting us.

COUNT YOUR GOLD AND SILVER: A STORY WITHIN A STORY

'A person who has today's bread in his basket and is worried, "What will I eat tomorrow?" – is a man of little faith,' declared Rabbi Eliezer. The Lord stands behind our own endeavours, and as He provides for the raven in the field, He provides for man also. In the words of the rabbis: 'He who created each day provides for the needs thereof.'

— The Wisdom of the Talmud

THIS STORY WAS NARRATED BY RABBI SHLOMO HALBERSTAM, AT A community gathering.

A young man from Chernobyl once came to see Rabbi Mottel to request a blessing. Rabbi Mottel asked the visitor to recount his typical daily schedule. The young man explained that he was a shopkeeper; he began each day by buying goods for his business from the local landowner. After this, he would recite the morning prayers; and then he opened his shop and began to sell his wares.

Rabbi Mottel was somewhat dismayed to hear this routine. 'Why do you go out to buy your goods before you recite the morning prayers?' he asked the young man. The young man explained that if he went after his prayers, either all the merchandise would have been sold out, or only the most inferior quality products would be left for him to buy; the best ware would have been sold much earlier.

'Ah, I see,' said the rabbi. 'May I tell you a story?'

There was once a teacher of Jewish studies, who was forced to travel far and wide to find Jewish children whom he could teach in return for cash payment. Not all his clients were rich; some paid him in gold coins; some gave him a few silver coins; the poorer ones who could not afford much, gave him copper or nickel coins. He did not reject any offers to teach. All the year he travelled from city to city earning as much as he could. He was away from home for longer than a year, at times. While he was away, his wife and children had to make do with whatever they could, living on borrowed money or credit, till he returned.

The teacher had made for himself a broad leather belt with four bags attached; one to store gold coins, one for silver, and the others for copper and nickel coins.

Having completed a full year of wandering, he was returning home with his four coin bags heavy with his earnings. He had a long way to go before he reached home. On the way, the Sabbath intervened, and he was constrained to stop and attend the prayers. He knew very well that it was forbidden to carry money on the Sabbath. So he decided that he would remove his belt and safely bury the money somewhere before he joined the prayers.

He dug a deep hole under a tree and counted the coins hurriedly. He was about to bury the coin bags, when he heard someone approaching. Panic stricken, he took the money out and hastened to a nearby inn where he handed the money to the innkeeper for safe custody while he went to say his prayers; it was the custom in those days, for several innkeepers to offer this service to people on the Sabbath. The money was safely stowed in the innkeeper's locker; and the man rushed away for prayers.

The prayers began; but the teacher was beside himself with anxiety. He had handed over his entire year's savings to a strange innkeeper without even taking a receipt for the amount deposited. How could he have been so careless! What if the innkeeper were to steal some of the coins! How could he prove the theft? And how would his wife and children survive for a whole year if the money fell short? How could they repay the creditors from the previous year? His concentration was wholly diverted from the prayers as he frowned unconsciously even as his eyes remained closed.

The innkeeper was a sensitive man; he understood what was going on in the mind of the teacher, and to reassure the man and allow him to continue his prayers in peace, he took the bags and placed them in front of the teacher and quietly went away to say his own prayers.

As he was about to begin his supplications, he was amazed to see the teacher frantically opening one of the bags and beginning to count the gold coins. To his immense relief, they were all there. He opened the second bag and began to count his silver coins. These too were exactly as he had left them.

'Surely, he will now give up this unholy business of counting money during the prayers,' the innkeeper thought to himself. But that was not to be! The man counted out his copper coins and then his nickel coins. When every coin had been accounted for, he returned to his prayers.

To say that the innkeeper was shocked and disgusted would be an understatement. He was seething with rage when he met the teacher after the prayers.

'You counted your gold and silver coins and you saw that they were safe,' he said to the teacher. 'How could you think after all that I would have stolen your coppers and nickels? Were not the gold and silver coins far more valuable? When you saw that I had not touched them, you were still suspicious that I would have stolen your worthless coppers and nickels? Is that not a ridiculous supposition?'

Rabbi Mottel finished his story and asked the young man from Chernobyl the following question: 'Every single morning, as you awake, you become aware that you are still alive and God has given you back your soul, your body and your brain, and your very life and limbs too! These are the equivalent of gold and silver coins. Whatever makes you imagine that he would take away your copper and nickel coins – the merchandise you wish to buy for the day?'

The young man bowed his head in shame.

'You should cultivate greater trust in God and believe that He who has given you back your life will also give you your physical sustenance,' the rabbi continued. 'I suggest that you do not rush out to buy your goods before your morning prayers.'

THOUGHT FOR REFLECTION

Begin the day with God! The first thing we do on getting up in the morning shapes the entire day. Does it not stand to reason that we should begin the day right? Every morning, when you wake up, there is a choice before you: you can choose optimism, faith, positive thinking and right attitude; or you can choose pessimism, defeat, negative thinking and despair. What would you choose? Begin the day well – and God will take care of the rest of the day!

Every day, as you wake up in the morning, let there be a prayer on your lips, a simple prayer. Let me share with you the prayer that I offer to God: 'O Lord! This new day comes to me as a gift from Thy spotless hands. You have taken care of me throughout the night, and I am sure You will keep watch over me throughout the day. Praise be to Thee, O Lord. Blessed be Thy Name. Blessed be Thy Name. Blessed be Thy Name!'

You can reword this prayer if you like, in your own way. But make sure you begin the day by remembering God – with a prayer on your lips. Leave off fretting and worrying about every little problem. Leave it to God to take care of you and the others. Put God first. He will automatically free us from our worries, and take care of all our 'concerns' and 'problems'.

There is a beautiful line in Sri Sukhmani Sahib, a Sikh scripture which I love to meditate on: *Avar tyag tu tisay chitar* ... Renounce everything; throw out everything; don't think of anything – but meditate on Him; i.e., concentrate on Him; think of Him, dedicate all your work to Him! *Avar tyag tu tisay chitar* ... If you wish to think of Him, you must empty your mind of all else. So long as you hold worries and anxieties in the mind, so long as your mind is not empty you cannot think of Him – and you will not be at peace. Therefore, empty your mind of all worries and anxiety.

Why should we carry heavy burdens on our minds and hearts, when we can easily cast our burdens at the feet of Him who is strong enough to bear all the burdens of all the worlds? Therefore, empty your mind of all worry and anxiety. Cast your burdens at His feet and He will give you the calmness, courage and confidence to face the challenges of life!

SIKHISM

BRIEF INTRODUCTION

$\mathcal{S}$IKHISM IS A FAITH, A WAY OF LIFE, A RELIGIOUS PHILOSOPHY AND a set of practises based on belief in one God, known as Waheguru; adherence to the teachings of the ten great Gurus or teachers of the faith, starting with Guru Nanak up to Guru Gobind Singh; and complete faith in the Adi Granth or Primary Volume. Adi Granth is revered as the Guru Granth Sahib, which is also thought of as the last and eternal Guru. It is not without significance that the word Guru should occur so often when we talk of Sikhism; the word *sikh* is derived from Punjabi (Sanskrit original *sishya*) and means a 'disciple' or a learner.

Many people believe that this religion is a reformed version or re-purification of the Hindu faith; some historians regard Sikhism as a symbiotic blend of Hindu, Islamic and Sufi influences, along with the inspiration of the Bhakti Movement of the India of those days; but many Sikhs reject this view and assert that their religion is a direct revelation from God, and has nothing to do with Hinduism or Islam.

The history of Sikhism may be said to begin with Guru Nanak, who was born in 1469. It continued for the next two centuries with his nine successors, and this initial phase came to an end with the death of Guru Gobind Singh, the tenth Guru, in 1708. This was a period of crucial importance in the history of Sikhism, when the new faith developed most of its distinctive and unique features. By the declaration of the tenth guru, the succession of personal Gurus came to an end, and the authority of the Guru was vested in the holy scripture of the Sikhs, the Guru Granth Sahib, thus contributing to the stability, strength and spiritual cohesion of the Sikh community.

All true Sikhs believe in the one and only one God, who has infinite qualities and names. He is the same for all religions, and is the universal Creator, Sustainer and Destroyer. He manifests everywhere, in every aspect of creation. He is fearless and without enmity. His form is indestructible. He doesn't need to take up any living form. He is without birth or death. He is enlightened with his own light. He has and will exist forever. In the words of the Adi Granth, He is *nirankaar, akala,* and *alakh* – formless, shapeless, timeless and beyond sight. He is omnipotent and omnipresent and is signified by the opening term of the scripture: *Ek Onkar.* In the beginning, He alone existed; and the creation of the cosmos was at His will or *hukam.*

God is knowable only to the spiritually awakened. In the task of knowing God and attaining salvation, the role of the Guru is indispensable. The Guru is the voice and light of God, and the source of all wisdom and salvation. The Sikhs believe that the Spirit of Guru Nanak was passed from one Guru to the next, 'just as the light of one lamp, which lights another and does not diminish'. Outward practises, rites and rituals are irrelevant to this pursuit: inward remembrance of the Name and the *shabad* (Divine Word) are essential.

Simran and *jap* – remembrance and recital of the name Divine – are fundamental to the Sikh way of life. Only by keeping the name of God in mind, can the soul progress towards salvation. Therefore, the Sikh Gurus ask the devotees to meditate with single mindedness, dispel doubt, remain focused, and subdue their ego. This is the way to perfection and liberation.

Sikhism also insists on the brotherhood of all humanity, the equality of all people. 'We are all sons and daughters of Waheguru, the Almighty,' proclaimed Guru Nanak. Thus discrimination on the basis of birth, caste, social class or gender, is strictly forbidden to the Sikhs.

Sikhism emphasizes *sangat* and *pangat* – that is congregations of the faithful, and fellowship meals shared by all devotees irrespective of caste, creed, colour or social status.

Thus we can say that universal humanism is at the heart of the Sikh faith. Social inequalities, sectarianism and distinctions of caste and creed are swept aside to emphasize community living, social consciousness and brotherhood of all men. This gives dignity and respect to each individual, and asserts the individual's right to faith and liberation through good work. Devotees sing, 'O Lord! I am neither high, low nor of the middle; I am God's devotee and seek His protection.' The principles of universal equality and brotherhood are essential beliefs of Sikhism.

Even when it was founded, Sikhism was a progressive and boldly liberal religion. The famous saying of its founder, Guru Nanak, 'There is no Hindu, there is no Muslim,' is still one of the basic tenets of the Sikh faith.

Sikhism insists that service to one's fellow men is one of the greatest good actions that human beings can perform. It insists equally, that seva should be offered to everyone, over and above any distinction of caste and creed. Seva is regarded as one of the best methods of inner cleansing and purification, along with simran, remembrance of the Name. In the gurdwara, service may take any form: sweeping the floor, fetching water, cooking food in the community kitchen, washing the dishes, and collecting the footwear of devotees. Each of these tasks is done with love and devotion, as an offering to God and Guru. Sikhs are exhorted to infuse this spirit of love and devotion in all their actions outside of the gurdwara.

From the idealism, the missionary zeal and the deep and devout mysticism of Guru Nanak, Sikhism had evolved into a militant faith of trained warriors by the time of the tenth Guru. This was undoubtedly due to the constraint of political, historical conditions, under which Sikhs were severely persecuted and killed, with many of their own Gurus becoming martyrs to the cause. However, the basic religious beliefs and convictions of Sikhism, were always adhered to, uncompromisingly.

Even today, in Punjab, many Hindu families give their first born son to the Gurus, to be baptized as a *Khalsa Sikh*, or a soldier of the Guru's army of protectors. It is said that this tradition started from the time of the tenth Guru, Guru Gobind Singh, who made a clarion call to all the Hindu families to offer their eldest sons to fight for the protection of dharma, against the forced conversions to Islam prevalent under the Mughal rule. Since then, Sikhism is traditionally regarded as a religion of warriors who were protectors of those who could not defend themselves.

GURU NANAK'S GROWING YEARS

Sing the songs of joy to the Lord, serve the Name of the Lord, and become the servant of His servants.

– Guru Nanak

THERE WAS GREAT REJOICING IN THE HOUSEHOLD OF KALYAN DAS Mehta, popularly known as Kalu; and this meant general rejoicing in the whole village, for Kalu was a *patwari* or accountant to the Muslim landlord, Raei Bhullar of the village Rai Bhoeki Talwandi. Kalu's wife, Tripta Devi was delighted. The couple already had a daughter called Nanaki, and now, their little family was complete!

Little did the simple village folk realize then that into this family was born the *yugapurush*, who would become teacher to millions across the ages. It is said that the child's birth saw the mud-built house filled with a golden glow of light, and the village midwife who delivered the baby swore to the people that the infant smiled at her!

Wonderful accounts of the infant's early days are given in the *Meherban Janmasakhi*, (local accounts of the Guru's life and birth, which have come down to us from ancient manuscripts). When he was barely a month old, he could focus his eyes on the person who held him; when he was three months old, he could hold his neck straight; at four months, he began to lisp, and when he was seven months old, he actually began to sit up; at eight months, he started creeping on one knee, and at ten months, he began to crawl and stand on his feet. When he was two he began to play with other children of his age, his favourite game was to gather up old family ledgers and manuscripts, wrap them up in a silk cloth and walk about with this bundle of papers held under his arm; occasionally, he would open the bundle and pretend to read from it to his bewildered friends!

Like many fathers of today, Kalu had his own ambitions for the child: he wanted him to learn to read and write and count, and acquire enough education to be able to inherit his post as the revenue official of the village. To his delight, Nanak was indeed a very intelligent child. He was sent to a school where he was taught Hindi; the village pandit taught him Sanskrit; and a maulvi schooled him in Arabic and Persian.

Pandha Gopal, the schoolteacher, wrote down a few letters of the alphabet on the slate and gave it to Nanak to learn from. Child Nanak asked his teacher, 'Does the knowledge of the alphabet have any significance without love?'

'Speak to me,' said Nanak, 'about the Creator and His creation. For all learning is in vain without any knowledge of Him. And to know Him, to realize Him, we need to love Him.'

Child Nanak's words left his teacher astonished! The teacher met the father and said, 'Your son is far wiser than I! I will certainly teach him all that I can, but to my mind, I am not capable of teaching him all that he wants to learn, for he is a great sage.'

When Nanak was 11, his father arranged to have the sacred thread ceremony performed for his only son. Elaborate arrangements were made for the ceremony, and the entire village was invited to Kalu's house. A yagna fire was lit, incense was burnt and all the sacred mantras were uttered by the priest. When the sacred thread was about to be put across the boy's shoulders, Nanak stopped the priest, and spontaneously recited the following lines:

'Let mercy be the cotton, contentment the thread, continence the knot and truth the twist. O priest! If you have such a thread, do give it to me. It'll not wear out, nor get soiled, nor burnt, nor lost. Says Nanak, blessed are those who go about wearing such a thread.'

The pandit stepped back in shock, and the entire crowd stared open-mouthed. This was quite unheard of in living memory, that a young boy from a pious Khatri household, should reject the *janeu*, one of the oldest and most sacred traditions of the Hindu religion. As for Kalu, he was deeply disturbed by his son's attitude.

In the days to come, his disquiet grew. He was anxious for his son's future. He often had long discussions with his son about his future occupation and means of livelihood. While the father was down-to-earth and tried to suggest occupations that might interest his son, Nanak seemed to dwell in a world apart, a transcendental world in which such mundane things did not matter.

The father was at a loss to understand his son! In despair, he said to Nanak, 'My son, it looks as if you are going to be an utter failure in life! Wouldn't you like to be someone in society? You must do something or the other to earn wealth. Why don't you take to farming? Be a farmer and plough the fields.' Nanak responded:

'Make body the field, good actions the seed, and water the truth. Let the mind be the cultivator; sow the seed of the Lord's Name; with deeds of love the seeds will fertilize.'

'Perhaps you would like to have a shop of your own,' Kalu suggested:

'Make this frail body thy shop and stock it with the merchandise of the True Name.'

The father did his best to interest his son in worldly matters. He asked Nanak to take the cattle to the grazing ground. Nanak let the buffaloes graze as they pleased while he sat down to meditate! The buffaloes strayed into the neighbouring field, making a feast of the ripe wheat which was ready for harvest, and leaving the whole field devastated with their rampaging.

Nanak was woken up from his reverie by the desperate cries of the farmer. 'I am ruined, I am ruined!' he cried out in despair. Nanak's heart melted in compassion for the loss inflicted on the man. 'Do not despair! Do not despair!' he called out. 'God will surely put a blessing on your field.' The Bhatti landlord was beside himself with rage and went directly to Raei Bhullar with his complaint. 'I am ruined, sire!' he wailed. 'My crop is utterly destroyed! I want justice!'

Raei Bhullar was a just and compassionate chieftain; he sent for Kalu and told him that he would let off Nanak without punishment; but the farmer's loss had to be compensated. Footmen were sent to the damaged field to estimate the loss. They returned to report that they could see no damage whatsoever. If at all the cattle had gone on rampage, it must have been elsewhere.

The complainant was taken aback. He said, 'Sire, I am no liar! With my own eyes I saw my entire crop flattened, and the cattle chewing the cud after they had gorged themselves on the wheat. I do not know what miracle has been brought about after I came to you.'

On another occasion, when Raei Bhullar was out on horseback with his servants surveying the crops, he was startled to see a hooded cobra holding itself perfectly still, in the midst of a field. He approached the cobra with his men, and saw with amazement that its hood was sheltering Nanak, who was fast asleep on the field. On hearing the men approaching, the cobra slithered away quietly. Bhullar awakened Nanak, who, rubbing his eyes, stood up and saluted the landlord with folded hands. Raei Bhullar embraced the boy and kissed him on the forehead.

'God's favour rests on this youngster,' he said to his companions. 'He is indeed a blessed one.' He did not mount his horse again, but walked home, overwhelmed by what he had seen. Summoning Kalu, he said to him, 'Your son will be the pride and honour of this village. You will become exalted, and I will become exalted, because he was born here amidst us.'

The father, then, put him in charge of a shop, but the son distributed the groceries among the sadhus and the poor and the needy. When the father protested, Nanak responded: 'My shop is made of time and space. Its store consists of the commodities of truth and self-control. I am always dealing with my customers, the sadhus and mahatmas, contact with whom is very profitable indeed.'

No matter how hard the father tried, he could not bring his son down to earth. Indeed, on one occasion he said: 'It would be easier to catch hold of the rays of the rising sun!'

One day, Kalu gave his son 20 rupees and sent him to a nearby market to make a profitable investment. 'Buy whatever goods you like, and come and sell them to the locals at a good profit,' he advised his son. 'Be sure you strike a good bargain,' he urged Nanak as he saw the boy off with an assistant, his former schoolmate Bala. On the way Nanak found a group of sanyasis who looked starved. Nanak spent all the money purchasing food items, despite the protests of Bala, who had been sent to keep an eye of him; he fed the sanyasis to their satisfaction. They felt happy and blessed Nanak profusely. Bala, in the meanwhile, ran away from the scene, fearing Kalu's outburst.

When his father asked him what he had done with the money, Nanak replied: 'I struck the most profitable bargain! I fed the poor ascetics who were starved to death. What better bargain than this, father?'

Kalu was dumbfounded. He began to realize that his son was no ordinary youth!

———◇◆◇———

THOUGHT FOR REFLECTION

I would like to say to all parents: Your children are your greatest treasures. Don't get so busy gathering silver and gold, that you neglect your richest treasure! Your children need your time, attention and love – for without love and attention, no child can grow up in the right way.

Today, parents are busy doing so many things. The father is a jet-setting executive, hopping across continents, playing golf on weekends, constantly talking on the cell phone at the dining table. As for the mother, she is a glittering socialite, the secretary of the exclusive ladies' club, attending coffee mornings, arranging kitty parties, visiting her beauticians for extended sessions and spending the evenings at dinners, parties, concerts and ballets.

Let me say to all parents – your children need your love, above all else. The nature of the soul is love – and without love, no child can grow up in the right way. You must give them your time! You must try to sow in their minds seeds of character, without which life can have no meaning or value. You must help them to grow in the love and fear of God.

GURU NANAK NOMINATES HIS SUCCESSOR

Guru Nanak displayed such power when he tested so great a man,
He put his umbrella over the head of Lehna, and exalted him to the skies.
Guru Nanak's light blended with Guru Angad's and one became absorbed in the other.
He tested his Sikhs and his sons, and all followers saw what he had done.
It was when Lehna was tested and purified that Guru Nanak consecrated him.

— Satta and Balwand

BHAI LEHNA WAS BUSY MAKING PREPARATIONS FOR HIS ANNUAL pilgrimage to Jwalamukhi. He was not only an ardent worshipper of Durga Mata but also the chief pujari of Khadur, where all the people, with the sole exception of one individual, were pious Hindus, and worshippers of Ma Durga.

The one exception was an equally devout Sikh, by the name Bhai Jodha, who would soulfully recite the hymns of Guru Nanak every day. Lehna was profoundly moved by the hymns and enquired of Jodha as to their origin: he was told of the First Sikh Guru, and an aspiration was kindled in his heart to meet Guru Nanak.

Lehna had been born to a comfortable inheritance. His father was a prosperous trader, and Lehna grew up in the ancestral house of his grandfather. It was from his mother, Mata Ramo, that he imbibed great devotion to Goddess Durga. It was his custom to lead his fellow devotees from the village to Jwalamukhi, the shrine in the Himalayas where Adi Shakti is worshipped in the form of nine flames.

Once again, this year, Lehna set out on his annual pilgrimage to Jwalamukhi, leading a band of fellow devotees. They passed by the town of Kartarpur, where at that time, Guru Nanak was in residence. Hearing of the Guru, Lehna decided that he would seek his darshan, before proceeding on the pilgrimage. But God had other plans for Bhai Lehna: the glance of the Guru, a few words with him, and Lehna had found the meaning of his life, the purpose of his existence! He declared that the objective of his pilgrimage had been accomplished; he would proceed no further. He had come under the magnetic spell of the Master, and fell at his feet with a prayer from the heart: 'Master, accept me as thy disciple!'

'What is your name?' asked the Guru.

'Lehna,' he replied humbly.

'Welcome Lehna,' smiled the Master. 'You have come to me at long last! Now, I am to pay your *lehna*!' (In Punjabi, *lehna* means 'the dues to be collected'. The Master thus indicated the karmic relationship between himself and his first successor.) From then on, Lehna started making frequent trips to the Guru's residence, to be in constant touch with his grace and his presence.

In those early days, Bhai Lehna, being the son of a well-to-do merchant, used to dress himself in the rich yellow silks of Bhukhara. In these resplendent garments, he went to see the Guru, who was then working in his fields.

The Guru greeted him cordially, and bade him carry a heavy load of wet grass home with him. The load was put on Lehna's head and he happily followed the Master. The muddy water from the wet grass dripped on to his expensive clothes, staining them. But Lehna was blissfully indifferent to it all.

As they entered the Master's home, the Guru's wife saw Lehna's condition and said with great concern, 'Is this the consideration you show to your disciples? Why is this guest of ours made to do such menial work? Why, his fine clothes are soiled with mud!'

'You do not perceive right,' replied Guru Nanak, 'he is bearing the burden of faith, the burden of his brothers, and those are not mud stains, but the sacred saffron anointing of Heaven. He is God's chosen one. He is chosen to be one who is fit to carry the burden.'

For the remainder of his Master's life, Bhai Lehna lived and served Guru Nanak, living in Kartarpur and Khadur, by turns. He served the Master faithfully, tirelessly, becoming a labourer in his vineyard. He walked the way of perfect obedience, forgetting his wealth and trade, his servants and his business. The Master was all-in-all for this faithful disciple!

Many are the stories that have come down to us of Lehna's obedience and devotion to the Guru. Each of these incidents speak volumes for his patience, his unquestioning obedience and his utter and complete dedication to the service of the Guru.

One dark winter night, it rained so heavily in Kartarpur that the walls of the dharamshala collapsed. The Guru expressed the desire that the walls should be mended immediately. The Guru's sons and many of his disciples assured him that they would send for a team of masons and labourers in the morning so that the damaged walls could be restored. But the Guru insisted that the work should begin at once. So they began repairing the wall.

When the work was partially complete, the Guru ordered the newly built up portion to be demolished, as it was not satisfactory. He instructed them to rebuild that part of the wall. They tore down what they had built, but decided that the rest of the work could wait and went off to get some sleep. Lehna alone toiled on, following the Guru's orders. And this was not just for a day or two! As the Janmasakhi tells us, 'For days and nights on end he worked on and on, alternately building the wall and then pulling it down as the Guru commanded.'

One of the disciples told him he was mad; Lehna's reply was simple: 'These hands can become pure only by doing the Master's work.'

***

There is yet another event reported by a few sources, which, according to some scholars, clinched the issue of succession. It is said that Guru Nanak once led his close followers into a thick jungle. Here he made gold and silver coins appear out of the blue before their astonished eyes. Alas, the followers ran helter-skelter after the coins, eager to grasp as many as they could. Only Lehna and another disciple, Bhai Buddha, remained unmoved by the gold and silver!

Guru Nanak now led them to a funeral pyre, and commanded both of them to lift the shroud on the corpse and eat its flesh! Horrified by this command, Bhai Buddha is said to have fled in panic. Unflinching and resolute as ever, eager to obey the Master's word, Bhai Lehna lifted the shroud, only to find that what lay underneath was not dead flesh, but Guru Nanak himself! A disembodied voice then spoke out as follows: 'This, thy successor, shall be part and parcel of thy own being!'

The word *lehna* in Punjabi means 'what is due to one from another'. One day, Guru Nanak called Lehna near and said to him, 'Your *lehna* is from me: you have to receive from me!' And, embracing his dear, devoted disciple warmly, the Guru said to him: 'From today, you are no longer Lehna; you are Angad, a limb of my body, a breath of my being, one with me in spirit, blended with my soul!' In his own lifetime, the Guru nominated Angad as his successor.

Thought for Reflection

Gurudev Sadhu Vaswani once said, in words of unsurpassed lyrical beauty:

The waking ones, alas, are not awake:
And the sleepers sleep—
Until Thy Light on them doth shine!
Awake are many called:
But they are not the waking ones.
Nor do the sleepers truly wake
Until they learn in silence and in love
To sing the Name Divine!

Most of us need someone to awaken us, an evolved soul, an awakened one – the Guru. The Guru is the Great Awakener. 'The Guru,' Gurudev Sadhu Vaswani says, 'is the lift to raise us to the heights, the lift which may take little ones to the kingdom of God.'

Awakening comes to the chosen souls in diverse ways! The Guru in his grace, calls the disciple to himself in a mysterious way, and the soul of the chosen one is transformed even by a touch, a glance, a word!

BABA BUDDHA

I am neither a child, a young man, nor an ancient; nor am I of any caste.

– Guru Nanak

'BHAI BUDDHA' TO THOSE WHO ARE FAMILIAR WITH HINDI OR Punjabi, sounds a contradiction in terms: a combination of 'brother' and 'old man'. Baba Buddha seems more logical, as it means a venerable elder. Both terms refer to an amazing Sikh devotee, one of the early legends of Sikhism, who came to Guru Nanak as a young boy and stayed on to become a venerable elder at whose hands successive Gurus were consecrated.

Bura, as he was originally named, was the only son of Bhai Suggha, a Jatt of Randhava clan, and Mai Gauran, born into a Sandhu family. As a small boy, he was grazing cattle outside the village when Guru Nanak happened to pass by. The little boy went up to him and, offering a bowl of milk to the Guru, prayed to him in the following words: 'O sustainer of the poor! I am fortunate to have had a sight of you today. Absolve me now from the circuit of birth and death.'

Guru Nanak was delighted and surprised at the wise words coming from such a young lad. He said to Bura, 'You are only a child. But you talk so wisely.'

Bura replied, 'Master, some soldiers were camping by our village, and they mowed down all our crops – ripe as well as unripe. And it occurred to me then that when this could happen to our crops, surely no one could restrain death from laying his hand upon us, at any time in our lives, whether we are young or old.'

Hearing this reply, Guru Nanak pronounced the words: 'You are not a child; you possess the wisdom of an old man.' From that day onward, Bura came to be known as Bhai Buddha (*buddha* in Punjabi meaning an old man), and later, when advanced in years, as Baba Buddha.

From that first meeting, Bhai Buddha became a devoted disciple of Guru Nanak. Neither his marriage nor his family could distract him from his chosen path and he spent most of his time at Kartarpur where Guru Nanak had taken up his abode than at Katthu Nangal, his own village. Such was the eminence he had attained in the Guru's congregation that, at the time of installation of Guru Angad, the second Guru, Guru Nanak asked Bhai Buddha to apply the ceremonial tilak on his forehead.

Bhai Buddha lived up to a ripe old age and had the unique honour of anointing all of the four Gurus. All his life he continued to serve the Gurus with complete dedication and remained an example of holy living for the growing body of disciples. He devoted himself zealously to tasks such as the digging of the *baoli* at Goindval under the instruction of Guru Amar Das and the excavation of the sacred tank at Amritsar under Guru Ram Das and Guru Arjan. The ber tree under which he used to sit, supervising the excavation of the Amritsar pool, still stands in the precincts of the Golden Temple.

It is significant too, that Guru Arjan had placed his young son, Har Gobind, under Bhai Buddha's instruction and training. When the Adi Granth was installed in the Harmandir on 16 August 1604, it was Bhai Buddha who was appointed the *granthi* by Guru Arjan. Thus he had the distinction of becoming the first high priest of the sacred shrine, now known as the Golden Temple.

One legend associated with Baba Buddha tells us that Guru Arjan and his wife Mata Ganga did not have a child for a long time, until Mata Ganga sought the blessings of Baba Buddha for an offspring. It is said that Baba Buddha told her that she would indeed give birth to an extraordinarily chivalrous son. Shortly after, Guru Har Gobind was born.

Baba Buddha subsequently retired to the forest, where he tended the livestock of the *Guru ka Langar*. What is left of that forest is still known, after him, as Ber Baba Buddha Sahib. When Baba Buddha left his mortal frame on 16 November 1631, Guru Har Gobind was at his bedside. It is said that the Guru gave his own shoulder to the bier and performed the last rites, as a mark of respect to the venerable soul who had anointed his grandfather, his father and himself, at the time of their accession to the sacred *Guru gaddi*.

―――◁◆▷―――

THOUGHT FOR REFLECTION

Age does not matter; circumstances and situations do not matter when the time is ripe for the grace of the Guru to descend on us! The true purpose of our life is liberation and self-realization – and we become aware of this only when we attain the feet of the Guru. It is the Guru who reveals to us our true identity – the atman within us.

Once we have handed ourselves over to him in full faith, he will see to all else – indeed, it will be his responsibility to ensure that we attain the goal of this human life!

THE MARTYRDOM OF
GURU TEGH BAHADUR

With power, fetters break, availeth all in grace Divine;
Nanak, everything is in Thy power, it is only Thou Who canst
assist.

– Slok Mohalla 9 (54), p. 1429, Guru Granth Sahib

A PALL OF GLOOM HAD DESCENDED ON INDIA. CONDITIONS WERE rapidly deteriorating for people under the tyrannous rule of Emperor Aurangzeb. After ten years of rule, Aurangzeb's dream now was to purge India of all 'infidels' and convert the whole country into a land of Islam. He was an intolerant ruler who had no respect for other religions and launched a brutal campaign of repression. Famous Hindu temples throughout the country were demolished and mosques built in their place. Aurangzeb issued a number of harsh decrees. He forbade Hindus from displaying illuminations at Diwali festivals.

He forbade Hindu *jatras*; he issued an order that only Muslims could be landlords of crown lands, and called upon provincial viceroys to dismiss all Hindu clerks. He then issued a general order calling upon all governors of all provinces to destroy the schools and temples of the 'infidels'; and they were told to put a stop to the teachings and practicing of idolatrous forms of worship. Under his dark regime, killing a *kafir* (non-believer) was thought of as the sacred duty of a Mussalman. The law laid down by the sacred scriptures of Islam was misinterpreted to sanction the indiscriminate killing of all those who refused to accept the authority of Islam.

In those days, Kashmiri pandits were among the most devout and orthodox Hindus in the land. Aurangzeb felt if they could be converted, the rest of the country would easily follow. He did not want to see the *tilak* (holy mark on the forehead) or *janeu* (sacred thread) on any of his subjects. Unable to withstand the torture meted out to their community by the Muslim viceroy of Kashmir, the pandits came in a delegation to meet Guru Tegh Bahadur at Anandpur Sahib.

They said to him, 'Guruji, Aurangzeb has sworn that he would behead us if we do not accept Islam. We have asked for a month's time so that we could discuss the issue amongst us. As the revered Sikh Guru of our days, we have come to you to seek your counsel. Please help us.'

Guru Tegh Bahadur was deeply moved by their plight. He pondered deeply over the fate of the country that was being subjected to such intolerance and brutality. What could be done to alleviate the people's misery? How should he find a way out of the crisis for the people who had sought him out with such hope and faith?

As the Guru was pondering over the issue, his 9-year-old son, Gobind Rai, walked into the room. Struck by the serious and gloomy mood in the room, the young Gobind asked his father what was happening. Guru Tegh Bahadur replied, 'Dear, son, the Hindus of our country face a deep crisis. Unless a holy man is willing to lay down his life for the sake of religion, there is no hope for their escape from imperial tyranny.'

Young Gobind replied instantly, 'Revered father, who would be better equipped for this than yourself?'

Guru Tegh Bahadur hugged his son and wept for joy. 'I was only worried about the future, for you are far too young,' he said to his young son. 'Leave me to God,' Gobind replied, 'and accept the challenge of the Mughals.'

On hearing these words from his son, Guru Tegh Bahadur was assured that he no longer needed to worry about his son's future. He then decided to sacrifice his life for the freedom of belief, the freedom to protect people's faith, and to help his Hindu brothers. He told the Kashmiri pandits to inform Aurangzeb that if Guru Tegh Bahadur adopted Islam, then they and the other Hindus would be ready to follow suit.

On receiving this message, Aurangzeb ordered his soldiers to capture the Guru and bring him to Delhi. Guru Tegh Bahadur said that he would definitely come to Delhi, but only when the time was right for such a visit.

The Guru bid farewell to his family and followers and dictated that his son Gobind Rai should be installed as the next Guru. Accompanying the Guru on this final journey, and prepared to accept the consequences of whatever happened, were his devout disciples, Bhai Mati Das, Bhai Dayala and Bhai Sati Das. Thousands of devout Sikhs were waiting to see him and hear his teachings. He sent the soldiers away and took the road to Delhi with his followers, stopping en route to meet as many devotees as he could. It is said that the path to the capital was covered in flowers showered on their Guru by the faithful.

Finally he reached Agra. As soon as Aurangzeb heard the news he ordered the immediate arrest of the Guru. Guru Tegh Bahadur and his party were captured soon after they reached Agra and taken in chains to Delhi. Aurangzeb now gave him the final ultimatum: 'Accept Islam, or prepare to die!'

To this the Guru replied, 'The people, the subjects are to the king as the roots are to the tree. He draws his very sustenance and nourishment from the subjects; if he crushes and oppresses them, he cuts his own foundation beneath himself! Therefore, let him be just to the Hindus, Sikhs and the Mussalmans alike. Tyranny is suicidal. That is why I have come here to tell him that I won't accept Islam. I would rather sacrifice my life happily instead.' Thereafter, the Guru was thrown in prison. He was locked up in a very tiny cell where he could not even walk around freely.

Guru Tegh Bahadur spent 15 long days in the prison. After 15 days, a Kazi came to Guruji and said, 'You are the supreme leader of the Sikhs as well as the Hindus. I give you 3 options, of which you will be allowed to choose only one. The first one is, accept Islam. The second one is, demonstrate a miracle to prove your faith, if you are not willing to accept Islam. The third one if you reject the other two options is, accept death.'

The Guru calmly replied, 'I will never accept Islam. I won't change my religion. As for your second option, showing miracles is not our job. Miracles are the manifestation of God's powers that are seen through his grace in certain states and conditions. They are not just conjuror's tricks that I can perform them before you like a magician to save this body that is perishable any way. Do not forget that I come here, led by God's will. We do not have the sanction of my sacred Masters to perform miracles for public show. All Sikh Gurus were miraculous, but they never showed miracles and lived a normal human life. The third option you offer me is death. That is what I have come here for. I am willing to die. The Mughal Empire is today thought to be the most invincible .... My death will bring along with it, the death of this Mughal Empire.'

The Guru suffered endless torture at the hands of the jailors. The faithful followers who willingly went with him to jail, also suffered. Mati Kama was sawn asunder. Bhai Dayala was boiled to death in an iron pot. It was such inhuman and barbarous tortures which the followers of the Guru had to suffer at the hands of the emperor's jailors.

It was announced throughout the city that people should get together at Chandni Chowk to witness Guru Tegh Bahadur's death. The next morning, Guru Tegh Bahadur was brought out of the cell. He wished to take a bath before he was executed. So he was taken to a nearby well where he took his bath. He was then brought to Chandni Chowk. At that moment he recited *shlokas* from the Guru Granth Sahib:

Ek Omkar, Satnam, Karta Purakh,
Nirbhav, Nirvain, Akaal Murat, Ajuni Saihib,
Guruprasad, Jap, Aadh Sach, Jugaad Sach,
Hai Bhi Sach, Nanak Ho Si Bhi Sach.

As he sat under a banyan tree, reciting the Japji Sahib, the order was given by the Kazi to behead him. The Guru was beheaded in one stroke. But it is believed by the faithful, that before the sword was lifted to behead Guruji, his head was already miraculously detached from his body. As Guru Gobind Singh puts it:

'It was the day of sorrow on this earth,
And it was the day of rejoicing in Heaven.'

It is said that the Guru's body was left in the dust as no one dared to pick up the body for fear of the emperor's reprisal.

A severe dust storm swept through the city that evening, turning the sky blood-red. Under the cover of darkness, a devout Sikh named Bhai Jaita managed to collect the Guru's sacred head and carried it off to Anandpur Sahib to the Guru's son. Another devout Sikh, Bhai Lakhi

Shah who had a cart, was able to smuggle the Guru's headless body to his house. Since a public funeral would be too dangerous, Bhai Lakhi Shah cremated the body by setting his house on fire. Meanwhile the head of the Guru was taken to the grief stricken young Guru Gobind Singh and the widow Mata Gujari.

On 16 November 1675 at Anandpur Sahib, a pyre of sandalwood was constructed, sprinkled with roses and the head of Guru Tegh Bahadur was cremated by young Guru Gobind Singh.

THOUGHT FOR REFLECTION

Have you ever asked yourself the question, 'What is the difference between an ordinary man and the saints of God?' The difference between an ordinary human being and a man of God is that the ordinary man goes about doing his work without awareness. But, men of God, whatever they do, right from their daily personal chores to their spiritual disciplines, do so with awareness. A saint or *siddha purush* is one whose thoughts are pure and lives constantly in the awareness that God is Omnipresent.

Let us put a question to ourselves – 'Do we love God? Do we love saints and sages?' If the answer is 'Yes', then our answer to all else must be 'No'. The mark of a man who loves God and His saints is sacrifice. If our love is devoid of sacrifice, it is selfish. Such love is a barter, a bargain with God. There is exchange of love and devotion in return for something. It is love which is conditional and 'expectational' if I may use such a word.

Love is selfless. It accepts sacrifice. Men of God take birth on this earth, become teachers and mentors, ascetics and *fakirs*, all for the sake of humanity. They come to mitigate human suffering. They come to heal us and lead us on to the path of Light. They put up with criticism; they go through many worldly trials. Some of them have even become martyrs for our sake. But they have done all this with a smile on their face and with gratitude to God. Unless and until man is willing to sacrifice, he is unable to give love either to God or to mankind.

THE KHALSA IS BORN:
HISTORY AND HER STORY

O beloved Khalsa, let him who desireth to behold me, behold the Guru Granth. Obey the Granth Sahib. It is the visible body of the Gurus. And let him who desires to meet me, search for me in the hymns.

– Guru Gobind Singh

$\prec\!\!\succ\!\!\prec$

IT WAS AN ERA OF DARKNESS, OPPRESSION AND HUMILIATION FOR Hindus and Sikhs when Aurangzeb took over the reins of the Mughal Empire in India. Not for nothing was Aurangzeb known as the scourge of Hindus and Sikhs, for he was indeed one of the most hated kings of the Mughal dynasty. His cruelty and tyranny were in a sense, inconsistent with some of his human traits; for he was in many ways, a man with many good qualities. He lived a simple life, he ate simple food, lived a pure life, kept away from all temptations of the flesh and kept busy all the time. He would make caps with his own hands, read books and would read the Holy Quran daily.

But alas, he was embroiled in religious persecution and forcible conversions. He was a man given to fanatical beliefs. He failed to understand that the Divine light of God shone in all religions, all faiths and all scriptures. He was against the Hindu faith. He was fanatical about converting Hindus and Sikhs to Islam. The Jats, the Rajputs, the

271

Satnamis, the Marathas and even the unorthodox Muslims like the Sufis and the Shias were oppressed and tortured under his cruel regime.

As the darkness of religious persecution spread all over India, people everywhere began to groan under the tyranny and oppression unleashed on them. At this time, it was to the tenth and last Guru of the Sikhs that they turned. Guru Gobind Singh was well aware of what was happening around him, and recalled the words of the Adi Guru, likening the emperors of his day to tigers and dogs: two hundred years later, it seemed as if nothing had changed! Peaceful co-existence was just not possible under such circumstances: as for the age-old Indian ideals of non-violence, submissiveness and tolerance, such approaches simply could not work against the 'mad dogs and wild tigers' that roamed the land. Tyranny was bad, the Guru knew; but submission to tyranny was equally unacceptable!

On one occasion, while meditating on the mountaintop, the Guru heard a voice, 'My dear one, now it is time for you to come out on to the battlefield.' Leaving his meditation, he followed the voice. He realized that it was his duty to stand up against these tortures inflicted by Aurangzeb. He took to the battlefield to protect the faithful. In so doing, he initiated a mighty movement.

Sikhs, he had instructed, should come to Anandpur straight without any intermediaries, thus establishing a direct relationship with his devout followers. The Sikhs had gathered at Anandpur in large numbers for the annual festival of Baisakhi. Thousands of faithful Sikhs congregated to hear him and carry out his commands. To the gathered multitudes he made the most stirring oration on saving their religion which was in great peril, and about his Divine mission to build a Sikh military force. He told them that they were now required to perform great and valorous deeds. But every great deed was preceded by equally great sacrifice, he pointed out. The holy Sword could create a heroic nation only after supreme sacrifice, for the establishment of Dharma required sacrificial blood. Records tell us of the stirring events at this historical meet:

'Who are you?' he asked them.

'We are your faithful disciples,' they answered.

'Who am I?' he asked them.

'You are our Beloved Guru and we will carry out your hukam,' they replied.

All of a sudden Guru Gobind Singh drew out his sword and demanded a devotee in whose heart he could plunge his sword. This sent a thrill of horror in the audience. He repeated it in a sterner and more sonorous voice. All were terror-stricken and there was no response to the first and second call. There was only an uncomfortable silence and then one man rose up! He was Daya Ram, a Khatri of Dalla village near Lahore. He expressed willingness to lay down his life.

The Guru led him into an enclosure. After a while, the Guru emerged out of the enclosure, his sword dripping with blood, and asked for a second sacrifice. Similarly a third, a fourth and a fifth man responded to his fiery call.

Then the Guru came out and declared that with these five dear ones who came forward to offer their lives as a sacrifice, the *Khalsa Panth* had been established. The five volunteers now emerged unscathed, safe and sound from the enclosure, and were proclaimed as the *panj piyare* – five dear ones.

Overcome by their devotion and sacrificial spirit, the Guru declared that Baba Nanak had found only one devoted Sikh in Guru Angad, whereas he had been blessed by the Guru to find five such Sikhs. Through the devotion of one true disciple, Sikhism had flourished all these years. By the consecration of five Sikhs his mission was bound to spread all over the world!

The Guru anointed his team with holy water called *amrit* and named the men Singh or lion, and the women Kaur or princess. This was when he came to be known as Gobind Singh. Individually each disciple was called a Singh and collectively they were given the name of Khalsa. He commanded the Khalsa to adopt the 5 Ks:

1. *Kirpan* or sword
2. *Kara* or iron bangle
3. *Kesh* or uncut hair
4. *Kanga* or comb
5. *Kaccha* or underpants

From the Master's tent on that fateful day emerged the new incarnation of the disciple as saint-soldier. The saint-soldier had committed his life for the Guru's cause; he accepted death in love. Clad in saffron-dyed garments and a saffron-turban, his tresses tied up in a crowning knot on the head, covered by the turban, he emerged as a lion, a Singh, ready to lay down his life for God, the Guru and for his brethren! The Guru also made each of them take the vow that they would read from the Guru Granth Sahib daily and would regard all men as their brothers – and be ever ready to extend their hand of help to people.

The Guru asked them to utter the following call after him: *Jo Bole So Nihal, Sat Sri Akal!* (Whoever utters 'The Immortal God is True' will be blessed.) It was thus that the great Sikh salute was first uttered. The Khalsa was born!

The initiation of the Khalsa alarmed the Rajput chiefs of the Shivalik hills. The Guru had, at the very outset, invited them all to join the Khalsa so that it could become stronger against the oppressive empire; but in their narrow perception, they saw a growing Sikh army as a threat to their power. They rallied under the leadership of the Raja of Bilaspur, in whose territory lay Anandpur, to forcibly evict Guru Gobind Singh from his hilly citadel.

The story of the Khalsa is not just about history. It is also about HER story for the brave women of the Khalsa played a crucial role in its early stages.

Forty of Guru Gobind Singh's men turned disloyal to him and deserted him at Anandpur. Not only were they afraid to die, afraid for their lives, desperate and starving; they preferred the ignominy of flight to defeat and death. They were so obsessed with their own survival, that they actually wrote and signed a letter denouncing their Guru. Having committed this ignominy, they rushed home to their families, fondly imagining that their wives would be overjoyed by their return, and happy that they were alive.

What they found in reality was the reverse. Their wives were appalled by their cowardice, and horrified that they had deserted their Guru. The wives looked them in the eye and said to them, 'We do not rejoice that you have returned to us alive, if you have abandoned your Guru. You are dead to us, no matter what. Go back and stand with your Guru. Or consider us dead as far as you are concerned.'

The male side of this story is often repeated, that the men returned to fight for the Guru and died in the battle, liberating their souls in the process. But the hidden story is that the consciousness of their Khalsa wives is what inspired them to do it.

The Khalsa women consciously chose widowhood over disobedience to the Guru. They chose to bear the terrible burden of seeing their husbands dead, of being left in deep sorrow and loneliness as widows, of raising their children alone, of having to find their economic security in the absence of a husband – they would have rather endured all this than to see their husbands walk away from their destinies and betray their Guru. These women knew – the duty and role of a Khalsa wife is to serve the soul of her husband and deliver him to his destiny and to God and Guru no matter what.

Thus it was the grace, security, wisdom and blessing of their wives that allowed the men to become liberated. These Khalsa women understood non-attachment, security in the Divine, living in the will of God, loyalty to the Guru so well that they could fearlessly send their husbands to their death, knowing that it was better for their husbands to die in service of the Guru than to live any other way. And the pain of losing their husbands was less to them than the pain of seeing their husbands lose their path to God. Publicly, the valour of the men prevailed. Privately, the wisdom of the women prevailed. And it was this joint consciousness, valour and wisdom, male and female, which displayed the true power of the Khalsa.

THOUGHT FOR REFLECTION

In recent times, a great deal of interest has been evinced in understanding and evaluating the role that women have played in history. This includes not only the study of women's status in society and women's rights throughout recorded history, but also the examination of individual women whose lives and works have had historical significance; and on the other side of the same coin, the effect that historical events have had on women, down the ages. Many scholars have expressed the view that conventional readings of history have tended either to minimize or ignore outright the contributions of women and the effect that historical events had on women as a whole; thus women's history is looked upon as a form of historical 'revisionism', which seeks to challenge or expand the accepted consensus of history.

The problem is this, that more often than not, we are so bedazzled by the remarkable and well-documented 'achievements' of the modern woman, that we tend to ignore the substantial contributions made by women of earlier ages. Bringing out a special *Guide to Women's History*, the *Encyclopaedia Britannica* noted that since the dawn of civilization, women have left their mark on the world, at times changing the course of history and at other times influencing small but significant spheres of life. But it is only in the past century, that we have begun to make concerted efforts to represent women's contributions more fully in history books. Consequently, the dramatic events that changed the status for many women in modern times, such as the right to own property, to vote, and to choose their own careers, may obscure the accomplishments made by women of earlier eras.

We would do well to realize and appreciate that this contribution has been tremendous, though the history books we read in school have failed to record the same.

I strongly believe that the world would learn a great deal from the lives of great Indian women starting from our divine Sita and Radha, through sages like Maitreyi and Gargi, singer-saints like Aandal, Mira and Jana Bai, heroines like Rani Padmini of Chithorgarh and Lakshmibai of Jhansi, to modern legends like Savitribai Phule, Sri Sarada Mani, Kasturba Gandhi and others.

SUFISM

Brief Introduction

Sufism, referred to as *TASAWWUF*, in Arabic, is understood by many scholars and Sufis to be the inner, mystical, or psycho-spiritual dimension of Islam. It is founded on the pursuit of spiritual truth as a definite goal to attain. This very logical principle is based on a typically succinct saying of Prophet Muhammad: 'Whoever knows oneself, knows one's Lord.' Most scholars agree that it is impossible to relate Sufism to any religion outside of Islam.

Although lay people refer to this tradition as Sufism, believers refer to it as the Sufi Way. This is because the use of the term 'ism' relates more to a philosophy or a school of thought like capitalism or socialism, and many believers feel that the Sufi Way is a more suitable term as it refers to a practical path, a way of living to follow.

Sufism is thought to have originated in the time of Prophet Muhammad. The first Sufis were actually contemporaries of the Prophet. Etymologically, the origin of the word *sufi* is thought to be from *ahl-al-suffa,* which literally means 'Companions of the Porch', or 'Companions of the bench'; the early Sufis were actually a group of devout but impoverished Muslims, who spent their days and nights on benches outside the mosque where the Prophet worshipped. They kept away from the world and worldly activities. They were men of non-possession. They ate what was given to them, and wore simple, coarse garments.

Gurudev Sadhu Vaswani referred to the Sufis as 'Friends of God'. He asserts that these men of poverty and purity were greatly admired by the Prophet. They walked the way of love to find God in the heart within. And love, as a great Sufi mystic says, lies in this, that you account yourself very little, and God very great. Love means giving all that you are and all that you have to Him whom you love, so that nothing remains to you of your own! As you tread the path of love, you find that the 'you' in you has vanished and alone the Lord, the Beloved remains.

In pursuit of their goal of worshipping Allah, Sufis belong to different *Tariqas,* or orders, established in the first few centuries after the Prophet's death. These orders have a master or *murshid* who will teach sacred knowledge to others in the group.

The faith of the Sufi rises above all creeds and all denominations and religions. It is a way of life – the life of faith and freedom and love. It seeks to set men free from the bondage of creeds and dogmas, of rites and ceremonies, calling them away from all things extern to the interior life of the Spirit. The Sufi emphasis is on the inner experience and ecstasy, rather than on deductive reasoning or practical rituals. It is the way of the heart – the heart which turns, at all times and in all conditions, to the one and only Beloved.

The Sufi emphasis on intuitive knowledge and the love of God increased the appeal of Islam to the masses and made possible its extension beyond the Middle East into Africa and East Asia. Sufi brotherhoods multiplied rapidly across the continents and their success was due primarily to the humanitarian attitude of their founders and leaders, who not only ministered to the spiritual needs of their followers but also helped the poor of all faiths.

Sufism exercised a tremendous influence, partly through mystical poetry, for example, that of Jalal ad-Din Rumi, and partly through the formation of religious brotherhoods. The latter grew out of the practise of disciples studying under a mystical guide (*pir,* or saint) to achieve direct communion with God.

Sufi psychology has influenced many areas of thinking both within and outside of Islam, drawing primarily upon the three concepts: a lower self called the *nafs*, a faculty of spiritual intuition called the *qalb* or, spiritual heart, and a spirit or soul called *ruh*. These interact in various ways, producing the spiritual types of the tyrant (dominated by nafs), the person of faith and moderation (dominated by the qalb), and the person lost in love for God (dominated by the ruh).

Sufi mysticism has always exercised a fascination upon the Western world, and its Orientalist scholars. Figures like Rumi have become household names in the United States, where Sufism is perceived favourably as quietist and apolitical.

The Islamic Institute in Mannheim, Germany, which works towards the integration of Europe and Muslims, regards Sufism as particularly suited for inter-religious dialogue and intercultural harmonization in democratic and pluralist societies; it has described Sufism as a symbol of tolerance and humanism – undogmatic, flexible and non-violent.

The sufi tradition of qawwali music is an ecstatic singing and listening experience that transports participants to a state of *wajad*, where they feel one with the Divine, attaining to a spiritual ecstasy. Originally performed mainly at Sufi shrines or dargahs throughout South Asia, it has also gained mainstream popularity throughout the world.

CHANGE THE WORLD

They will become Godly when they will have God in their hearts.

– The Religion of God

$\mathcal{B}$AYAZID, A SUFI MYSTIC, TELLS US IN HIS AUTOBIOGRAPHY, 'WHEN I was young I thought of one thing all the time; and I said this to God, and in all my prayers this was the base: "Give me energy so that I can change the whole world." Everything and everybody looked wrong to me. I was a revolutionary and I wanted above all else to change the face of the earth. ... When I became a little older and a little more mature I saw that what I wanted to accomplish was not so easy after all. I started praying: "This seems to be too much. Life is going out of my hands – almost half of my life is gone and I have not changed a single person, and it is much too much to expect to change the whole world." So I began to say to God, "My family will be enough. Let me change my family."'

'And when I became old,' says Bayazid, 'I realized that it is no mean task to try to change one's family; even the family is too much, and who am I to change them? Then I realized that if I can change myself that would be enough, more than enough. So I prayed to God, "Now I have come to the right point. At least allow me to do this: I would like to change myself." God replied, "Now there is no time left. This you should have asked in the beginning. Then there was a possibility ..."'

THOUGHT FOR REFLECTION

What is heaven? What is hell? Heaven and hell are our own creation. To create heaven, all we need to do is change the pattern of our mind. Change your mind – and you change the world.

May I offer you Four Golden Rules for a peaceful life?

1. Seek not to please men: seek only to please God.
2. Take serious things lightly and light things seriously.
3. Laugh as much as you can.
4. Cultivate the Spirit of acceptance.

RABIA AND HASSAN

Someone asked where God was before earth, skies, and Divine Throne existed. We said that the question was invalid from the outset because God is, by definition, that which has no place.

– Hazrat Rumi

RABIA, THE GREAT SUFI MYSTIC, LIVED A REMARKABLE LIFE. Throughout her life, her love of God, poverty and self-denial were her constant companions. She did not possess much more than a broken jug, a rush mat and a brick, which she used as a pillow. She spent all night in prayer and contemplation, chiding herself if she slept because it took her away from her active love of God.

As her fame grew, she had many disciples. Farid-ud-din Attar, who has recorded her life, tells us that she held discussions with many of the renowned religious people of her time. Though she had many offers of marriage, and one (according to legend) even from the Amir of Basra, she refused them as she had no time in her life for anything other than God.

Her concept of Divine Love was truly elevating. She was the first to introduce the idea that God should be loved for God's own sake, not out of fear – as earlier mystics had done. Thus she prayed, 'O, Allah! If I worship you for fear of hell, burn me in hell, and if I worship you in hope of paradise, exclude me from paradise. But if I worship you for your own sake, grudge me not your everlasting beauty.'

One day, Rabia was passing through a street on her way to the marketplace. It was her habit to go to the marketplace every day, and tell people about the truths she had sought and attained through her prayers and reflections. And for many days she had been watching a mystic, a well-known mystic, called Hassan, sitting before the door of the mosque and praying to God with intense devotion, 'God, open the door! Please open the door! Let me in!'

On that day, Rabia could not take it anymore. Hassan was crying in a heart-rending wail, tears were rolling down his cheeks, and he was shouting again and again, 'Open the door! Let me in! Why don't you listen? Why don't you hear my prayers?'

Every day, as she had passed by, Rabia had laughed to herself; she had laughed quietly, whenever she had heard Hassan uttering his plaint. But it was too much for her to take today. Hassan was weeping his heart out. She went up to him, shook him up and said, 'Stop all this nonsense! The door is open – in fact you are already in!'

Hassan looked at Rabia, and that moment became a moment of Divine revelation for him. Looking into the eyes of Rabia, he bowed down, touched her feet, and said, 'You came in time; otherwise I would have spent my whole life just calling God in vain! For years I have been doing this – where have you been before? Why did you not come earlier to take me out of my misery? I know you pass this street every day. You must have seen me crying and praying. And yet you did not come to me until now!'

Rabia said to Hassan, 'Yes, but truth can only be said at a certain moment, in a certain space, in a certain context. I was waiting for the right moment, the ripe moment. Today it has arrived; hence I came close to you. Yesterday if I had told you, you would have felt irritated; you may have even become angry. You may have reacted antagonistically; you may have told me, "You have disturbed my prayer!" – and it is not right to disturb anybody's prayer.'

Rabia said, 'I had wanted to tell you this long time back, but I had to wait for the right moment. It did not come till now.'

Thought for Reflection

Who is a true Sufi? The answer to this I found in one of my visits to a holy place. It was at a dargah that I saw, engraved on a tablet the thought provoking words: *Be silent and behold the Beloved!*

A true Sufi speaks but little. A true Sufi ever remains silent. My dear devotees of the Lord, write these words on the tablet of your heart and practise it. Control the urge to speak more than necessary. Avoid being garrulous. Whenever you are tempted to speak more than necessary, remind yourself of the adage: A true Sufi speaks less. If you want to say something in one sentence, then say so in a few words. If you want to convey something in a few words, compress it and reduce the number of words to the minimum.

My dear ones, be precise. Be concise. Let silence be your hallmark; let silence be your watchword.

Use the silence for imagining illumination. Think of the light, the cosmic radiance present everywhere. Sit in silence, imagine the source of all light – your Guru, your deity, your prophet; bring that radiant picture before the mind's eye, and see the miracle happen. You will be engulfed by light. You will be transformed. You would avoid worldly affairs, for the beauty of silence has touched you; and you do not want to spoil it by smearing it with mundane happenings. Try it and experience the change within you.

Beholding the Face of the Beloved

*Your task is not to seek for love, but merely to seek and find all
the barriers within yourself that you have built against it.*

– Rumi

Saint Farid once visited a city, where his discourses and
teachings captivated the hearts of all seekers. Many people flocked to
see him, hear him and receive his blessings. Among them was a young
man, who fell at the saint's feet and said, 'Please help me see the face
of the Beloved! Please help me commune with Allah, for my heart is
smitten with longing for the Lord!'

Saint Farid smiled at the young man, and asked him, 'Have you
ever fallen in love? Have you ever experienced *ishq*, which has enslaved
a million hearts?'

'Alas! No,' the young man replied, 'till now I have never experienced
that strange emotion you speak of.'

'In that case,' Saint Farid said, 'I suggest that you fall in love! Fall in
love with someone, learn the ways of love and then come back to me. I
will show you how you may realize God.'

So determined was the young man to realize God that he set about
following the saint's command. He walked the streets of the city, but he
saw no one with whom he could fall in love. As he wandered through
the city, he happened to cross the palace gates. Glancing at the upper
storey, he saw a beautiful girl standing near a window. 'Here is the girl
I was looking for,' he said to himself. 'I shall fall in love with her. I shall
gain the experience of love that the saint spoke to me of.'

Straightaway he positioned himself outside the palace in such a way that he could look at the window directly. And he stood there, trying to catch a glimpse of the girl.

Now, the girl happened to be the princess of the realm, the only daughter of the king. She saw the young man standing beneath her window staring at her, whenever she happened to pass before her window. At first, she dismissed him as a curious passer-by; but when he continued to stand there day after day, she became annoyed. She sent her waiting women to chase him away.

The palace maids approached the young man and said to him, 'Leave this spot at once, or you will be in trouble! The princess is upset by your constant presence. We were sent to drive you away. If you do not leave, she may complain to the king, and you will be sent to prison or thrown out of the kingdom!'

The young man was unabashed. 'A holy man has sent me here to learn the experience of love,' he said to the women. 'I am determined to learn the lesson thoroughly. Come what may, I shall remain here, looking at the girl I love.'

When the princess was told of this, she was taken aback. What kind of madness was this? How could one deal with a man who was set on such a foolhardy mission?

Before she could decide on how best to deal with this 'lover', news reached the king's ears that a young man was standing outside the palace, staring at the princess's window. The king's blood began to boil! Why, the scoundrel must be stoned to death! He summoned his minister and ordered him to put the man to death.

By now, the minister had been apprised of the whole story. Earnestly, he said to the king, 'Let us not act in haste, Your Majesty. The young man has spoken of true love. A lover has to be treated with caution. His sighs, his tears and his anguish have the power to move heaven. Many empires have been destroyed because of the pain of lovers. If the young man curses us, God will hear the curse, and send disasters upon us!'

The king was alarmed. 'You may be right,' he said, 'but I urge you to do something – anything! – to drive the man away. The sight of him standing there with that intense look in his eyes unnerves me! I do not want those eyes to behold my daughter. Please do whatever you can to spare us from those eyes.'

The minister thought carefully, and worked out a strategy. He went to meet the young man and heard him out.

'I understand your wish,' he said to the lover. 'You are determined to go through the experience of love. I will tell you how your desire may be accomplished, come with me.'

The minister took the young man to the entrance of the watch tower just inside the palace gates. 'Climb this tower,' he said to the young man. 'When you reach the top, you will see the princess standing below. If you truly wish to attain your beloved, then jump down from the top of the tower, and she will be yours.'

The young man accepted the minister's challenge. In a matter of minutes, he had climbed the steep steps of the tower and reached the top.

The minister now persuaded the king and the princess to walk down to the foot of the tower. He explained to the king, 'This youth is either a mad man, or a true lover. I am now going to ask him to jump down. If he is smashed to smithereens, our problem is solved. If he survives, then he is a true lover, and we should deal with him carefully.'

And so it came to pass. The princess stood below, and the minister cried to the young man, 'If you truly love her, jump down now! But consider carefully, whether you really want to do this. Think of the risk, the danger involved. Retract, before it is too late.'

The young man replied, 'This tower is nothing! I would jump into an ocean, walk into a fire, and fall from a cliff for the sake of my beloved!' He looked down at the princess, who appeared to be a tiny speck below him. Calling the name of God, he jumped down.

There was a furore! The young man lay, lifeless, at the feet of the stunned princess. She began to weep bitterly. The king and the minister were too shocked to react.

At that very moment, Saint Farid arrived at the palace. At a glance, he took in what had happened. Taking stock of the situation, he said to the princess, 'Go near the lifeless form of this young man and call out his name – Salim. If he is a true lover, he will open his eyes at your voice.'

The princess did as she was told. She drew close to the young man and whispered, 'Salim! Salim!'

A miracle came to pass! The young man not only awakened, he was up on his feet when he saw Saint Farid.

Saint Farid then said to him, 'Behold, young man, the princess is here by your side. You are free to marry her and become the lord of this vast kingdom.'

'But what will I do with this kingdom?' cried the young man, 'you know I came here to prove myself. My one and only desire is to see the face of Allah. All the rest is of no interest to me!'

'Look at the princess,' said Saint Farid softly, 'is she not beautiful? Would you not be a lucky man to marry such a girl?'

The young man stared at the princess. 'True, she is very beautiful,' he agreed. 'But her beauty is not without blemish, and, as for me, my heart is set on meeting Allah.'

Pleased at the answer, Saint Farid beckoned the young man to follow him. 'Come with me and I shall get you a glimpse of true beauty, beauty which is pure and blemish free.'

THOUGHT FOR REFLECTION

A Sufi does not care for worldly affairs. He wants to drink the wine of love and go into the rapturous beauty of the Beloved. A time comes in his life when, he looks for his Beloved everywhere; in every nook and corner; in every flower and tree; in clouds and rain; he searches for His face in the sky and on the earth his obsession takes him to the deserts and the mountain peaks.

A Sufi is like a moth who wishes to burn itself in the flame of love. He thinks nothing of destroying himself (his ego) in his magnificent obsession for the Beloved. At first it is the obsession to have the vision of the Beloved, then it becomes an intense longing to annihilate oneself and merge with that powerful attraction, the Beloved.

It is for this experience that a Sufi wanders like a mystic. His flame is kindled and he goes about in the quest of *Ishq Illahi*, which promises to take him to new horizons of experiences. The mystic experiences deny the rationale of mind; the mystic experiences are beyond description. They are the experiences of the spirit, they are subtle and esoteric.

A Lesson in Humility from Bayazid al-Bistami

There came one and knocked at the door of the Beloved.
And a voice answered and said, 'Who is there?'
The lover replied, 'It is I.'
'Go hence,' returned the voice;
'There is no room within for thee and me.'
Then came the lover a second time and knocked and again the voice
demanded, 'Who is there?' He answered, 'It is thou.'
'Enter,' said the voice, 'for I am within.'

— Rumi

HERE WAS A CERTAIN ASCETIC WHO CLAIMED TO BE AMONG THE holy men of Bastam. He had his own group of followers; but he was never absent from the circle of Bayazid al-Bistami (or Abu Yazid al-Bistami). He attended all Abu Yazid's discourses and sat with his companions.

One day he said to Abu Yazid, 'Master, for 30 years I have kept regular fasts; I stay awake every night to pray; I hardly ever sleep. But I have not seen even a glimmer of the Light you speak of; I discover no trace of this knowledge that you promise will come to all seekers. And please believe me, when I say to you, I thirst after that knowledge; I yearn to see the Light; and I love your discourses.'

Abu Yazid said to him, 'Even if you fast every day and pray every night for 300 years, you will never realize one atom of this discourse.'

'But why?' demanded the ascetic, in consternation.

'Because the veil that hides you from the Light is your own self,' replied Abu Yazid.

'Then I beg you to give me a remedy for this, that I may tear this veil and get to see the Light,' the man said to Abu Yazid.

'I can, indeed, offer you a remedy; but I am afraid you would never accept it,' answered Abu Yazid.

'I assure you, I most certainly will,' said the man. 'Just tell me the remedy and I shall do exactly as you suggest.'

'In that case, here is my prescription for you,' said Abu Yazid, 'I want you to go this very minute and shave off your hair and your beard. Remove all the fine clothes you are wearing and tie a loincloth of goat's wool about your waist. Hang a bag of nuts around your neck; go out into the marketplace; collect as many children as you can and tell them, "I will give a nut to everyone who slaps me." Go all over the city doing this; go especially to places where you are well-known. This will be your remedy.'

'Glory be to God! There is no God but God,' cried the ascetic on hearing these words.

'If a nonbeliever uttered those words, he would become a believer,' remarked Abu Yazid. 'But by uttering the same, you have become a polytheist.'

'How is that possible?' the man demanded to know.

'Because you consider yourself too grand to do what I asked you to do,' replied Abu Yazid. 'You uttered these words to express your own importance, not really to glorify God.'

'But I cannot bring myself to do what you have suggested,' the man protested. 'Give me another remedy.'

'There is only one remedy for your condition, and that I have given to you,' Abu Yazid declared.

'I cannot do it,' the man repeated.

'I said to you that you would not do it, that you would never obey me, did I not?' said Abu Yazid.

(From the *'Memorial of the Saints'* of Fariduddin Attar.)

———⟨◆⟩———

THOUGHT FOR REFLECTION

The wise ones tell us that there are many veils that keep God hidden from our consciousness. Perhaps the most troublesome one is the veil of the ego. Gurudev Sadhu Vaswani often said to us, 'Remove the veil of ego, and you will behold the light divine.' He, the omnipresent one is right here, standing before us. We are unable to see Him due to this stubborn, unyielding veil of the ego.

'God is right there, bright and illuminated. But the ego blurs our vision and we are unable to see the shining Divine Light,' Gurudev Sadhu Vaswani added. 'An egoless man is one who walks the little way. His is the way of acceptance. He accepts everything. If he is asked to be the president of the country, he accepts it and holds the reins of the country. And when he is asked to be sweeper, he accepts that too, in the same measure. A humble man asks no questions.'

May I say to you, my dear brothers and sisters, if we can remove the veil of the ego we would truly have the vision of the Beloved!

ALLAH IS HERE!

Whoever loves to meet Allah, Allah verily loves to meet him.

– Anonymous

THERE WAS A DEVOUT MAN, WHO ALWAYS HAD ALLAH'S NAME ON HIS lips and in his heart. Every night, he cried 'Allah! Allah!' until his lips became sweet with the name of God.

Satan was not at all pleased about this. So he whispered in the man's ear, 'Why now, you chatterbox! You have cried "Allah!" till your voice is hoarse. May I ask you, have you ever heard an answer to your constant cry? Has ever an answer come from the Throne to tell you, "Here I am!" Then why do you persist with your fruitless cry? How long will you go on crying, "Allah! Allah!" Isn't it time you stopped?'

The poor man was heart broken; he felt desolate and abandoned; he wept tears of anguish, as he laid his head on his pillow the following night. Why hadn't Allah, the Merciful and the Benevolent ever answered the cry of his overflowing heart?

As he fell into a disturbed sleep, he had a vision of the Mystic Shaikh Khazir in a green garden.

'Look now, good soul,' Khazir called to him, 'why is it that you have desisted from the mention of God tonight? Can it be possible that you regret having called upon Him?'

'I have called upon God repeatedly,' the man said to Khazir, 'and not once has he answered "Here I am" to my repeated calls. I therefore fear that I may be refused from His door.'

Shaikh Khazir answered, 'Ah, son! Don't you know that God says "Here I am", every time you utter His holy name? Verily, Allah says to you: Your cry of "Allah" is itself My reply to you, My answering call, "Here I am"; your pleading and agony and fervour are My messages to you. All your twisting and turning to come to Me are My drawing you towards myself, so that your feet may be set free. Your yearning and love are the lasso to catch My grace. Your attempts to reach Me are in essence, My attempts to reach you! In the inner silence that surrounds the call of "Allah", you may hear Me whisper, "Here I am".'

THOUGHT FOR REFLECTION

Every true seeker wishes to behold the vision of the Beloved in his lifetime. His longing is intense and deep. His yearning is unbearable. He wants to tear apart all the veils between him and his Beloved. He wants to have the Vision Beautiful. A seeker will always beseech the Lord, 'O, Lord, I am unable to reach You. But surely You can reach me and bestow me with the grace – so that I may become worthy to witness Your Divine Self.'

There are three principles to be followed to attain to a vision of the Lord:

The first is – be detached – this world is an illusion.
The second is – ignite the flame of Love Divine.
The third is – seek refuge in Him and ask for His Grace.

TAOISM

BRIEF INTRODUCTION

*T*HE FOUNDER OF TAOISM IS THOUGHT TO BE LAO-TSE (604–531 BC), whose life overlapped that of Confucius (551–479 BC). However, many historians feel that he is actually a mythical figure, or a popular synthesis of a number of historical figures. Such scholars point out that the Chinese term Laozi literally means 'Old Master' and is generally used as an honorific reference or title. Lao-Tse is revered as a wise man in philosophical forms of Taoism, but regarded as God in more religious and 'practising' forms of Taoism, much like the Buddha in some schools of Buddhism.

The *Tao Te Ching* or *Dao De Jing* is a Chinese classic text. Its name comes from the opening words of its two sections: *dào* or 'way', *dé* or 'virtue', and *jing* or 'classic'. According to tradition, it was written around the sixth century BC by Lao-Tse, although many people say that it was compiled by his disciples later. Many artists, from China and other countries, as well as poets, painters, calligraphers, and even gardeners have used the Tao Te Ching as a source of inspiration. Its influence has also spread widely outside East Asia, aided by hundreds of translations into western languages.

Tao (pronounced 'Dow') can be roughly translated into English as path, or the way. As Chinese scholars say, it is basically indefinable. It has to be experienced. According to the followers of the faith, it 'refers to a power which envelops, surrounds and flows through all things, living and non-living. The Tao regulates natural processes and nourishes balance in the Universe. It embodies the harmony of opposites (i.e., there would be no love without hate, no light without dark, no male without female).'

One of the key concepts of Taoism is *wu wei*, literally 'non-action' or 'not acting'. The concept of wu wei is complex and reflected in the word's multiple interpretations: it can mean 'not doing anything', 'not forcing', 'not acting' in the theatrical sense, 'creating nothingness', 'acting spontaneously', and 'flowing with the moment'. Lao-Tse is thought to have used the term in conjunction with simplicity and humility as key virtues, often in contrast to selfish action. On a political level, it means avoiding violent events such as war, harsh laws and unjust taxes. Some Taoists see a connection between wu wei and esoteric meditation techniques, such as 'sitting in oblivion' (i.e., emptying the mind of bodily awareness and thought).

The concept of a personified deity or God is foreign to Taoism, as is the concept of the creation of the Universe. Each believer's goal is to become one with the Tao, the force which flows through all life and is the first cause of everything.

Taoism started as a combination of psychology and philosophy but evolved into a religious faith in 440 CE when it was adopted as a state religion. At that time Lao-Tse became popularly venerated as a deity. Taoism, along with Buddhism and Confucianism, became one of the three great religions of China. But by the end of the Ch'ing Dynasty in 1911, state support for Taoism ended. Much of the Taoist heritage was destroyed during the next period of warlordism. After the Communist victory in 1949, religious freedom was severely restricted. During the 'cultural revolution' in China from 1966 to 1976, much of the remaining Taoist heritage was destroyed. Some religious tolerance has been restored in China under Deng Xiaoping from 1982 to the present time.

Taoism currently has about 20 million followers, most of who live in Taiwan. Over 30,000 Taoists live in North America and Canada as well. Taoism has had a significant impact on North American culture, especially in areas such as acupuncture, herbalism, holistic medicine, meditation and martial arts.

Pan Ku: The Tao Myth of Creation

God (the great everlasting infinite First Cause
from whom all things in heaven and earth proceed)
can neither be defined nor named. For the God
which can be defined or named is but the
Creator, the Great Mother of all those
things of which our senses have cognizance
yet the spiritual and the material, though known to us
under different names, are similar in origin, and
issue from the same source, and the same obscurity
belongs to both, for deep indeed is the darkness
which enshrouds the portals through which we have
to pass, in order to gain a knowledge of these mysteries.

– Tao Te Ching (Tr. G.G. Alexander)

IN THE BEGINNING OF TIME, THERE WAS NO COSMOS AS WE KNOW IT today; there was only elemental chaos. The varied components of the heavens and earth mingled freely together. The organizing principle lay dormant somewhere inside this elemental chaos, for the transformation of chaos into cosmos was yet to happen. This primeval mass was shaped like an egg.

For thousands upon thousands of years, the unborn, unmade universe remained in this condition. When the time was right, when the time was ripe, the egg hatched. The lighter, pure substances floated upward; these were called yang, and they formed the heavens. The heavier, more impure substances dropped downward, and formed the earth. These were named yin.

From these two substances was created a third force, the giant Pan Ku. As Pan Ku grew, his enormous size divided the heavens from the earth. The giant lived for thousands of years. Helped by four creatures, a tortoise, a phoenix, a dragon, and a unicorn, he laboured day after day to mould and shape the earth. Together, Pan Ku and his companions created the earth as we know it today.

When the earth was fully forged and operational, Pan Ku passed away. His body was totally transformed. His left eye became the sun and his right eye became the moon. His blood became the rivers and oceans, his breath became the wind, his sweat became the rain, and his voice became the thunder. His flesh became the soil, and from the fleas living on his body, the human race was generated. Thus the stage was set for the drama of human civilization to unfold.

The story of Pan Ku is the Tao myth of creation. Like all myths of creation, it points to the fact that the One gives rise to the many; that there is an organizing principle behind creation; that when this creative force is set in motion, opposing forces, binary opposites are formed; such as heaven and earth, black and white, day and night, good and evil. These are the ideas of the yang and the yin, of the masculine and feminine. These opposing qualities are, by their fundamental natures, equal in all respects but forever separate entities.

THOUGHT FOR REFLECTION

You, who are looking for miracles, open your eyes and see! All around us are the miracles of God. A tiny seed grows into a huge banyan tree. A caterpillar becomes a butterfly.

The world of Nature, all the aspects of the wide and vast Universe that God has created, is full of the most potent energy and the most positive vibrations. If ever you are feeling 'low' or mentally exhausted, go out to breathe the fresh air outdoors. Breathe in the fresh air, and as you inhale, tell yourself, 'I am connecting to the Universe God has made. Let its positive energy flow into me.'

Look around you with new, fresh vision. Notice the trees and plants and creepers which you take for granted. Were they always there? Have you witnessed the miracle of their growth?

Express your gratitude to God for the Miracle of creation – for the blue sky, the life-giving warmth of the sun, the enchanting silvery light of the moon, the myriads of stars, the birds, the flowers, the grass, the butterflies and all that makes up the unparalleled beauty of creation!

This simple activity will make a great difference to your well-being and attitude!

FOLLOWING THE WAY

The Formless Way
We look at it, and do not see it; it is invisible.
We listen to it, and do not hear it; it is inaudible.
We touch it, and do not feel it; it is intangible.
These three elude our inquiries, and hence merge into one.

Not by its rising, is it bright,
nor by its sinking, is it dark.
Infinite and eternal, it cannot be defined.
It returns to nothingness.
This is the form of the formless, being in non-being.
It is nebulous and elusive.

Meet it, and you do not see its beginning.
Follow it, and you do not see its end.
Stay with the ancient Way
in order to master what is present.
Knowing the primeval beginning is the essence of the Way.

— Lao-Tse

Tao means 'the way'. Here is a Tao short story that reflects the importance of the way.

There was a young man who had an overwhelming desire to take a look at the life-size statue of Lao-Tse, the Tao Master, which stood atop a steep hill. He set out one night, determined to make it to the hilltop for a vision of the statue.

It was a long journey, for the hill was a great distance away from his village. The path was rough and steep and rugged. Having travelled a few miles, the young man was fatigued and lonely. He decided to wait until daybreak to pursue his journey.

As he sat wearily by the roadside, he saw an old man coming up the path. The old man stopped by on seeing him and made a few enquiries. Where was he coming from? What was his destination?

When he heard that the young man had set out to see the statue of the Master, the old man said to him, 'Let us travel together. I have made this journey before, and I would love to do it again.'

'But I get tired so soon,' said the young man. 'I need to rest every now and then.'

'So shall it be!' said the old man cheerfully. 'Come. Let's go!'

The young man got up and the two set off on the journey. The path was unbelievably beautiful and the two walked on steadily. Whenever the young man complained of aching feet or stiff knees, the old man agreed to rest until he felt better. Before he realized where he was, the young man found himself at the top of the hill, and the statue of the Master stood before them in all its majesty.

Speechless with wonder, the young man stood before the statue and gazed at it till his heart overflowed with a sense of happiness and achievement. His desire was fulfilled; his goal was accomplished. He felt he could stand there forever!

'Come on, let's go,' said the old man.

'Where to?' asked the young man. 'Our journey is over. We have reached the destination.'

'But that does not mean you can rest,' said his sprightly old companion. 'The journey does not end with this. Look ahead of you! The path is beautiful. You will have to pursue it. There is nothing called the destination, there's only the way!'

THOUGHT FOR REFLECTION

In the endless adventure of existence, God and man are comrades. God is our one unfailing companion. He will never leave us. We may try to run away from Him. But He will continue to follow us as our own shadow. Choose the kind of bond with Him that your heart desires, and you will never lose your way on the journey of life.

For one day, carry God in your heart, take Him with you, wherever you go. Involve Him in your day's activities. Talk to Him when you feel afraid, depressed or lonely. Seek His help when you feel lost or scared. Keep turning to Him for every little advice you need. If someone hurts you, tell Him about it and seek His comfort. In the night, thank Him for being with you throughout the day. As you retire to bed at the end of the day, you will surely feel you have drawn closer to God.

Good Luck, Bad Luck

Shape clay into a vessel;
It is the space within that makes it useful.
Cut doors and windows for a room;
It is the holes which make it useful.
Therefore benefit comes from what is there;
Usefulness from what is not there.

– Lao-Tse

THERE IS A CHINESE STORY OF AN OLD FARMER, WHO HAD A WEAK, ailing horse for ploughing his field. One day, the old horse ran away into the hills. The farmer's neighbours pursed their lips and offered their sympathy to him. 'Such rotten luck!' they remarked.

'Bad luck? Good luck? Who knows?' replied the farmer, philosophically.

A week later, the old horse returned, bringing with it a herd of wild horses from the hills. This time, the neighbours swarmed around the farmer to congratulate him on his good luck.

'Good luck? Bad luck? Who can tell?' was his reply.

Sometime later, while trying to tame one of the wild horses, the farmer's only son fell off its back and broke his leg.

Everyone thought that this was bad luck indeed.

'Bad luck? Good luck? I don't know,' said the farmer.

A few weeks later, the king's army marched into the village and conscripted every able-bodied young man living there. The farmer's son, who was laid up with a broken leg, was let off, for he would be of no use to them.

Now what could this be – good luck or bad luck? Who can tell?

THOUGHT FOR REFLECTION

Accept! Accept! Accept! When you cultivate the spirit of acceptance, you move towards the goal of *samatva* or equanimity. Samatva implies balance, serenity and tranquility, which are born out of spiritual understanding. And therefore, Sri Krishna declares in the Gita: *Samatvam Yoga Uchyate* – Equanimity is called Yoga.

It is not adversity, but also prosperity that topples our sense of balance. When we meet with success repeatedly, we grow egoistic and arrogant. We tend to overlook God's grace and develop a false sense of superiority.

Adversity on the other hand, brings out the worst of our negative emotions – fear, despair, misery and insecurity. We lose all sense of objectivity, and succumb to self-pity.

Something that seems to be bad on the surface may actually be good in disguise. And something that seems to be attractive and 'lucky' may actually be harmful to our best interests. The wise ones leave it to God to decide what is best for them. They know that all things turn out good for them. They know that all things turn out good for those who love God and accept His will unconditionally.

Work and Rest – Tao Mode

Fill your bowl to the brim and it will spill. Keep sharpening your knife and it will blunt. Chase after money and security and your heart will never unclench. Care about people's approval and you will be their prisoner. Do your work, then step back. That is the only path to serenity.

– Tao Te Ching

THERE WAS A FARMER, OVER 90 YEARS OLD, WHO WAS A GREAT ADMIRER and follower of Lao-Tse. One day, he was busy drawing water from a deep well in his field, assisted by his young son, a robust youth.

A wise old man from the city was passing by; he saw the old man and his son, yoked together, sweating it out to irrigate their field. Filled with compassion for the old man, the city-dweller remonstrated with him, 'You, old fool! Why do you break your back and exhaust your son in this fashion? Don't you know that a pair of oxen will do this job more efficiently than the two of you put together? Are you aware of how we pull water in the city? Don't you need to learn new ways of doing things? Why do you torture yourself and this young man?'

The old man said, 'Hush! Softly, if you please! You must be careful what you speak before young people! Hush! Please come at lunchtime, when my son takes a break with his friends, and I will talk to you then.'

Soon it was lunch time. The son went away and the old man sat down to eat his food. Now, the wise city dweller came forward to join him. 'You see, you did not want your son to hear me, because you don't want him to put up a resistance to your old style of working!' he said to the old man, accusingly.

The old man laughed. 'I am 90 years old, and I am still up and about and moving around and keeping good health. I sleep soundly at night, and I live by the labour of my own hands and feet. I would like my son to be even more healthy and fit, when he gets to be as old as I am! I would like him to work side by side with my grandson, when I am no more.'

'I know what goes on in the city. I too, can afford to engage horses or oxen to pull the water from my well. I know you have machines in the city to do all the hard work that we do here with our hands. But I want my son to be hale and hearty, healthy and fit and have the same strength and good health that I enjoy now, when he is 90. I want him to enjoy a well-earned night of sleep at the end of every day … so I let him work hard. Hard work will never ever cause him harm.'

What we do on one hand has an immediate effect on the other. He who works little during the day, loses repose at night. Rest is earned through labour.

———◁▷◆◁▷———

Thought for Reflection

The story goes that a hardworking man died and went to Heaven. When he met his Maker face to face, he asked Him outright: 'Lord, what is the idea of making men old? Why do you take away our physical gifts one after the other – our strength, our stamina, our speed, our agility – until we are left in a frail and decaying body?'

And the Lord replies, 'Dear child, ageing is not a curse – it is a gift that I have bestowed upon you, so you may become mature and wise, realize that you are not the body, that you do not belong to this world, but to Me, who am your Heavenly Father!'

The message of this story is indeed beautiful! The proverb says, 'What I gave, I got; what I lost, I gained.' We lose childhood to gain youth. We lose youth to gain adulthood. At every stage of life, we lose to gain!

Ageing may deprive us of physical prowess and energy. But it is a stage when we grow spiritually. We grow in maturity, wisdom, understanding patience and tolerance. The loss is physical – but the gain is spiritual. Need I tell you which is greater?

Experts say that irreversible ageing – i.e., loss of vital cells leading to gradual physical debility – starts at the age of 25!

It is in the nature of all matter to change with time. Wood, rock, stone, soil – you name it, it disintegrates with time. So does the body. But what is ageing to the body can be maturing to the mind and spiritual unfolding for the soul! If you believe that you are essentially a spirit, ageing should not bother you!

THE MAN WHO RAN AWAY
FROM HIMSELF

The Tao is in all things, in their divisions and their fullness. What I dislike about divisions is that they multiply, and what I dislike about multiplication is that it makes people want to hold fast to it. So people go out and forget to return, seeing little more than ghosts.

– Chuang Tzu

ONCE UPON A TIME, THERE LIVED A MAN WHO WAS DEEPLY DISTURBED by two things: the sound of his footsteps and the sight of his shadow. Wherever he went, his footsteps sounded in his ears; and wherever he went, whatever he did, his shadow followed him. He feared them, he hated them, and they would not leave him.

Determined to get rid of both, he decided that he would run away from them, as fast as his legs could carry him. So he got up and started running. But every time he put his foot down, he heard his footsteps; and the faster he ran, the faster his shadow caught up with him, following behind him effortlessly.

'That is just not fast enough,' he said to himself. 'I can't get rid of them, because I am too slow!'

He decided that the only thing he could do was to run faster. Faster! Faster! He ran so fast that he collapsed and died, exhausted and out of breath.

What he failed to realize was that if he had stopped running and just stepped under the shade of a tree, his shadow would have vanished; and if he had just sat down and stayed still, there would have been no more footsteps!

———————

THOUGHT FOR REFLECTION

Man's way of life in the modern age is one of the main causes of stress. Somehow modern life and stress seem to go together. The way we live, the way we work, the way we talk, the way we function every day, contribute to the building up of stress. People rush about all the time, as though they were carrying the entire burden of the world upon their shoulders. People rush about, accumulating what they think they need – only to realize that they don't need it at all. They resemble squirrels in a cage – running, all the time – but getting nowhere.

We seem to be in a hurry all the time! It is not only when we are on our feet that we are hurrying; when we are seated, at rest, our minds are rushing somewhere or the other. We may be waiting in an outer office, waiting for an appointment with a doctor, waiting for an interview call – but we are hurrying, rushing in our thoughts. This mental rush, this mental hurry is one of the main causes of tension.

We need to take it easy! Take it easy my brother! Take it easy, sister! There is a word which Spanish people use often. Whenever two Spaniards meet, they say to each other, 'Tranquilo! Tranquilo!' *Tranquilo* means – take it easy! This is the message which all of us need today – Take it easy! Take it easy!

ZEN BUDDHISM

BRIEF INTRODUCTION

THE JAPANESE WORD *ZEN* AND THE CORRESPONDING CHINESE TERM, *Ch'an* are derived from the Sanskrit word *dhyana,* meaning 'meditation'. Zen is a school of Mahayana Buddhism, which focuses on attaining enlightenment (*bodhi*) through meditation, even as Gautama, the Buddha, did. According to Zen belief, all human beings have the Buddha nature, or the potential to attain enlightenment within them; but the Buddha nature has been clouded by ignorance in most people. Zen Masters say that the way to overcome this ignorance is not the study of scriptures, or the performance of religious rites, devotional practices, and good works, but sustained meditation; this, they say, will eventually lead to insight and awareness of the ultimate reality. Training in the Zen path is usually undertaken by a disciple under the guidance of a master.

An interesting story is narrated in the early Buddhist scriptures of the origin of Zen. One day, a number of disciples had gathered around the Buddha, eager to hear his sermon. But on that particular occasion, the Buddha chose to remain utterly silent, only holding out a lotus flower for his disciples to see. Most of them were utterly puzzled by this silence. Only one of them, Mahakashyapa, gazed intently at the flower, and realized the inexpressible meaning of the Buddha's gesture. He had obtained inspiration directly from the Buddha's gaze and the flower that the Master had held. He smiled at the Buddha in gratitude, and the Buddha smiled back in recognition of his disciple's subtle sense of insight.

Thus, was born a new school of Buddhism, in which experiential wisdom took precedence over sermons and scriptures; and in which revealed transmission bypassed the need for words and rituals. Zen draws its inspiration from these words attributed to the Buddha: '*Bodhisattvas* never engage in conversations whose resolutions depend on words and logic.'

To this day, Zen Masters do not use words to transmit their wisdom, relying instead on intuitive thought processes and the grasp of unspoken truths. It is believed that Bodhidharma, the South Indian Pallava prince-turned-monk, was the one who first brought Zen to China; he himself is thought to have been in the direct lineage of the disciples of Mahakashyapa. The essence of Zen philosophy is expressed in the Bloodstream Sermon attributed to him:

> Buddhas don't save Buddhas. If you use your mind to look for a Buddha, you won't see the Buddha. As long as you look for a Buddha somewhere else, you will never see that your own mind is the Buddha. Don't use a Buddha to worship a Buddha. And don't use the mind to invoke a Buddha. Buddhas don't recite *sutras*. Buddhas don't keep precepts. And Buddhas don't break precepts. Buddhas don't keep or break anything. Buddhas don't do good or evil. To find a Buddha, you have to see your nature.

Although Zen rejects words as a channel of teaching wisdom, the early Zen Masters were well-versed in the various sutras of Buddhism; it was just that they felt that actual practise of the Buddha's ways was more worthwhile than reading or reciting from the scriptures. By the seventh century, Zen Buddhism, as taught by Bodhidharma, was well-established in China as a separate and distinct school.

It is often said in Zen history, that 'a five-petalled flower blossomed' in China. This Zen expression means that Zen opened up like a flower with five petals and spread throughout the whole country. These schools were Igyo, Hongen, Soto, Unmon, and Rinzai. Thousands of temples were constructed across the Chinese countryside, in forests and mountains, where tens of thousands of people devoted themselves to the study and practise of the Zen dharma. Zen philosophy and practise permeated and elevated Chinese culture, making its art and thought sublime, until it was systematically rooted out in the Communist movement of the twentieth century.

Although Zen Buddhism arrived in Japan as early as the seventh century, it did not develop significantly in that country until the twelfth century. The Rinzai sect of Zen was introduced to Japan by the Chinese priest Ensai in 1191. Rinzai Buddhism emphasizes the use of *koans*, paradoxical puzzles or questions that help the practitioner to overcome the normal boundaries of logic. Soto Buddhism was another Zen sect that was transmitted from China to Japan. It emphasizes the practise of *zazen* and tells the aspirant simply to clear the mind of all thoughts and concepts, without making any effort towards enlightenment, until enlightenment occurs naturally.

Zen has exercised a profound influence on the daily lives of the Japanese people. This influence can be seen and appreciated in many aspects of Japanese life, including eating, clothing, painting, calligraphy, architecture, theatre, music, gardening, decoration, etc.

Zen is perhaps the most well-known school of Buddhism in the West today. Its concepts have been influential on Western society since the latter half of the twentieth century. There are about 9.6 million Zen Buddhists in Japan today, and numerous Zen groups have developed in North America and Europe in the last one hundred years.

HEAVEN AND HELL

Holding on to anger is like grasping a hot coal with the intent of throwing it at someone else; you are the one who gets burned.

– Bodhidharma

HAKUIN WAS A FIERY AND INTENSELY DYNAMIC ZEN MASTER. Once, a Samurai warrior came to visit him. 'I want to know from you if there is really a heaven and a hell,' he said to Hakuin.

'Who are you?' asked Hakuin.

'My name is Nabushige,' said the man, 'and I am a Samurai.'

'So, you're a brutish soldier,' said Hakuin. 'You deal in violence; you are callous about causing pain to others; what makes you think you can understand heaven and hell? What gives you the right to pose such questions before me as if you are an insightful individual who can debate such matters? Have you ever looked at your face in a mirror? It is ugly! And why do you wear these ridiculous clothes? You look like a beggar. Go away from here and do not waste my time with your foolish questions.'

Nobushige was so incensed that he drew his shining sword out of its scabbard in a flash. His eyes glowed like red hot coals. Hakuin continued. 'So you have drawn your sword! Your weapon is probably much too dull to cut off my head.'

Nobushige uttered a vile curse; his face was crimson with rage, as he began to bring his sword down, teeth clenched and every nerve quivering with wrath. In just a fraction of a second, just before his head could be severed from his trunk, Hakuin remarked: 'Here open the gates of hell!'

The samurai was taken aback; he stood still and understanding dawned on him. Utterly humbled by the Master's wisdom and overwhelmed by his utter self-control, he sheathed his sword. His eyes were filled with tears of gratitude as he bowed in deep reverence before the Zen Master, who had risked his life to teach him the truth about anger and its hellish effect.

'Here open the gates of paradise,' said Hakuin, as calm and composed as ever.

THOUGHT FOR REFLECTION

A leading practitioner of meditation in the US points out that several cultures and religions simply do not teach people to focus on the world within them; their emphasis is often on words, rites and rituals; on a form or a Being or Spirit outside; thus the innermost spirit remains out of reach of most people.

The Indian tradition on the other hand, has always placed great value on meditation, reflection and contemplation – on the state of inner silence and inner stillness. For it is in this state that we will find tranquility, serenity, self-knowledge and true awareness. In this state, too, we will experience true freedom – freedom from fears, desires, tensions, insecurities and complexes that haunt us in the waking state. In this state of inner consciousness, we will also discover our own Divinity – that we are not the bodies we wear; we are not the insignificant, pathetic, frail creatures that we take ourselves to be; we will discover that we are the immortal atman, the eternal, infinite spirit that is *sat-chit-ananda* – pure, true, eternal bliss!

Winning the Debate

To talk much and arrive nowhere is the same as climbing a tree to catch a fish.

– Chinese proverb

It was the custom in Japan that a Zen temple had to offer full hospitality i.e., free boarding and lodging to any travelling monk, who could enter into a debate on Buddhism with the resident monks and win his argument. If he was defeated, he had to move on.

In a humble Zen temple in the north of Japan, two brother monks lived together. The elder one was both wise and learned, but the younger one was rather dull and blind in one eye.

A wandering monk came and asked for lodging, properly challenging them to a debate about the sublime teaching. The elder brother, who was tired that day from much studying, told the younger one to take his place. 'Insist that the dialogue must take place in silence,' he warned his dull brother.

So the young monk and the stranger went to the shrine and sat down. Shortly afterwards the traveller rose and went in to the elder brother and said: 'Your younger brother is an amazing fellow. He defeated me effortlessly. Let me offer you my congratulations. You have indeed taught him well.'

'Can you please relate your debate to me?' asked the elder monk.

'Well, it went this way,' explained the traveller. 'First of all, I held up one finger, representing Buddha, the enlightened one. In reply, he held up two fingers, signifying the Buddha and his teaching. So I held up three fingers, representing the Buddha, his teaching, and his followers, living the harmonious life. To this, he shook his clenched fist in my face, indicating that all three come from one single realization. He won the debate hands down, so I really have no right to remain here.' The traveller bowed to the elder monk and left.

The younger brother walked in a little later and asked the senior monk, 'Where is that belligerent fellow?'

'Congratulations,' said the elder brother, 'I understand you won the debate.'

'Don't you believe anything of that sort,' the younger one replied, 'I've won nothing; but I'm surely going to beat that fellow up.'

'Why? What happened?' asked the elder monk. 'What was the dialogue all about?'

'Well, that fellow was sure aggressive. The minute he sat down before me, he held up one finger, insulting me by insinuating that I have only one eye. I must tell you I controlled my temper, as he was a stranger and a guest. Out of politeness, I held up two fingers, congratulating him for being blessed with two eyes. But he was not so gracious as me. The insolent wretch held up three fingers, suggesting that between the two of us we only had three eyes. I tell you, I got really mad and clenched my fist to punch him, but he was such a coward, he bowed and ran out and that ended it!'

———◁◇▷———

Thought for Reflection

A distinguished professor of comparative religion was being ferried across a river by an illiterate boatman. The professor began to chat with the boatman as he was leafing through the pages of the encyclopaedia that he was carrying.

'Tell me, my good man, have you read the Bible?'

The boatman had to answer in the negative.

'Ah! One-fourth of your life has been wasted!' sighed the professor. 'Have you at least heard of the Gita?'

'No, sir,' replied the boatman regretfully.

'One-half of your life thrown away!' exclaimed the professor. 'Surely, you have heard of The Book of Common Prayer?'

'What's that?' said the boatman and received the retort: 'You have wasted three-fourths of your life!'

As this discussion was going on, the boat sprang a leak and water began to enter the boat rapidly through the crevices. Now it was the turn of the boatman to ask the scholar, 'Sir, can you swim?' The professor replied, 'I have read several books on swimming and gathered a lot of information on it, but I cannot swim.' The boatman then commented, 'Then your entire life has gone to waste. The boat is about to sink!'

The professor's bookish knowledge was of no use to him. So too, if we wish to cross this vast ocean of worldly life and experience happiness through it, we should actually practise spirituality and not just acquire theoretical knowledge.

THE ENIGMATIC LESSON

In what is seen there should be just the seen; in what is heard there should be just the heard; in what is sensed there should be just the sensing; in what is thought there should be just the thought.

– The Buddha

KUSUDA WAS A YOUNG PHYSICIAN IN TOKYO. HE HAD A FRIEND WHO was an ardent student of Zen. Kusuda asked him what Zen was all about.

'I wish I could tell you,' the friend said. 'But it's not easy! But let me tell you one thing for sure: if you understand Zen, you will no longer be afraid to die.'

Kusuda was intrigued. 'I would like to try it,' he said to his friend. 'Can you tell me where I can find a good teacher?'

'I suggest that you go to the Master Nan-in,' the friend told him.

Kusuda promptly decided to call on Nan-in. But he decided that he first had to find out if the master was really not afraid to die. So he took with him a miniature dagger, nine and a half inches long, to use in their first meeting.

When Kusuda walked into his room, Nan-in exclaimed, 'Hello there! How are you? It is a long time since we met, isn't it?'

Kusuda was completely thrown off guard. 'But … but we have never met before this!' he exclaimed, in confusion.

'You must forgive me,' said the teacher. 'You are right, of course. I mistook you for another student of mine, a physician who is also receiving instruction at the moment.'

319

Disarmed and taken by surprise, Kusuda had to abandon any idea he had of putting his teacher to the test. Rather warily, he asked Nan-in, 'May I receive Zen instruction?'

Nan-in said heartily, 'But of course! Zen is not at all a difficult thing. Since you happen to be a physician, just treat your patients with loving kindness. That is Zen for you.'

In the following weeks, Kusuda visited Nan-in three times. Each time Nan-in gave him the same instruction: 'There is really no need for a physician to waste his time around here. Just go and treat your patients with loving kindness.'

Kusuda was disappointed. He could not see how this teaching, excellent though it was, could make him unafraid of death. So, on his fourth visit he said to Nan-in, 'When my friend first sent me to you, he told me that Zen can help me lose the fear of death. But you have not taught me to be unafraid to die! Each time I have come to you, you only tell me to take care of my patients with loving kindness. Of course, I am doing it. But if this is all the Zen you have to teach me, there is no point in coming to you any more.'

Nan-in smiled and patted the doctor kindly. 'I am sorry I have been too strict with you,' he said. 'I shall now give you a *koan* [Zen Riddle].'

He presented Kusuda with Joshu's Mu to work over, which is the first mind-enlightening problem in the book called *The Gateless Gate*. Most koans are the sayings of the great Zen masters of the past, who used them on their students to open their minds to the truth of Zen. This was the koan given to Kusuda: it is called Joshu's Mu.

A monk asked Joshu, 'Does a dog have Buddha nature?' Joshu said, '*Mu*.' (The literal meaning of the Japanese '*mu*' [Chinese '*wu*'] is 'no', 'does not have', 'is without', 'no-thing', etc.)

Joshu's answer was quite simply 'Nothing', which was not to say that a dog lacks Buddha nature. Both Joshu and the monk knew that Buddha nature is inherent in all creatures without exception, which is why Joshu's 'mu' should never be interpreted as a denial of this fact.

The only purpose of his response was to break the monk's habit of excessive rational and logical thinking in trying to understand the truth of Zen; once reason and logic are set aside, he could aspire to a higher understanding of reality beyond affirmation and negation, in which all contradictions disappear on their own. Thus Joshu's 'mu' is neither a yes nor a no. It is an answer that transcends the binary opposition of yes and no and points directly to Buddha nature, to the reality beyond yes and no.

Those who believe they can solve the koan 'mu' through deductive reasoning will only end up staring at a blank wall. Attempting to interpret and understand 'mu' intellectually is like trying to hit the moon with a stick, or trying to relieve an itch on your foot by scratching your shoe. The old masters have said, 'Attempting to solve "mu" by rational means is like attempting to break through an iron wall with your fist.'

Kusuda pondered this problem of 'mu' for two years. At length he thought he had reached certainty of mind. But his teacher commented: 'You are not in yet.'

Kusuda continued in concentration for another year and a half. His mind became tranquil. Problems dissolved. No-thing became the truth. He served his patients well and, without even knowing it, he was free from concern over life and death.

Then when he visited Nan-in, his old teacher just smiled.

THOUGHT FOR REFLECTION

Gurudev Sadhu Vaswani once asked a gathering of teachers: 'Knowledge is increasing: is happiness increasing too? Schools and colleges are multiplying; are happy homes multiplying?'

Is it not worth reflecting upon?

We have more 'graduates' and 'doctorates' than ever before. Has the nation grown in integrity, vitality and strength? Have our young people become more appreciative of the deeper values which alone can give meaning, and significance to life?

The spiritual component in education cannot come from without, it already exists within the teacher – in the choice the teacher has made to be an educator. Bring this spiritual light to bear upon all that you do – and you will become a true teacher in every sense of the word!

Theft or Gift?

Keep your mind alive and free without abiding in anything or anywhere.

– The Diamond Sutra

It was late evening. The senior Zen Master, Shichiri Kojun, was in *zazen* (seated meditation) when a thief entered the temple. Unable to get past the people there, he decided to enter the Master's room at the back of the temple complex. He had a sharp sword ready, drawn in his hand. The Master, who had started reciting the sutras by then, was disturbed from his evening devotion, when the thief brandished his sword and shouted, 'Your money or your life!'

The Master was not in the least scared by the sight of the intruder. But he was most certainly annoyed by this rude interruption, and said to the man, 'Please do not disturb me! All the money I have is in that drawer. Just help yourself.' And he resumed his recitation.

To say that the thief was startled by this unexpected response would be an understatement. But he proceeded with his business anyway. As he was hurriedly helping himself to the money, the Master stopped and called, 'Please don't take all of it away. I need to pay a few bills tomorrow. Leave some money for me.'

Bemused, the thief left some money behind and prepared to leave. Just as he was leaving, the Master suddenly shouted at him, 'Where are your manners, my good man? You have taken my money and you don't even have the courtesy to thank me?'

This time, the thief was really shocked for he realized that the Master was not in the least afraid of him or his sword. The very idea made him uncomfortable and somewhat nervous. He mumbled his thanks and left the place as fast as his legs could carry him. Later that night, he confessed to his friends in the profession that he had never ever been so frightened in his life.

A few days later, the thief was caught by the police and confessed to many of his recent crimes, including the theft at Shichiri's house. When the case came up before the Magistrate, the Master was called to testify against the criminal.

'Do you recognize this man?' he was asked. 'He has confessed that he stole money from your room.'

The Master replied, 'No, this man did not steal anything from me. I gave him some money. In fact, he even thanked me for it.'

The thief was so moved that he decided to turn over a new leaf. When he was released from prison, he became a disciple of the Master and many years later, he attained enlightenment.

THOUGHT FOR REFLECTION

The secret of inner peace is in three words: 'Let it go!'

Let it go! Let go of your fears, your anxieties, your problems and your frustrations. Let go in God's name; for He is the support and sustenance of your life. There are no obstacles on your path that He cannot clear; no problems that He, in His mercy and wisdom, cannot solve!

If you want to be at peace, if you want to feel that God is watching over your life, if you want to feel the abundant love of God in your heart, if you wish to live in the present moment, then just let go of all your anxieties and worries, let go of all the constraints which are oppressing you; hand your life over to God, and watch miracles happen!

Let go, let go, let God!

Sounds so simple doesn't it? And yet most of us know that this is not as easy as it sounds.

The solution to most of our problems is to let go, in the name of God. Trust his wisdom to solve your problems when you feel that you can't cope and can't handle them yourself. It is particularly important to let go of petty resentments and losses. In the larger context of life, these issues are so petty and trivial. If you wish to nurture relationships, letting go of small irritations is a must. When you let go of your bitterness and anger, you will be surprised to realize how much more valuable life is, and how necessary it is to build lasting bonds with those you love.

The Invisible Sutras

Before you change reality, let reality change you!

– Zen saying

$\Leftrightarrow\Leftrightarrow$

Tetsugen Doko was one of the best-known Zen Masters of the Obaku School in Japan. He lived in the seventeenth century, and it was his life's aspiration to publish the Buddhist scriptures in Japanese. In those days, the sutras were only available in Chinese translations. He discussed the project with a few friends in the publishing business; he was told that it would indeed be an expensive task, as it would involve making around 60,000 wooden blocks for printing.

Tetsugen was not discouraged by the cost. With dedication and energy, he started travelling all over Japan, collecting money for this 'dream' project. A few wealthy people were so inspired by his enthusiasm that they donated a large amount of gold and silver to him; but many not-so-well-to-do folks also gave him smaller amounts, for which he was equally grateful. At the end of 10 years, as the collection was inching towards the target amount, however, tragedy struck.

The River Ujiin, the Kyoto prefecture, was in spate, and overflowed its banks. Floods devastated the province. Many people were left homeless and starving. Without a second thought, Tetsugen used all the money he had collected to offer what relief he could to the people.

Did this mean that he gave up his dream of publishing the sutras? Not at all! When he had finished with the relief and rehabilitation operations, Tetsugen started his collection drive for the second time, with renewed energy and drive. Once again, people came forward to give whatever they could. When he was close to saving the amount required, another tragedy occurred; this time, it was an epidemic which spread throughout Japan, affecting thousands of people. Once again, Tetsugen spent all the money he had collected to aid the suffering victims.

Once again it was back to zero, for this indefatigable monk. More years passed as he resolutely approached people to collect funds. Finally, it was 20 years after he started that he was able to publish the sutras! And this dream was achieved barely a year before the brave and devoted Master breathed his last. The original printing blocks he used are preserved today in the Obaku Monastery in Kyoto, Japan.

The Japanese people often tell their children that Tetsugen's efforts were not wasted at all; he has left behind him three editions of the sutras; the first two editions, they say, are invisible but far superior to the third edition which is the published version!

What are the two invisible sutras? Why are the invisible sutras of greater value? This is a *koan* (riddle) that Zen students love to discuss.

THOUGHT FOR REFLECTION

Service, it has been rightly said, is the rent we have to pay for being tenants of this body. Every morning, as we wake up, we must ask ourselves this question: What can I do to help? What can I do to make a difference? For indeed, each one of us can and must make a difference. There are so many tasks to be accomplished by us – there are hungry ones to be fed; there are naked ones to be clothed; there are elders to be cared for; there are children to be taught. There is so much work to be done! And every one of us – from the youngest to the oldest – can make a difference.

There are many people who say to me, 'We would love to make a difference. We would love to serve others. But we have so little money, so little time, so little energy, what can we do? Our resources are, alas, limited. How can we be of service to others?' 'There is not much that I can do on my own,' is what many of us think. We are mistaken. The tragedy for many of us is not that our aim is too high and we miss it – but rather that our aim is too low and we reach it!

As Herschel Hobbs says, 'The world measures a man's greatness by the number who serve him. Heaven's yardstick measures a man by the number who are served by him.'

ZOROASTRIANISM

BRIEF INTRODUCTION

ZOROASTRIANISM IS OFTEN DESCRIBED AS ONE OF THE OLDEST 'revealed' religions of the world, although perhaps one of the least known today. It is also regarded as one of the ancient monotheistic religions of the world, which first began as a widely accepted religion of the ancient Iranian people. Zoroastrians believe in the one universal and transcendental God, Ahura Mazda, the one uncreated Creator to whom all worship is ultimately directed. In some European languages, it is therefore referred to as Mazdaism.

The religious beliefs and philosophy of this ancient faith are based on the life and teachings of Zarathustra, or Zoroaster, as the Greeks referred to him. Thus, the religion may be described as the worship of Ahura Mazda, exalted by Zoroaster as the supreme divine authority. Though most adherents of this faith refer to themselves as Zoroastrians, some also call themselves Behdin, meaning 'follower of Daena', or the 'Good Religion'. It is one of the most widely respected religions of the world today, but its faithful adherents are very few in number, compared to the other major religions of the world. Most of the world's Zoroastrians today think of India as their home, although there are a few still living in Iran.

In fact, the Zoroastrian religion is first described recognizably in The Histories by Herodotus, as the culture and faith of the Persians, as Iranians were called at the time. Both the famous Persian emperors, Cyrus II and Darius are thought to have been worshippers of Ahura Mazda, and their faith encouraged them to be liberal rulers, who practised tolerance towards all faiths. However, the Zoroastrians, who once enjoyed great prestige and political power in Iran, came under severe economic and political pressure to convert when Iran was brought under Arab Muslim rule.

Many scholars believe that Mazdaism pre-dated Zoroaster, and was part of the society and culture of Persia for thousands of years. But modern history regards Zoroaster as the founder of the faith, and the Prophet of Ahura Mazda.

His biographers tell us that when he was 30 years old, one early morning, he went to fetch some water from the river. The sky had just turned its colour and the sun was about to rise. As he had gone into the waters of the river, Vohu Manah (the Angel of the Good Mind) appeared to him, and opened the portal to the Divine Light of Ahura Mazda. This was the first moment of Illumination and the first Revelation of Zoroaster.

Soon, he decided to move out of the land of his birth along with his chosen disciples, but wherever he went, he faced opposition. It was King Vishtaspa, who was a wise and just man, who gave the prophet an opportunity to expound his views in a court-debate, and so convinced was the king by Zoroaster's powerful arguments, that he willingly embraced the faith. This was a major turning point in Zoroaster's life and a remarkable breakthrough in the spread of his faith. He was now free to preach extensively, and successfully propagated his faith in the neighbouring countries as well. It was at the court of King Vishtaspa that he is thought to have composed the *Gathas* – 17 beautiful and profound hymns, which are still venerated as the most sacred scriptures of Zoroastrians.

None of the stories of his life portray Zoroaster as a divine being, not even the most extravagant legends that have been built up later. He remained a man like all others, though divinely gifted with inspiration and closeness to Ahura Mazda. Unlike the Quran, the *Gathas* of Zoroaster are not 'channelled' – i.e., the *Gathas* are regarded as the inspired composition of a poet-prophet rather than a text dictated by a heavenly being. His life is an inspiration for all Zoroastrians, precisely for this reason: in his innovations, in his loving relationship with God, and spiritual courage, he is a model for all his followers. In fact, many Zoroastrians regard their prophet as the first priest of their millennia-old faith.

Zoroaster preached that there were only two gods, the 'wise lord', Ahura Mazda, and his eternal rival Ahriman. It was the duty of all believers to be on the side of Ahura Mazda. This supreme God is worshipped and his prophet is Zoroaster. Zoroaster is not worshipped but is followed as his directed path of truth and righteousness, *asha*, will lead men and women to God.

Zoroaster gave three important commandments to his followers to enable them to lead perfect lives and work for their own spiritual progress. These are *humata* (good thought), *hukhta* (good word), and *havarshta* (good deeds). Good thoughts are very important in the spiritual journey of man, because all else comes out of thoughts. Without good thoughts one cannot subject oneself to Divine will.

Thinking good alone is not sufficient, for one must have the courage to speak the truth all the time. One must be truthful to oneself and to others, for there is no place for hypocrisy or duplicity in the life of a true Zoroastrian. Performance of good deeds is equally important. The supreme power of God, in the aspect of *Khshathra Vairya*, comes to Him who engages himself in good actions. Good actions also include *sraosha* or service, obedience and devotion to God. When we cultivate this virtue we will be able to see the path of salvation clearly in front of us.

ZOROASTRIAN CREATION MYTH

Now the two primal Spirits, who reveal themselves in vision as Twins, are the Better and the Bad, in thought and word and action. Between these two the wise ones chose aright; the foolish not so.

– Zoroaster

THE ZOROASTRIAN MYTH OF CREATION IS TOLD TO US IN THE *Bundahishn,* an ancient text which dates from the sixth century AD. According to this text, in the very beginning, there was nothing in the world except for the 'wise lord', Ahura Mazda, who lived in the endless light; and there was also the 'evil spirit', Ahriman, who lived in the absolute darkness. Between these realms of light and darkness lay emptiness.

Then, one day, Ahura Mazda decided to make different creations. First, out of shining and bright metal, he shaped the sky. Then, he created pure water. Third, he created the earth, which was flat and round, with no highs and lows, no mountains and valleys. Fourth, he created plants, moist and sweet with no bark or thorn. Fifth, he created the animals, big and small. Then he created the first man, Gayomard, who was tall, bright and handsome. Lastly, he created fire and distributed it within the whole creation. The wise lord ordered fire to serve mankind in preparing food and overcoming cold.

The evil spirit saw from his realm of darkness the beginnings of an amazingly created world, new and wonderful beyond compare. The wise lord said to him, 'Evil Spirit! Aid my creatures and give them praise so that you will be immortal.' Incensed, the evil spirit snarled, 'Why should I aid your creatures? Why should I praise them? I am far more powerful! I will destroy you and your creatures.' Crawling back into the abysmal darkness, he began to shape demons, witches, and monsters to attack the endless light.

The all-knowing wise lord was well aware of what the evil one planned to do. He knew that there would soon ensue a great battle with the dark forces. Now, the wise lord fashioned the six spirits: these were the 'holy immortals', to guard his creations against the endless darkness. The holy immortals were shaped from his own soul, and to each he gave his own nature. These were the *Amesha Spentas*.

First he created *Khshathra*, the power of right and just rule, to become the guardian of the sky. Then he created *Haurvatat*, the power of wholeness and good health, and she was the protector of the waters. *Spenta Armaiti*, the power of holy devotion, serenity and loving kindness, was created to be the guardian of the earth. *Ameretat*, the power of long life and immortality, was made to become the protector of the plants. *Vohu Manah*, the good mind, was created to protect the animals. And *Asha Vahishta*, the power of truth and justice became the guardian of the fire. Lastly, the wise lord made his own holy spirit, the protector of mankind.

Ahriman saw the wise lord's holy immortals and was enraged. He cried, 'Ahura Mazda! I will destroy you and all your creations. You will never be victorious!'

So, he and his demons began to attack the wise lord's creations one by one. They tried to destroy the water but they could only bring bitterness to it. They tried to destroy the earth but they could only put mountains and valleys. They tried to wither the plants but the plants only grew thorns. The evil spirit and his demons brought into the world sadness against happiness, pain against pleasure, pollution against purification and death against life. They attacked Gayomard, and gave him sickness and death. The evil spirit thought he was victorious; he imagined that he had destroyed mankind and triumphed against the light! But he was ignorant and foolish and quite mistaken.

When Gayomard died, from his bones grew a rhubarb plant. After

40 years, a man and a woman, Mashya and Mashyana, grew out of the rhubarb plant. Mashya and Mashyana promised the wise lord that their children would help him in his battle with Ahriman. Mashyana gave birth to 15 twins and every pair scattered around the world and became a race.

Thought for Reflection

Zoroaster preached that there were only two gods, Ahura Mazda and Ahriman. It was the duty of all believers to be on the side of Ahura Mazda, who is:
Omniscient
Omnipotent
Omnipresent
Impossible for a normal human being to conceptualize
Unchanging
The creator of everything
And the source of all the goodness and happiness in the world.

Amesha Spentas are God's divine attributes. By knowing them, man can know God. These aspects are like the rays emanating from the single eternal source of light. The first three aspects represent the Father-aspect of God while the remaining three represent the Mother-aspect.

Combating the goodness is God's adversary, *Angra Mainyu* who resides in hell. This dualism is twofold – cosmic and moral. There is the cosmic dualism between God and the *Angra Mainyu* who is the destructive spirit that introduces the evils of death, sickness, etc., into God's pure and beautiful world. There is also a moral duality that points towards the inherent good and evil sides of a human being.

Zoroastrians believe in the duality of existence – i.e., the presence of good and evil in the world. They also believe in the divinity of all creation, which God created out of His own astral body.

Human beings are born pure and have a choice either to follow the teachings of God and remain righteous or follow the ways of the evil and be damned. Depending upon their choices and their actions, God decides their fate in the spiritual realm. God offers knowledge of righteous conduct and provides instructions for the expiation of sin.

The Life of Zoroaster

On three noble ideals be ever intent:
The good thought well thought,
The good word well spoken,
The good deed well done.

– Zoroastrian Creed

ZOROASTER, ALSO KNOWN AS ZARATHUSTRA, IS SALUTED AS A Messenger of God by many. According to one report, he was born approximately one thousand years before Christ, in what was then known as Persia.

As we all know, every child is born into this world with a cry, a wail. Of Zoroaster, it is said that the new-born babe greeted this world with a loud burst of laughter! All nature seemed to rejoice at his coming: the rivers and the running brooks, the woods and the hills, the lilies of the field and the lotuses in the lake, seemed to sing in joy.

The baby was beautiful to behold. The light of purity shone in his eyes; a benevolent smile played upon his lips. They named him Zarathustra – which means 'lover of camels'. He would live up to that name, by feeding other people's cattle from his father's barn.

As he grew into boyhood, it was obvious that he was quite different from other children. Many were the wonderful deeds he did, even at that age. Often, he would give away his food to a passing beggar, while he himself stayed hungry. He would distribute all his playthings amongst his friends, keeping nothing for himself.

At the age of 7, Zoroaster was sent to study under a teacher well-renowned for his knowledge and wisdom. For the next eight years, Zoroaster sat at the feet of his Master, to receive the knowledge of the sun, moon, stars and celestial bodies in their orbits, the cycle of the seasons, the light, the wind and the rain, of men, birds and animals – and the great Creator of the Universe.

As he grew in years, he grew also in the quality of compassion. His heart flowed in a stream of sympathy to all living creatures. It is said, that he once bought bread to feed a dying dog, and offered the creature some comfort in its last hours.

When he was just 15 years old, he moved away from the world of men, to meditate in the seclusion of the forest, in a cave on the Mount Sabalon. He meditated for long on the mystery of life, and the wonder that is the world. He communed with Ahura Mazda. He beheld Him face-to-face, and spoke to Him, as a son would speak to his father.

From time to time, he descended from the mountain heights to the plains below. He mingled with men. He shared his food with the hungry; he gave away his clothes to the needy; he served the aged and the infirm. He healed the sick. He lightened the loads of the burden-bearing camels and horses. He comforted the forsaken and forlorn with his loving words: he offered them hope and cheer on their lonely way, blessing them and healing their broken hearts.

For 15 years, he continued to live this life – a life of meditation and communion with the highest, and of service and compassion to the least of the little ones. When he was 30, he came back to live among his people. His face shone as molten gold; in his eyes was the light of wisdom; he had been illumined by a Divine Revelation, initiated by a series of seven blessed visions!

For the next 10 years, he moved through the towns and the villages of his native land, proclaiming the Truth that had been revealed to him. Not once did he get an eager, receptive audience, willing to listen to him. The people were just not ready to receive from the prophet the revelation meant for them and the rest of mankind. He was greeted with jeers and howls wherever he went; they even pelted stones at him, inflicting wounds on his pure, sacred body. He bore in gentle and loving patience the pain and the scorn heaped upon him. On his lips was the smile of mercy and in his heart was the prayer: 'O, Ahura Mazda! Have mercy on them and lead them out of the darkness of the Evil One, into the Light of thy Truth!'

At last, he found someone who would stand by him and accept the truth of his teachings. His cousin, Metyoma, came up to him, saying, 'Zarathustra, I believe in thee and thy mission! Permit me to follow thee!'

Together, they moved, from place to place, two lone pilgrims of Ahura Mazda. Together they preached, together they served and suffered, knowing fully well that triumph would always belong to Truth. And indeed, Truth triumphed, ultimately! The day arrived when Zoroaster was hailed as a Prophet by the very people by whom he had been persecuted earlier.

In the course of his wanderings, Zoroaster came one day to Balkh, the capital of ancient Iran, where King Vishtaspa held his court. There was something about the Prophet, some glow in his looks, some magic in his words, which cast a spell on the king. Clad in pure white, flowing garments, bearing in one of his hands a staff of cypress wood, and in the other, the sacred fire, Zoroaster's appearance worked a transformation on the king. This conqueror of many lands and many armies was conquered by the Truth of the prophet. He was happy to surrender himself to the Messenger of God, whose only weapons were love and righteousness.

The Truth of his faith was now triumphant. Wherever he went, crowds of people followed him – no longer to pelt him with stones, but to revere him and touch the hem of his garment in love and devotion. For this prophet was also a healer of souls – he reclaimed lost souls with the holy word of God. In his sacred text, the *Vendidad*, Zoroaster tells us, 'There are healers of different types; there are those who heal with the knife: and there are those who heal with herbs. But the best is even he who heals with the holy word.'

Such was his power, that Zoroaster cured men afflicted with diverse deadly diseases. He gave sight to the blind. It is said that he even brought the dead to life.

The influence of Zoroaster's teachings spread as far as Greece and Rome. Socrates was said to have a Zoroastrian instructor named Gobyras. It was said that Plato, too, wished to visit Persia to study with Zoroastrian teachers, but could not undertake the proposed journey due to the outbreak of a local war.

What were Zoroaster's teachings? He looked around him and saw all creation burdened by anxiety, groaning in pain and misery. He felt the agony and anguish of human hearts. He perceived the unshed tears in the eyes of birds and animals. He called upon every man to enlist himself in the Army of God.

'Be ye warriors of Light!' he said to all who heard him.

'What may we do to belong to the Army of God?' people asked him.

'Walk the way of righteousness!' was his simple answer.

'How may we walk the way of righteousness?' they persisted.

Clear and simple, direct and profound was his reply: 'Build your life in good thoughts, good words, good deeds!'

The root cause of man's suffering, he taught, was ignorance – what the Gita calls *avidya*. 'It is ignorance,' said Zoroaster, 'which drags many men to their ruination. For men, in their ignorance, do not realize that when they injure another, they cause harm to themselves. All humanity is one family and I can be happy only when my brothers and sisters are happy.'

'Banish ignorance with the light of wisdom,' he urged, again and again.

'What are the primary duties of man?' he was asked.

'These three,' he replied, 'First, to convert an enemy into a friend; second, to teach righteousness to the wicked; and third, to spread the light of wisdom, where ignorance abounds – for wisdom is richer than all the wealth of the world.'

Zoroaster moved, from place to place, with his message of righteous living. His message brought about a revolution in the hearts and minds of his people. It called them away from a life of sordid selfishness to a larger, higher, more beautiful life of loving fellowship and service of the needy. It infused in their hearts a new faith in God and goodness.

For 47 years, Zoroaster continued to pass on his message to rich and poor, princes and peasants. Then came the day, which cometh in the life of all men, wherever they may be – the Day of Farewell from this earthly pilgrimage.

It is believed by some of the faithful that the prophet was carried away by a stroke of lightning; yet others believe that he was assassinated while conducting worship in his temple.

I do not know how it was – I only know that such a One as Zoroaster can never die! The seasons may tire and the years may grow old, but the life and teachings of this great Messenger of God will continue to spread their radiance, far and wide!

———❧◆❧———

THOUGHT FOR REFLECTION

Gurudev Sadhu Vaswani said to us: 'Blessed is the Truth seeker. For his life is tragedy and tears.' Every suffering is a gift from God. It is the gift that will help you in self-growth. To avoid suffering is to shut yourself away from 'the life beautiful'. The supreme vision of beauty comes from the cross!

Sorrow, grief, hardship, loneliness and insecurities are given to us to make us strong in spirit, to endow us with moral courage, or what I call muscles of the spirit. Difficulties give us courage and strengthen our will power. They put us through a process of cleansing and purification.

Long ago, we were sitting out with him in an open courtyard in Hyderabad, Sind. It was a clear starry night, and we felt blessed to be in his presence. He said to us, 'The great Saints and Prophets of humanity come into this world to do the job of a dhobi. They come here to wash you, cleanse you, remove all the filth accumulated over your previous births and make you clean and pure and radiant and ready to enter His presence.'

My dear brothers and sisters, we have been collecting the accumulated impurities, the *vasanas* of past lives which are to the soul like household dust, filth and muck, over the cycle of previous births. It is difficult; nay, it is impossible for an individual working on his own to remove those layers of filth. It is only the Guru, who is a man of God, who can perform this job.

The Grain of Wheat

With an open mind, seek and listen to all the highest ideals.
Consider the most enlightened thoughts. Then choose your path,
person by person, each for oneself.

– Zarathustra

An ancient legend gives us a fascinating account of how King Vishtaspa first met Prophet Zoroaster.

One day, Vishtaspa was returning to his capital from a tour of the provinces, when his entourage passed by a rich and fertile orchard of exceptional beauty. The land around the orchard was desolate, but the orchard itself was well-cultivated, well-tended and rich in natural beauty. It was obvious that the task of planting, cultivating and growing the orchard to its current state must have been a task well beyond the abilities of ordinary men. The people tending the orchard must have worked under a great man with foresight, wisdom, dedication and diligence.

Vishtaspa asked one of the ministers accompanying him to enquire about the orchard and its owner. The minister returned to tell the king that it was none other than the renowned sage Zoroaster who owned the garden. The king had heard of this wise man and his growing fame, for at that time, Zoroaster had already begun spreading the word of God among his people. Impulsively, the king decided to invite Zoroaster to his palace to answer a few questions to which he had thus far been unable to obtain satisfactory answers from his advisers and counsellors.

When Zoroaster came to greet the king and welcome him to the orchard, the king promptly extended an invitation to the prophet to visit the palace. But Zoroaster asked the king to forgive him, since his task of tending the orchard could not be neglected. However, Zoroaster reached in to the satchel he was carrying and took out something; it was a small grain of wheat. Offering the grain of wheat to the king, Zoroaster told him that the grain had taught him a lot of valuable lessons, which had provided answers to many of the questions that had troubled him earlier.

Perhaps the king was a little displeased with Zoroaster's response. However, he had to be content with the sage's offering and returned to his palace, with the grain. The king was convinced that the grain had magical properties; else how could the sage have offered it to him with such assurance? He decided to place the grain of wheat safely and securely in a valuable, ornamental gold box. Every day he would open the box and stare at the grain, hoping to find the answers to his questions. Days passed; but he felt he was none the wiser.

After a few months, the king grew frustrated and impatient and decided to go back to the orchard to meet Zoroaster. He showed him the gold box with the grain in it, and told the sage that thus far, he had failed to imbibe any special wisdom from it. He demanded to know from Zoroaster what lessons the grain was supposed to teach him.

Zoroaster placed a simple question before the king: what would have happened if the king had sowed the grain of wheat in the soil and nourished it with food and water instead of placing it in a gold box?

Together, the king and the sage reflected on the many lessons they could learn from that simple act. First, in order to grow and transform, the grain would need to be removed from the gold box and grounded in the earth. As with the grain, the king realized he needed to step out of his golden cage, his comfortable surroundings. Then, in the same way as the vital, life-giving and life-sustaining forces of nature would act on the grain to nurture its growth, so would he be nurtured with knowledge and understanding.

In short, the king understood that the grain could only teach him what he was ready to learn!

The answers to the many questions that had troubled him were to be found all around him. The ability to imbibe them and grow in wisdom lay within him. Instead of just seeing, he would watch and observe;

instead of hearing, he would listen and reflect; instead of demanding answers from others, he would develop his own mind and seek answers through insight.

King Vishtaspa's quest for wisdom had begun!

———◁◇▷———

THOUGHT FOR REFLECTION

Man came to the earth as a pilgrim, but has become a wanderer. Even in our spiritual quest, we wander from creed to creed, from one school or thought to another, from one teacher to another, and are filled with unrest. We move to temples and churches and places of pilgrimage, and meet with disappointment. For, not until we turn within, will we find that which we are seeking.

Truth is within! Wisdom is within! The source of all strength is within! Therefore, turn within!

A beginning has to be made somewhere. Every day, preferably at the same time and at the same place, let us sit in silence and pray, meditate, do our spiritual thinking. It is our daily appointment with God. We keep a number of appointments, every day. Alas! We neglect this most important of all appointments – our daily appointment with God. He is not far away from us. He is wherever we are. He is here: He is now! All we have to do is to close our eyes, shut out the world and call Him – and there He is in front of us. In the beginning we may not see Him: let us be sure, that He sees us. We may not be able to immediately hear His voice: but He hears us. The tiniest whisper of human heart, the smallest stirring of the soul is audible to His ever-attentive ears. Speak to Him: open out your heart to Him: place all your difficulties before Him: and you will find wonderful things happen to you.

SADDA MAMA

Hearken with your ears to these best counsels,
Reflect upon them with illumined judgement.

— Ahunuvaiti Gatha

DID YOU KNOW THAT THE CHAMELEON IS REGARDED WITH GREAT reverence among the Parsis and is never killed? In fact, it is affectionately called 'Sadda Mama' in Gujarati.

The legend of *Sadda Mama* goes back to the ancient history of Iran, when the Zoroastrian Empire had begun to collapse. The last Zoroastrian ruler, Yazdegard III had been defeated by the Arabs, in the battle of Nihavand in AD 641 and he and his army were in hiding as they scattered across the land. The poorer people who wanted to follow their religion were persecuted and forced to give up their faith. The few who refused were trying to escape the Arab army and make their way to safety.

One day a group of tired Zoroastrians, who had become refugees in their own land, were crossing a large desert. They hoped to cross the barren and empty stretch so that they could reach the sea coast. It was a long and tiring journey and the sun beat fiercely down on the refugees. One of them sighted a well far away in the desert; they started moving towards it, hoping to get cool fresh water.

What they did not know was that just behind the well a great danger lay for them; a group of Arab soldiers had laid an ambush for them, and were hiding in the sand behind the well with their weapons ready to kill the tired refugees.

A small chameleon, perched near the well was watching all that was happening and was very anxious to prevent the massacre of the innocent Zoroastrians. It wondered how it could help these poor people and indicate to them the danger into which they were walking. All of a sudden, it had an idea. In the desert everything is arid, dull brown in colour and dry, but the Arabs were wearing brightly coloured clothes.

The little chameleon jumped on to the back of the first soldier and, true to his nature, turned a bright blue. Far away in the desert the refugees saw a flash of blue and stopped in puzzlement. What could that bright blue flash mean? Near the well, the chameleon jumped on to another man and turned a bright red. And forthwith, it kept hopping from one soldier to the other as they lay in ambush and the red, yellow and green colours sparkling across the expanse of the brown desert alerted the Zoroastrians.

They decided to stop and send out a scout party by another route. The scouts approached the well from behind and saw the Arabs waiting to ambush them. They also saw the little chameleon that was busy jumping from one soldier to another, creating a many coloured splash; they understood that it was trying to warn them not to fall victims of the ambush. The chameleon, they saw, was vigorously shaking its head from right to left, trying to tell the refugees that it was not safe to proceed to the well.

When the scouts returned to tell their people about the ambush, the Zoroastrians were forewarned and forearmed. They managed to gather their weapons together and actually took on the ambushers and defeated them. They looked at the chameleon that had saved their lives and were filled with gratitude and reverence for the animal. As for *Sadda Mama*, it nodded its head up and down, as if to tell them that they must always heed the voiceless messages of animals, whenever they were in danger and needed help.

The Zoroastrian scholar who has narrated this legend for us adds that to this day, Zoroastrians, especially children turn to their *Sadda Mama* whenever they are in doubt about any issue and want to know the Truth. They ask a question and if the *Sadda Mama* shakes its head from right to left, they take it as a warning and change their plans accordingly. When it nods his head up and down, they take it to mean that it is blessing them and encouraging them to go ahead and act with the power of Truth behind them.

THOUGHT FOR REFLECTION

The world stands today, at the threshold of a new age; we have been fortunate to witness the birth of a new millennium – we, who are the children of two centuries. A new era is knocking at the doors of our hearts. Are we going to open the door to the new age?

It is my firm belief that we are now standing on the threshold of a new age of love, which will bring the spirit of brotherhood among all creation. As the new age dawns, materialism will have to give place to spirituality. People will live the vedanta in their daily lives. And what is the vedantic concept if not spiritual? One life flows in all things. Therefore, I believe, that future civilization will be built on *reverence for life*.

It is my earnest appeal to my brothers and sisters; let us show reverence for everything – for fellow human beings, for the vast universe around us, the earth, the sky, the trees, stones, rivers, flowers, birds and animals! Truly, the time has come when man must either make friends with nature – or perish.

Vedanta teaches that there is but One Life in all. The One Life sleeps in the mineral and the stone, stirs in the vegetable and the plant, dreams in the animal and wakes up in man. Creation is one family, and birds and animals are man's younger brothers and sisters in this beautiful family. Is it not then, our duty to guard our younger brothers and sisters from the cruel knife of the butcher?

Let us therefore, cultivate what Gurudev Sadhu Vaswani calls 'Cosmic Consciousness' – to commune with the earth-spirit, to have a new feeling for the 'animal' world. For the so-called 'lower' animals are also children of Mother Earth. To treat them harshly is wrong. To take them to the slaughterhouse is a sin.

How Zoroastrians came to India

By fate the days of Zoroaster ended:
no one could even trace the Noble Faith.
When Zoroaster's thousandth year had come,
the limit of the noble faith came too.
When kingship went from Yazdegerd the king,
the infidels arrived and took his throne.
From that time forth Iran was smashed to pieces!
Alas! That land of Faith now gone to ruin!

– Qissa-i Sanjan

THE LINES QUOTED ABOVE NARRATE THE *NADIR* OF THE ZOROASTRIAN faith in Iran, their native land. The victory of the Arabs over Emperor Yazdegerd III and the fall of the Sasanian Dynasty mark the end of the era of Zoroastrian ascendancy in Iran. It was then that the transition of the Zoroastrians from Iran to another homeland began. Persecuted on account of their faith, and often forced to convert, Zoroastrians first moved to the mountainous regions of Kuhestan, until their *dastur* (chief priest) warned them to move south.

A small group of Zoroastrians living around the town of Nyshapour near the Fort of Sanjan in the province of (greater) Khorasan, decided that Iran was no longer safe for Zoroastrians and their religion, and decided to emigrate to India. They travelled to the island of Hormazd (Hormuz) in the Persian Gulf, and after three years' preparation set sail for India. Thus began the Zoroastrian migration to India. The story of this historic migration is told in the *Qissa-i Sanjan* (The Story of Sanjan) an epic poem in the Gujarati language, which is the only surviving document of the Parsis' early days in India.

It is said that they set sail for India, landing at first in the island of Diu, off the coast of Gujarat. Some accounts state that about 18,000 Parsis had set out in different groups, landing at Diu, Vairav and Cambay.

Encouraged by their *dastur*, they approached Jadi Rana, the local Hindu ruler, asking for asylum (*panahat o maqamat* meaning 'refuge and home'). The Rana was at first suspicious of the foreigners. He made them give an account of the tenets of their faith in great detail. He then imposed certain conditions on them:

1. They should adopt the local Gujarati language.
2. Their women should were saris like the local womenfolk.
3. The men should lay down all weapons.
4. Their marriages should be performed in the evenings, in the manner of the local Hindus.

The refugees graciously accepted the demands made on them. They expounded on the teachings of their faith, and when the Hindu Raja heard the oration, his mind regained perfect ease. Having been granted asylum, the emigrants established the settlement of Sanjan in Gujarat, (named after the hometown from where they had set out decades ago) which was soon flourishing.

Sometime thereafter, the priests of the fledgling community approached the king with a request to establish a Fire Temple. Their wish was granted, and a temple was subsequently installed and consecrated.

***

A beautiful story is told to us of the arrival of the first Zoroastrians in India. Fleeing from Arab occupation, persecution and forced conversion in their homeland, Persia, they had fled eastward, arriving at the port of Navsari in Gujarat in the ninth century CE. An emissary was sent to the local ruler, Jadi Rana, requesting him to offer patronage and sanctuary to the newly arrived refugees.

The Rana sent them an unusual welcome gift: a bowl brimming over with milk. It was a gesture meant to communicate to the intelligent community that his kingdom was full; and he would find it difficult to accommodate the new arrivals. The Parsi high-priest received the bowl graciously; he sent for some sugar and mixed it thoroughly with the milk and sent it back to the Rana, who was absolutely delighted with the gesture.

For the return-gift indicated to him symbolically that the newcomers would not only blend smoothly and harmoniously with the local population, but also add sweetness by way of their loyalty and respect for the land of their adoption. To this day, the Parsi community in India has remained true to the 'sweet' promise that their ancestors made all those centuries ago.

THOUGHT FOR REFLECTION

Zoroastrians in India remember their traditional story of The Crisis: how, once upon a time, Mother Earth was in trouble. She asked God (Ahura Mazda) if He could send her a prince, with warriors, to stop the people from hurting her, using force. But Ahura Mazda said He could not. Instead He would send to earth a holy man, to stop the people from hurting her, through His words and inspirational ideas. And thus was born the Prophet, Zoroaster.

India is considered to be home to the largest Zoroastrian population in the world. Like the Sindhis, the Parsis also constitute a minority community that has contributed richly to Indian education, industry, economics, philanthropy and culture. They are, today, one of the most prosperous, peace-loving, philanthropic and friendly communities in the country, having achieved wide acceptance, even while maintaining their unique cultural and religious identity. They have never sought special privileges, but always contributed to their adopted country through their philanthropy and entrepreneurial spirit.

EPILOGUE

Sadhu Vaswani

Brief Introduction

*I*F WE ARE BLESSED IN OUR LIFETIME, WE MEET JUST ONE OR two persons who enter into our consciousness and bring about a transformation in our lives. And the whole direction of our lives is changed, because of them. One such was beloved Gurudev Sadhu Vaswani. He brought about a transformation in the lives of many by the power of his love, which opened up our cribbed, cabined, stuffy souls and let the sunshine of God's grace flow in.

Today, thousands of aspiring souls in many parts of the world regard beloved Gurudev as the light of their life. His was a life of singular simplicity blended with selfless activity. His greatness lay not in doing extraordinary things but in doing ordinary things extraordinarily well. His life was a long chain of little deeds of love. His philosophy of life was simple. And his prescription for happiness was, 'If you want to be happy, make others happy!'

How can I even begin to tell you about Gurudev Sadhu Vaswani? My entire life, my work and my aspirations as a pilgrim on the path were inspired, influenced and moulded by him! I cannot attempt to give you a comprehensive account of his life; but an endeavour has been made, in the following pages, to bring together a few glimpses from the beautiful, inspirational life of the great Master. His life was a shining witness of God dressed in the form of a man.

In the great adventure of life, God and man are comrades. To the One Family, the One Brotherhood belong both man and God. To most of us, however, God remains invisible. We are unable to see him, to feel him, to touch him, to speak to him, and to hear his soft, sweet, flute-like voice. Man's heart yearns for a manifestation of God.

It was a Sufi *dervish* who said, 'You must meet God every day. And if you cannot meet him, go and meet someone who has met him and who lives in constant communion with him. The two are not separate from each other!'

Men of God have appeared in all climes and countries, in all races and religions. They have appeared to reveal God's love to humanity and to lead erring humanity back to God.

One such man of God was born on 25 November 1879 in Hyderabad-Sind, a town that has given birth to many saints, dervishes and fakirs (contemplatives and men of renunciation). He was called by many names. The name by which he was known across the length and breadth of India was Sadhu Vaswani. In his characteristic humility, he said, 'I am not a sadhu. I do but aspire to be a servant of the sadhus, the rishis, and saints.'

Tributes were paid to him by men and women of light and leading in East and West. In the West, they spoke of him as a 'Herald of the New Age', a 'Faraday of Spiritual Science', a 'Pioneer and a Path-pointer'. The Irish Poet, Dr Cousins, saluted him as 'India's modern Mystic', a 'Fore-runner of the New Age', and a 'Thinker and Revealer of the deep truths of the Spirit'. But he said, 'I know not much. I only know that the longing within me grows, day by day, to be consumed, more and more, in the flame of sacrifice to him, whose beauty blooms in all the worlds and whose love I see shining, shining everywhere!'

'By what name may we call you, beloved of our hearts?' we asked him once. 'May we call you a sadhu, a guru, a yogi, a rishi? Or may we call you Sache Padshah, for you are, verily, the uncrowned king of our hearts?'

In answer, he said, 'Call me by this simple name – Dada. For I am your brother on the pathways of life.' He never claimed to be more than a brother. Many regarded him as their master, their Guru. But he said, 'I am a Guru of none. I am a disciple of all!'

When saints walk the earth, there is an aura of sanctity and holiness about them, that draws the suffering, lonely, forsaken souls towards them, operating like a divine magnetism. Such was the aura around Sadhu Vaswani who had devoted his life to the service of suffering humanity. Men, women and children flocked to him, wherever he went – but the women outnumbered men, for is it not true that they had greater burdens to bear, and complex emotional responsibilities to handle? In their beloved Master they found someone who offered them sympathy and solace and guidance. It is true that women are more spiritually inclined and therefore felt drawn towards the holy saint who constantly urged them Godward.

During the last years of his earth-pilgrimage, crowds followed him wherever he went, eager to touch the hem of his garment and to listen to his words – more precious than pearls. But he gave himself no supernatural airs. He was one of the humblest of men that ever trod the earth. In him was the humility of one who had reduced himself to naught. Having everything, he chose to live as a fakir, a man who possessed nothing. Knowing everything, he lived as one who knew not. His humility was profound.

The word 'Dada' means 'elder brother'. He was, verily, a brother of all men, all races, all religions, all nations, a brother of the bereft and bereaved, a brother, too, of birds and animals, trees and flowers, rivers and rocks, stars and streams – a brother of all creation.

***

Once, a 'deputation' of friends and admirers waited on Sadhu Vaswani, with a request that he write his autobiography. 'Your life is radiant with the light of wisdom and rich in experiences known only to you,' they said. 'Share them with us and let hundreds and thousands benefit by your spiritual aspirations and achievements.'

In his characteristic humility, Sadhu Vaswani answered, 'There have been no achievements. The story of my life is a story of my abject poverty and God's abounding grace.'

After the 'deputation' left, Sadhu Vaswani said, 'To write an autobiography is to puff up one's ego! Such writing will bless neither him who writes nor him who reads.'

He added, 'If it be absolutely necessary to write an autobiography, let it be written after the pattern of St Augustine's Confessions.'

Sadhu Vaswani's life was a picture gallery – pictures that still have the power to attract, to teach, to inspire. Every picture has an experience to share, a message to give. Every picture is radiant with the love of God and the God-in-man, and with the light of the soul. It is hoped that the incidents narrated in the pages that follow may carry the reader on the wings of imagination, to witness in person, the real life story of this holy man of God.

Sadhu Vaswani never longed for the joys of the heaven-world. He did not aspire *mukti,* salvation, liberation from the cycle of birth and death.

The question was put to him more than once, 'Is there anything higher than mukti?'

He answered, 'I do not ask for mukti. I fain would be born, again and again, if only that I might be of some help to those that suffer and are in pain!'

***

Gurudev Sadhu Vaswani reminds us of a saint who, for the love of God, became a servant of humanity. After completing his mission of help and healing on earth – so the story tells us – he moves on to the heaven-world. He is about to enter the portals of paradise, when he hears a cry of agony, 'I am in anguish and pain: is there no one to help?' The cry comes from a corner of the earth. And the saint says, 'Not for me the joys of the heaven-world. Back to the earth must I go to help a brother or a sister in need.'

Such a one was Gurudev Sadhu Vaswani. Towards the close of his earth-pilgrimage, pointing one day to a street-dog, he said, 'I would not mind being reborn as a dog, if thereby I could give relief to some in suffering and pain!'

On one occasion, he said, 'I would wish to enter hell to give love to those that burn there in the fires of selfishness and greed!'

Heaven can wait!

WHERE IS YOUR FURNITURE?

(To the many people who spoke of him as a poet, a mystic, an educationist, a philosopher, a saint, a sage, a seer) ... I am none of the things they speak about me. I but aspire to be a bhakta, a lover of the Lord...

'What is the way of love?' I am often asked.

I say, 'The way of love is the little way.'

'What is it to tread the little way?'

'To tread the little way is to be humble as dust, is to realize your nothingness: for the heart must be emptied before it can receive the treasures of the Spirit.'

— Sadhu Vaswani

BEFORE EMBARKING ON HIS JOURNEY TO FOREIGN LANDS, Prof. Vaswani took two vows. In the spirit of a pilgrim, he said to himself, 'I leave the shores of India, to take to multitudes the message of India and her rishis, her sages and her saints.'

The very first vow, which Prof. Vaswani took, was the vow of simplicity. He would lead a simple life – in dress, in diet, in daily living. To this pledge, he remained ever true.

During his stay in Europe, one of Prof. Vaswani's friends, Bhojsingh Pahlajani, who came from Sukkur and who later became the Speaker of the Sind Legislative Assembly, came to meet him, one day, saying that he had bought two tickets for a concert. He asked Prof. Vaswani to join him.

'This I cannot do,' said Prof. Vaswani. 'I beg to be excused.'

'But I have already purchased a five-shilling ticket for you,' Bhojsingh persisted, 'I am sure you will not disappoint me.'

Prof. Vaswani, in a spirit of humility, explained to him that he had already pledged to avoid concerts and movies during his sojourn in Europe.

'In this foreign country, you will feel lonely, bored and lost, if you keep away from all entertainment. You need to move out with friends and not be confined to the four walls of your house,' Bhojsingh argued.

'I can never feel bored or lonely and lost,' replied Prof. Vaswani, 'because I have a friend who is always with me. I recite His Sacred Name: *Hari bol, Hari bol.* And this strengthens me, upholds me, uplifts me. I have need of nothing else.'

Prof. Vaswani remained true to his resolve. He lived a simple life – away from luxuries, pleasures and entertainment. Not all the allurements and enticements of the West could shake his resolve. He stood steadfast as a rock.

In later life too, Gurudev Sadhu Vaswani continued to be simple in his dress and diet and daily living and, as the truly great are, he was in his simplicity sublime. At one time, he lived in the Hari Mandir – a big hall in which a mattress was spread on one side. Sadhu Vaswani slept on the mattress at night, and during the day, sat on it and did his work. There was a small desk on which he did his writing, as he sat on the floor. And there were many books spread all over.

One day, a Frenchman visited him. He had learnt of Sadhu Vaswani through the writings of Paul Richard, who had said of the Master, 'I have been blessed, for amidst the deserts of Sind, I have found a true prophet, a messenger of the new spirit, a saint, a sage, and a seer, a rishi of new India, a leader to the great future – Sadhu Vaswani.'

The Frenchman had expected to see Sadhu Vaswani living in a beautifully furnished house. He was astonished to see that the Master's dwelling was a simple hall with a mattress, a desk and books.

He asked Gurudev, 'Where is your furniture?'

Gurudev asked him, 'Where is yours?'

The Frenchman said, 'I have no furniture. My furniture is in my home in France. I am only a traveller here.'

Softly, Gurudev Sadhu Vaswani answered, 'So am I!'

---<>◇<>---

THOUGHT FOR REFLECTION

Soon after he renounced his career and his worldly life, Gurudev Sadhu Vaswani went to dwell in a small town – Old Sukkur – in silence. The entire day, he spent in silence and when evening came, he came out for about an hour to take a walk. That was the time when the people could meet him and put to him questions in regard to spiritual life.

That was a period of utter simplicity. He, who as principal of several colleges, had lived in big, beautiful bungalows, now lived in a small, tiny room. He permitted himself to spend the meagre amount of ten rupees a month from his savings. Five rupees were spent on food, three rupees on rent of the room which he occupied, one rupee on postage stamps (for correspondence), eight annas on sugarcane (he had a sweet tooth) and the remaining eight annas on soap, oil and other miscellaneous items. During this period, a wealthy man gave him a donation of Rs 3,000. Gurudev Sadhu Vaswani immediately passed it on to the members of the panchayat, requesting them to utilize the amount in building a shrine of silence where spiritual aspirants could come and spend their time in silence and meditation. For this purpose, the panchayat received a free grant of land from the municipality.

In the compound, they had a pipe where Gurudev Sadhu Vaswani came every day and took his bath, and washed his clothes. In his heart, there was a deep yearning to live, in his own words, 'a hidden life in the Hidden God'.

Is not the Thief Your Brother?

Without Thee
Who else will forgive
The multitude of sins
I have committed,
Birth after birth?
If Thou wilt judge me,
By my deeds,
I will forever
In bondage lie!
Alas, I have erred,
Unceasingly!
Do Thou, O Shyama,
Kindle the flame
That will never die!

– From Sadhu Vaswani's Nuri Granth

SADHU VASWANI ALWAYS RETURNED LOVE FOR HATE. 'WHY DO YOU DO so?' he was asked. He answered, 'Each man giveth what he hath. God has given me nothing but love!'

Sadhu Vaswani blessed those that blamed him. He prayed for those that persecuted him. He was free from desire, free from passion and anger. He was the very picture of Peace. To see him was to recall the immortal words of the Gita:

Forsaking all desires,
Abandoning all pride of possession,
Selfless and without egoism,
He moves onwards,
And enters into Peace!

It is the peace of God. The Gita calls it *Brahma-Nirvana.*

During the early days of the Mira School in Sind, one of his associates was very upset and angry with Gurudev just because his niece was not appointed as the head of the school. He wrote a number of falsehoods against Sadhu Vaswani and his organization in the newspaper, purchased copies of the same and distributed them free among many of those very devotees who attended Sadhu Vaswani's satsang. Sadhu Vaswani heard about it; but he chose to remain silent. He spoke not a word in self-defence.

After a few years, the man realized the grievous fault he had committed. He came and fell at Sadhu Vaswani's feet and, weeping like a child, said, 'You are a true Saint of God! I am a sinner. I spread falsehoods against you. Not once did you utter a word against me. Pray forgive this repentant sinner and tell me what I may do to repent.'

Sadhu Vaswani lifted him up and, holding him in a warm embrace, said, 'Weep not, brother. If you would repent aright, forget all that you have done – and remember God!'

Once, a thief entered the compound of the Mira School building and broke some water-pipes. The thief was about to carry away the pipes when he was caught by the night watchman and handed over to the police.

Sadhu Vaswani learnt of this incident only the next morning. When he heard that the thief had been handed over to the police, he felt sad. He felt that the man could have been let off with a warning. When some of the brothers protested that the man was after all only a common thief, Gurudev said, 'He, whom you call a thief – is he not your brother? Can you disown him? Don't you see your face in his face?'

He did not stop with expressing his anguish. He sent word to the magistrate in charge of the case, requesting him that he might be pleased to pardon the thief.

But before Sadhu Vaswani's message reached the magistrate, the thief had already pleaded guilty to the charges. The magistrate found himself in a predicament. The accused had confessed his guilt; and sentence had to be passed accordingly. But the magistrate said to himself, 'How can I disregard the words of a saint of God?' And the thief was let off!

The thief came running to the mission campus and fell at Gurudev's feet. The light of repentance shone in his eyes, even as he shed tears of gratitude. 'I am a poor man,' he said to Sadhu Vaswani. 'My children were starving. In vain I sought for work to earn an honest rupee. It was in utter desperation I broke into your compound, little knowing that therein dwelt a saint of God. Pray forgive me! Forgive me!'

There were tears in the eyes of the thief. Sadhu Vaswani's eyes also glistened with tears. He blessed the thief, gave him some new clothes and a few rupees, and asked a brother to arrange to get him some form of regular employment.

On another occasion, Sadhu Vaswani said, 'Even a harlot is not alien to us. Have faith in her and you will save her!'

Thought for Reflection

Forgiveness is an attitude of compassion and understanding with which we choose to react to the world around us. We stop seeing others as insensitive and unfeeling or rude and boorish, or cold and selfish. We try to understand their weaknesses, their fear and insecurity, which made them behave in a way that hurt us. In a sense, it is a scared and confused and hurt child inside each one of us which is responsible for such outbursts. This child lurks even within the adult, getting out of hand at times.

Forgiveness is not a one-off action. It is a constant and ongoing process. Mistakes and rash judgements occur again and again in our life. Sometimes we bear the brunt of others' wrongdoing; occasionally, we wrong others. Each time this situation occurs, we need to change our attitude, change our perception and move beyond our habitual prejudices. Each time we make this shift in perspective, we grow in the spirit of understanding and compassion, until forgiveness is no longer a difficult and painful business!

Forgiveness is not only for saints and sages. How often have we not come across people, who, when urged to forgive and forget, will retort with passion, 'I am not a mahatma ... I am not a saint ... I am only human!'

So many of us believe that we cannot forgive; that it is too difficult, that it is the prerogative of saints and other evolved souls – not for the likes of us.

Forgiveness need not be a feat of supernatural power. It is just a way of putting the past behind you – once and for all. It is a way of moving on. It is a way of seeing things differently; looking at life from a new perspective. It is the realization that we cannot stay bitter and angry for the rest of our lives.

To Live is to Give!

I have but one tongue. If I had a million tongues, with every one of those million tongues, I would still speak the one word: Give! Give! Give!

— Sadhu Vaswani

Sadhu Vaswani, was once asked, 'What is your religion?' His reply was truly significant. He said, 'I know of no religion higher than the religion of unity and love, service and sacrifice.'

For him, indeed, to live was to serve, to live was to love, to live was to bear the burdens of others – to live was to share his all with all.

One evening, as we were taking a walk on the roadside with Sadhu Vaswani we saw a poor man lying underneath a tree. His clothes were tattered and torn; his feet were covered with mud. Sadhu Vaswani stopped at the sight of this man. He asked for a bucket of water to be brought. And when it was brought, this prince among men – he had but to lift up a finger and hundreds of us would rush to find out what his wish was – with his own hands he cleansed the body of the poor beggar and passed on to him his own shirt to wear! The poor man pointed to the cap on Sadhu Vaswani's head, and without the least hesitation, the Master passed on the cap to him. On that occasion he spoke certain words, which I can never forget. He said, 'This shirt and this cap and everything that I have, is a loan given to me to be passed on to those whose need is greater than mine.'

Mark the word loan – everything that we have is a loan given to us, to be passed on to those whose need is greater than ours. Nothing belongs to us; nothing has been given to us absolutely; everything has been given to us as a loan – our time and our talents, our knowledge, our experience, our wisdom, our prestige, our influence in society, our bank accounts, our property and possessions, our life itself is a loan given to us to be passed on to those whose need is greater than ours. In these simple words of the Master, as it seems to me, are enshrined the seeds of a new humanity, a new world order, a new civilization of service and sacrifice.

THOUGHT FOR REFLECTION

The following *subhashita* (gem of speech) is attributed to Sage Ved Vyas:

All the wisdom that is taught through innumerable books may be summed up, in half-a-verse, thus: 'To serve humanity is meritorious, and to harm anyone is sinful.'

Indeed, it is this caring spirit that we all need. When I go to big cities like Mumbai, Delhi, Kolkata and Chennai, I find that people seem to have stopped caring. They have become insensitive, indifferent to the needs of those around them. Their attitude towards the suffering and misery they see around them is defined by the words: 'It's none of our business.'

Surely, it's our business! Mankind is our business. The Vedas give us the wonderful concept of *Vasudaiva Kutumbakam*. Humanity is one family; and in this one family of humanity, every man is my brother; every woman is my sister. It is my duty to do all I can to help them – to the best of my ability, to the best of my capacity. I must do all I can, to help as many as I can, in as many ways as I can, to lift the load on the rough road of life. I often say to people: the opposite of love is not hatred; the opposite of love is apathy – indifference to the needs of those around us.

We are all born with the spirit of caring and sharing. But somewhere along the way, as we grow older, we lose this wonderful spirit!

SERVICE OF THE POOR IS WORSHIP OF GOD

Man's knowledge of the world has vastly increased. Science has made rapid advances. But has science listened to the voice of the saints, 'To do violence to another is to violate my own integrity: for my brother's blood is mine'? And this day, I pray that the aspiration may grow within me that I may possess the twofold treasure: inner life, and humble service of little, lowly ones!

— Sadhu Vaswani

GURUDEV SADHU VASWANI WAS VISITING A SMALL VILLAGE. HE STAYED as a guest of a village schoolmaster. In the school, there studied only a few students. Their eyes sparkled with the light of love.

One day an educated man came to the village. He could speak English fluently, and he was humble and loving. The students felt happy in his company.

Suddenly, a rumour spread that this highly educated man had attended the evening satsang of the untouchables and had dined with them. The elders of the village, the temple priests and the members of the panchayat were shocked. They said that they would have nothing to do with such a man. He must be regarded as an outcast. The poor village-folk loved this man beyond words, but what could they do?

Sadhu Vaswani saw the predicament of the village-folk. That evening, he went and participated in the satsang of the untouchables. They all rose up to greet him with deep love and respect. 'Is there anything we can do for you?' they asked him.

Sadhu Vaswani said, 'Bring me a broom.'

In obedience, they bought a broom. He took it, and with it he started sweeping the floor of some of the dirtiest cottages in the colony. As he swept the floor, he kept on repeating the words. 'Service of the untouchables is worship of God.'

One and all, the Harijans in the colony took up these words and sang them as a kirtan-song. The entire colony resounded with the words, 'Service of the untouchables is worship of God.'

The news spread like wildfire in the village that a holy man of God – Sadhu Vaswani – had swept the cottages of the untouchables and sung the words, 'Service of the untouchables is worship of God.'

In a quiet way, the agitation, which was about to flare up against the educated man, died down.

THOUGHT FOR REFLECTION

On the material plane we judge people by their affluence. We ask people, 'How much have you studied?' 'What are the academic degrees you have acquired?' 'How much wealth have you amassed?' or, 'What is your salary?' These are all questions relating to worldly, material considerations.

The man who is wealthy and affluent, enjoys a high status in the society, but in the heavenly world all these things are of no significance. There, the only question asked is, 'How much do you love God? How much love do you have for God's broken images, the poor and the needy?' God does not want to know about your bank balance, your qualifications, your designation, your caste or your creed. He asks you about love.

God does not care about birth, status, caste or creed. All He wants from you is the gift of a loving heart.

Let us all kindle the light of love in our hearts.

His Name was Compassion!

If I meet a hungry man, let me not ask why he is hungry, when so many others feast at their banquet tables. Let me give him food to eat.

If I meet a naked man, let me not ask why he shivers in the cold of wintry nights, when so many have their wardrobes filled to overflowing. Let me give him garments to wear.

And if I meet a man lost in sin, let me not ask why he is lost, but with a look of compassion, with a song or syllable of love, let me draw the sinner to the spirit.

Let me draw, by awakening, the longing that lies latent in all.

Let me lead some out of darkness into Light!

– Sadhu Vaswani

In Gurudev Sadhu Vaswani's life, two streams flowed side by side – the stream of detachment and the stream of compassion. At heart, he was utterly detached. Nothing could keep him tied to the external world. At a mere wish, he could enter the depths within. His life was a beautiful blend of the contemplative spirit and of reverent, loving service to the poor and downtrodden, the broken, bleeding ones of humanity.

Even as a child, Sadhu Vaswani was very different from other children. His face was beautiful to behold. As he grew in years, a far-away look entered his eyes. He became more and more aloof. He felt no joy in mixing with others. He spent much of his time in the silence of an upper room that no one ever used.

Sometimes, as he sat down to his meals and heard the cry of a passing beggar, he would take away his food to share it with the hungry one. From the beginning of his days, he was filled with the spirit of compassion for all who were in suffering and pain.

Again and again, his mother found him awake in the middle of cold, wintry nights.

'What keeps you awake, my child?' she would ask him. 'Is it the cold of the winter? Then let me wrap around you one more blanket or quilt.'

He said to her, 'Mother, the cold I feel cannot be overcome by a hundred blankets or quilts!'

'I do not understand you, my child,' said the mother. 'Speak to me in plain words, not riddles!'

He said, 'Mother, I am thinking of hundreds of homeless ones who, in this severe cold, are lying on the roadside. Their cold seems to pierce my frame.'

Throughout his life Sadhu Vaswani had this sense of identification with the poor and destitute. In later years, once when he was ill, he was unable to take solid food. He felt that he would like to taste an orange. Several oranges were brought to him. As he looked at them, his thoughts moved out to the sick people who lay in the poor patients' wards of the government hospital. Without tasting a single orange himself, he sent them all to the poor patients. And he said, 'I feel satisfied. I feel as though I have eaten all the oranges!'

Many said to him, 'When you give to the poor, you do not discriminate, you do not make sure if the person to whom you give is deserving or otherwise.'

Sadhu Vaswani said, 'The Lord gives without hesitation to an undeserving person like me. Who am I to enquire into the deserts of others?'

On one occasion, Sadhu Vaswani said in good humour, 'The man who gives only to those whom he considers deserving has reason to pray that the Lord, in judging him, will not follow his example.'

THOUGHT FOR REFLECTION

Compassion does not require a hefty wallet, strong limbs or heroic deeds or great and austere sacrifices. A helping hand, a friendly word or gesture, a kind smile will more than suffice!

It has wisely been said: Giving is living! For the health of the human body depends on its exhalations as well its inhalations. It is reported that a young boy, who was to don the role of a shining angel, was covered with a coating of fine gold leaf. The coating closed all the pores of his skin, and he died as a consequence of this disastrous make-up.

This must serve as a warning to all of us, who have the tendency to cover ourselves with our wealth! Let not the pores of our compassion, benevolence and generosity be clogged by wealth! Let us not be constrained to die a spiritual death, smothered in the wealth of this world!

All that we give, in love and compassion, we give to the Lord Himself. The first beneficiary of such service is not the receiver, but the giver – for it takes him closer to the Lord.